What People Are Saying about Leslie Montgomery and *The Faith of Mike Pence*...

Leslie Montgomery has written an intimate and fascinating portrait of our nation's vice president. Through dozens of interviews with those closest to him, Montgomery details the challenges and opportunities Mike and Karen Pence have faced and how their faith has guided them. *The Faith of Mike Pence* is an inspirational, unflinching, and compelling story for anyone who wants to know the truth about who Mike Pence really is as a Christian, husband, father, friend, and politician. For anyone interested in politics, faith, and the Trump-Pence partnership, this book is a must-read.

—*Ralph Reed*
Founder, Faith & Freedom Coalition

There are some in the nation who call Mike Pence a zealot and a theocrat, but they don't know him like I do. He is a man of integrity who lives by the principles of his faith in government, where many are more comfortable with politicians who use religion to sway votes. From Pence's rich, spiritual heritage as an Irish Roman Catholic, born and raised in Columbus, Ohio, to becoming a born-again Christian and leading our nation as our vice president, Leslie Montgomery hasn't missed a beat. If you've been as curious about our vice president's faith and his life as a husband, father, and leader as the rest of the nation has been, then I insist that this book is a must-read!

—*Dr. Robert Jeffress*
Pastor, First Baptist Church, Dallas, Texas; *Fox News* contributor

As someone privileged to know our vice president, it is my opinion that Leslie Montgomery has captured the essence of what has the been the centerpiece of the life and times of Mike Pence. It has been said that one is only qualified to lead to the degree that he is willing to serve. This encompasses Mike Pence.

—*Andrew Phipps*
Radio/TV host, *Phipps Gospel Sing*

Christianity often receives a bad rap from politicians and the media. However, the basic principles of the faith, if practiced by those who lead our nation, could produce a gentler and kinder society. Christian principles demonstrated by the political leaders of our nation could go a long way in unifying a nation that has been blessed by God beyond measure and yet, divided by those who abuse our society with derogatory language and behavior. *The Faith of Mike Pence* demonstrates how such principles can be demonstrated in the life of one willing to set the example regardless of the cost. Leslie Montgomery has written an objective analysis of a life being lived by those principles, who is unwilling to compromise. Her motive seems obvious. Not only does she portray a life, but promotes a faith whose principles, if practiced, could change a nation. I have felt deeply honored to be among the interviewees for the book and even more blessed to have been Mike and Karen Pence's pastor for more than a decade.

—*Dr. Charles Lake*
Executive director, Growth Ministries

Perhaps no public figure since John Kennedy has been attacked for their faith by the misinformed and politically prejudiced as much as Mike Pence. Leslie Montgomery's book is one of the few profiles to portray Pence's faith story in a fair manner. Unlike other accounts, Montgomery uses the testimonies of many who know him the best, not those with political or personal agendas.

—*Bill Smith*
Former chief of staff

Finally, a book that gets to the crux of the misrepresented "feud" between Vice President Pence and the LGBT community. Through interviews with key staff members, family, friends, and close associates, Leslie Montgomery has proven that from day one, Mike Pence has been a vice president for all Americans.

—*Gregory T. Angelo*
Former president, Log Cabin Republicans

I hope that every American who is turned off by bare-knuckle, negative politics will read Leslie Montgomery's wonderful book about Vice President Pence's pure motives, solid values, and personal humility. This book is a "must read" for Christians who feel a call to seek public office or who currently serve in an elective capacity. For them, it is more than a profile of a man who holds the second highest office in the land. They will be encouraged and inspired by this book. It will serve as an invaluable roadmap for how they should maintain and reflect a strong Christian witness in the rough and tumble profession that they have chosen.

—*Ed Simcox*
Former secretary of state for Indiana

There has never been a vice president like Mike Pence in the history of the United States, and I believe there will never be one like him. He is a man of true conviction, if there ever was one. Most men check their faith at the door, but not Mike. Whether he is at home, at a peace summit halfway across the world, or the Oval Office, his faith informs everything he does. America is blessed to have him as our vice president—and we are blessed to get a glimpse of this side of his extraordinary life through Leslie Montgomery's *The Faith of Mike Pence.*

—*Jack Graham*
Pastor, Prestonwood Baptist Church
Founder, PowerPoint Ministries

Leslie Montgomery has produced the book that best captures the real Mike Pence. By doing her homework and numerous personal interviews, she has captured the fundamental decency and genuine Christian commitment of Mike Pence.

—*Dan Murphy*
Friend and fraternity brother

Vice President Mike Pence is a man worth writing about, reading about, and learning from. Leslie Montgomery has managed to pull back the curtain on the faith of the Pence family with inspirational true stories that will fortify and embolden every reader to stand strong in his or her faith with courage and joy. If you are a father, read *The Faith of Mike Pence* and be encouraged. If you are a husband, open the pages and see how to be a godly husband who loves his wife like Jesus loves us. And if you feel called to be involved in politics, this book will prepare you in a unique way to go forward with a steady gait.

—*Dr. Jay Strack*
President, Student Leadership University

When Mike Pence walks into a room or steps onto a stage, you immediately sense that he is a man who walks with the Lord. You can see it through the compassion in his eyes and the confidence in his step. He knows who he is and he knows who guides him. There are few men I admire more than our current vice president. I would do anything Mike asked of me and I know he would do anything within his power for me. He is a man who is passionate about his family, his friends, his sacred charge as a public official, and his mission as a servant of God. Leslie Montgomery has intricately captured that passion and reveals the heart of our nation's vice president in such a manner that it leaves you encouraged, inspired, and challenged in your own journey of faith. You simply must read this book!

—*Doug Deason*
President, Deason Capital Services, LLC
Advisor for prison reform

The Faith of Mike Pence provides deep insight into the formative role Mike Pence's faith has played, not just in his journey to the vice presidency, but in how he lives his life on a daily basis. During the years that I worked for him, Mike was never ashamed of the gospel and that comes through clearly in Leslie's well-researched and clearly-written book. I highly recommend *The Faith of Mike Pence* to anyone who wants to understand the central role that Vice President Pence's personal relationship with Christ has played from the time he was a young man and how it impacts his decisions today.

—*Stephen C. Piepgrass*
Communications director, U.S. Rep. Mike Pence, 2001–2002

I've known Mike Pence since he was relatively unknown in the community and I can say with certainty that he's the same man today as he was then: a man of faith, integrity, and fortitude. Reading *The Faith of Mike Pence* gave me tremendous insight into both Mike and Karen through the stories others shared, including those by the Pence family. If you're someone who is curious about how this simple couple from the Midwest developed their faith, values, and the leadership skills to guide our nation, this book is a tremendous read.

—*Howard Hubler*
Indiana businessman

Reading *The Faith of Mike Pence* is more of an experience rather than a recounting of events and information. Through her creative ability to organize countless first-hand interviews into a seamless narrative, Leslie Montgomery has chronicled decades of Mike Pence's life to provide insight into how his faith and personal relationship with Jesus Christ has molded and shaped his heart and character to become a man who loves and serves God with all his heart, mind, soul, and strength. At times, the reader almost feels present in-the-moment as Mike's Spirit-filled faith and life is revealed through stories illustrating Mike's integrity, priorities, difficult choices, mistakes, patience, kindness, humility, generosity, spiritual growth, disciplines, and prayer life. Through life events, Leslie allows us to see Mike and Karen model a godly marriage characterized by an unbreakable bond of love, commitment, and partnership. You will be encouraged, challenged, enriched and blessed by this inspired classic.

—*Jim Dodson*
Pastor; former accountability group member

The purpose of *The Faith of Mike Pence* is not to persuade the reader to agree with Pence's positions, political or religious. Rather it is to document one man's spiritual journey—from his mother's womb to the present day. To this end, it succeeds splendidly. Pence's harshest critics will understand the man better after reading the book as will his most ardent fan and the many others in between.

—*Cecil E. Bohanon*
Professor of Economics, Ball State University

Since President Trump picked Mike Pence as his running mate, the media has caricatured Pence so badly, I hardly recognize him. As one who has known the vice president since 1994, I can confidently say that Leslie Montgomery has accurately depicted the real Mike Pence. If you want to know the heart of the man who is a heartbeat away from the presidency, you need to read Montgomery's account of *The Faith of Mike Pence*.

—*Gary Varvel*
Friend and former cartoonist for *The Indianapolis Star*

The Faith of Mike Pence is an authentic portrayal of the man I had the privilege of getting to know so well and is a must-read.

—*Ryan Reger*
Former field representative/scheduler for Mike Pence

Leslie Montgomery has done the nation a great service by introducing Americans to the real Mike Pence and his life's partner, Karen. *The Faith of Mike Pence* lets the reader see the true man of faith behind the headlines—the dedicated Christian, husband, father, and patriot—those of us who have had the privilege of working with him over the years have always known him to be. Mike Pence is indeed a man of absolute integrity who not only talks the talk, but walks the walk.

—*Dr. Richard Land*
President, Southern Evangelical Seminary

Leslie Montgomery captures the essence of the Mike Pence I have known for more than thirty years. His faith, his marriage, and his caring for allies and opponents alike are all documented in compelling prose.

—*Mike Murphy*
Senior vice president, Hirons, Indianapolis

Over the years, it has been inspirational to watch Mike build a morally coherent life in a political environment full of corruptible temptations. Leslie's work provides affirmation that he is on the right track.

—*Ken Blackwell*
American politician, author, and conservative activist
Senior Fellow for Family Empowerment, The Family Research Council

Mike Pence wields enormous influence—perhaps more than any previous vice president. Montgomery has been able to peer into the world view of the man who is a heartbeat away from becoming president and use that vantage to draw a lucid and insightful portrait of the man, his faith, and his vision for America. A must-read for anyone interested in 21st century American politics.

—*David M. McIntosh*
President, Club for Growth

I have great respect for my friend Vice President Mike Pence and the genuine values he demonstrates wherever he goes, whether speaking at a governmental briefing or surveying a hard-hit community after a natural disaster. He made a statement that touched my heart and shows his strength and conviction: "I am first a Christian, second a conservative, and third a Republican." *The Faith of Mike Pence* clearly shows how our vice president's deep devotion to God has permeated his life and motivated his dedication to public service. This book reveals the heart of Mike Pence.

—*Apostle Guillermo Maldonado*
King Jesus Ministry International, Miami, FL

THE

FAITH

OF

MIKE

PENCE

LESLIE MONTGOMERY

WHITAKER
HOUSE

THE FAITH OF MIKE PENCE

Leslie Montgomery
Yeshu'a Ministries
P.O. Box 45104
Boise, Idaho 83711

www.authorlesliemontgomery.com

ISBN: 978-1-64123-225-8
eBook ISBN: 978-1-64123-226-5
Printed in the United States of America
© 2019 by Leslie Montgomery

Whitaker House
1030 Hunt Valley Circle
New Kensington, PA 15068
www.whitakerhouse.com

Library of Congress Cataloging-in-Publication Data
Names: Montgomery, Leslie, 1967- author
Title: The faith of Mike Pence / Leslie Montgomery ; foreword by Mike
   Huckabee.
Description: New Kensington, PA : Whitaker House, 2019. | Includes
   bibliographical references. |
Identifiers: LCCN 2019011066 (print) | LCCN 2019011677 (ebook) | ISBN
   9781641232265 (e-book) | ISBN 9781641232258 (hardback) |
Subjects: LCSH: Pence, Mike, 1959- | Pence, Mike, 1959—Religion. |
   Vice-Presidents—United States—Biography. | BISAC: BIOGRAPHY &
   AUTOBIOGRAPHY / Religious. | BIOGRAPHY & AUTOBIOGRAPHY / Political. |
   POLITICAL SCIENCE / Government / Executive Branch.
Classification: LCC E840.8.P376 (ebook) | LCC E840.8.P376 M66 2019 (print) |
   DDC 973.933092 [B] —dc23
LC record available at https://lccn.loc.gov/2019011066

2 3 4 5 6 7 8 9 10 11 ᵂᴴ 26 25 24 23 22 21 20 19

DEDICATION

To my Lord and Savior, Jesus Christ

PREFACE

There is a sea of negative books on the market about Mike Pence. Due to the positive nature of this one and the timing of its release, some will say that the vice president or those associated with him asked me to write it or influenced me in some other way. I want to set the record straight from the onset.

In 2006, I wrote and released *The Faith of Condoleezza Rice*, knowing it might be years before I published another book. My husband and I were undergoing fertility treatments and vowed that if I got pregnant, I'd take a few years off of working outside the home to raise my children until they were in school full-time. Well, I did get pregnant and we had two children in the span of two-and-a-half years.

In early summer 2017, with two kids getting ready to start school again, I prayed and asked God to send me a new book contract; it was time to get back into the thick of things. Two weeks later, I dreamt that I was to write *The Faith of Mike Pence*. The truth is, neither he nor his faith were even on my radar. I got out of bed and began doing a little research. I wrote a book proposal for different publishers and began to accumulate a list of people I hoped to interview.

Within the next couple of days, I sent my proposal to the publishers of my book on Condoleezza's faith. They got back to me right away to say they weren't interested.

The worst part of an author's life is courting publishers. It literally drains the life out of you. So I prayed to God, "If writing this book is really Your will, please send the right publisher to me."

The *next day*, I received an e-mail from Christine Whitaker, the author liaison at Whitaker House. I had sent her a fiction book proposal a year earlier and she was just getting back to me. She wasn't interested in *that* proposal, but she did invite me to send any non-fiction proposals I had. I quickly sent her my proposal for *The Faith of Mike Pence*. Within days, Christine let me know Whitaker House was interested. In the realm of book publishing, getting a contract within days is unheard of—it simply never happens.

I put a request in to the White House to interview the vice president and his wife. I asked for their permission to interview their families and closest friends. While I waited for an answer, I prayed and asked God to give me favor by opening the doors. In the meantime, I just kept doing research, interviewing people, and writing the book in faith.

As I proceeded, I had no idea what was going on behind the scenes. Without informing me, my requests for interviews and cooperation were denied. Unaware of this denial, I kept praying in faith and asked others to join me. I had faith that if God had really asked me to write this book, He'd blow open the necessary doors to get it done.

One afternoon as I was in my car, I received an unexpected call from a man who introduced himself as Jay C. Steger, a fellow believer and the vice president's best friend. He hadn't even been on my radar, let alone on my list of people to interview. Jay told me that although my request for the vice president's approval and assistance in this book was initially denied, he had since had a change of heart. Jay would connect me to the "inner-circle" of the vice president's friends to interview—and possibly family members as well.

As I interviewed different people, God gave me favor and they began referring to me other people to interview, opened doors to those who were often reluctant to speak, and encouraged the vice president and his people to participate in this project to the fullest extent possible.

While many participated, there was some resistance from others. The vice president, his family, and those closest to him had been burnt horribly by the media in the past, with their comments taken out of context, twisted, or used as weapons. I was facing an uphill battle. Yet I believe in the power of prayer and kept on storming the gates of heaven, asking for God to open the doors and give me favor.

Ultimately, I ended up with more than fifty interviews with many other people, some of whom wished to remain anonymous. While everyone supported this book and had great things to say about the vice president, not everyone shared his religious convictions or political views. This in itself revealed a lot about who he is as a man and Christian, as well as his ability to connect with people.

One afternoon, I had a unique interview with Rex Elsass, founder and CEO of the Strategy Group Company. Rex is a dear friend of the vice president's and his company has produced all of Mike Pence's campaign ads since he won his first congressional campaign. Rex and I connected spiritually and God showed him my heart for this project. It was clear to him that I wasn't writing a "tell-all" or out to hurt the vice president, but to share the truth about who he is as a man, husband, father, politician, and Christian. What I can only believe is a miracle from the hand of God, Rex became an avid supporter and, on several occasions, personally advocated on my behalf directly to the vice president to participate with his wife and family. While awaiting the vice president's response, Rex and his assistant, R. J. Richmond, linked arms with me in prayer and faith that God would indeed open the necessary doors to the West Wing at the White House. Miraculously, He did.

I'm not under the illusion that everyone who reads this book will be in agreement with the vice president's political views. I must point out, however, that this is not a book about politics, but about Mike Pence's faith and how it directly affects the rest of his life. As he likes to say, "I'm a Christian, conservative, and Republican—in that order."

Many people who do not support Mike's spiritual views will find ways to mock him or twist comments and stories about him. It saddens me that we live in a country where we strongly advocate for religious freedom, yet take offense and become angry with those who don't share our views. Regardless of one's religious beliefs, if we are mature, reasonable people, we should respect anyone who lives by their convictions as Mike Pence does.

My overall goal with this book is not to set the vice president up as a spiritual hero, but to show the heart of the real man—as a Christian, husband, father, and politician. In doing so, I tried to allow his own words and those of his family, friends, and colleagues tell his story while I served as a conduit to weave it together. My prayer is that it inspires, encourages, and challenges you.

To God be the glory.

ACKNOWLEDGMENTS

First and foremost, I thank my mother, Dianne Andrews, for being my best friend, confidant, rock, and prayer warrior. Your unwavering support and encouragement throughout this project have been invaluable. Thank you for celebrating with me all the miracles that took place to make this happen. I'm so thankful God chose you to be my mom.

A big shout-out to my kids, Paul, Isabella and Elijah, who sacrificed countless hours while their mom did interviews, research, and writing for this book. I am so amazed by your love. You take my breath away. Punka-doodle-popper, baby!

A special thank-you to my husband, Dallas, for listening to me for hours on end as I retold the inspiring and encouraging stories about Mike Pence that were shared with me in interviews. It was my pleasure to keep you awake all night talking when we traveled cross-country by car on vacation over the summer of 2018. Your gift of wisdom is something I admire the most about you. Your spiritual insight regarding Catholicism and Christianity as a whole was most beneficial. You're a wonderful leader and example to our kids. I love you for that.

This book is possible in large part due to the support, input, advocacy, and prayers of Jay C. Steger. I will always cherish the hours upon hours that we spoke, as well as the joy we share in our faith. You've been a blessing by helping me attain crucial interviews and sharing details and stories with me. Saying "thank you" seems insufficient to show my gratitude. Together, we have accomplished our goal with this book. I pray you're proud of all you've done to see it through and the final result.

A heart-felt thank-you to Dr. James Dobson for your generous and kind gift and the comments you shared with me regarding your relationship with Mike Pence. I respect and honor you for all you do on behalf of our Lord. It's been a privilege to write for Focus on the Family for over twenty years. Thank you for allowing me to be a part of the tremendous work you've done on behalf of families around the world.

To Rex Elsass, what can I say besides, "You're amazing!" You came from out of nowhere and went far and above the call of duty to help me get the vital interviews and information I needed to complete this project. I am eternally grateful to you for being my advocate, friend, and brother in Christ. I will never forget what you've done for me and pray God will bless you a hundredfold for your effort. I owe you big time! And a *big* thank you to R. J. Richmond of the Strategy Group Company as well. He was my fellow prayer warrior every step of the way. You guys are awesome!

A special thank-you to Bill Smith for committing to reading the manuscript for political accuracy and accountability purposes and joining me in prayer for its completion and success. Your assistance is so appreciated. You're a blessing to me.

Christine Whitaker jumped on this project so fast, my head spun. She saw the vision and she ran with it, doing everything in her power to make this book a success. I've never worked with a publisher who was so invested in a project for the sole purpose of sharing the heart of God. She's linked arms with me from day one in prayer and as a result, we've seen miracle after miracle occur. Thank you for listening to the Spirit to publish this book.

There are not enough words in the English dictionary to express my gratitude for my personal team of prayer warriors who daily storm heaven's gates on my behalf. Your intercession on behalf of my life and this book and all that has gone into it is priceless. I'm proud to call you my brothers and sisters in Christ, Susan Van Someren, Shirley Rosenvall, Cathi and Dana Danzer, and Mary Lou Phillips.

Pastor Jackson Cramer, you are an extraordinary man of God and I'm so blessed to call you my pastor. You have advocated and interceded for me from the moment I first stepped through the doors of Cole Community Church and I am overwhelmed by the love of Christ that you and the church have freely given. If every church in America loved their congregants as well as our church does, the body of Christ would radiate into the world and pierce the darkness in a way that has yet to be seen since the moment Jesus rose from the dead.

Special thanks to Jeanne Cramer for being my prayer and accountability partner. Your love and support is invaluable. For me, there was a kindred spirit between us from the moment we met. I praise God for you.

Dr. Kent DelHousaye with the DelHousaye Group has been instrumental as my life coach and communications strategist. You've changed my life with your encouragement, wisdom, and instruction from the first time we began working together. You've been a true gift from God.

I'd like to thank the editing team at Whitaker House. You've done extraordinary work and I appreciate your efforts and the expertise that only good editors have to make a manuscript presentable to the public.

My marketing and public relations team is simply the best. Thank you to Jim Armstrong, Karen Campbell, and Matt Palumbo for reaching the world and getting the word out regarding the truth of who Mike Pence is as a man of God.

To my friend and sister in Christ, Sarah Olson. You always have a listening ear, wise advice, a biblical perspective, and a loving and caring attitude. I love that we share joy in prayer, in raising our children unto Christ, and in servanthood. I also enjoy the fact that we can find humor in just about anything. Laughter doeth good like medicine (Proverbs 17:22). I'm so thankful the Lord brought you into my life "for such a time as this." You're simply the best.

Additional thanks go to many others who helped me in some manner or allowed me to interview them for this book, including those who wished to remain anonymous (you know who you are), as well as those who made significant contributions including, but not limited to, Franklin Graham, Richard Land, Ken Blackwell, Ralph Reed, Stephen Piepgrass, Doug Deason, Van Smith, Dr. Ronnie Floyd, Craig Fehrman, Scott Uecker, Dr. Jay Strack, Cecil Bohanon, Mark and Patricia Bailey, Tony Suarez, Congressman John Carter, Dr. Jack Graham, Andrew Phipps, Ryan Reger, Reverend Johnnie Moore, Mike Murphy, Gary Varvel, Garry Smith, David McIntosh, Pastor Harry Jackson, Pastor Jim Dodson, Howard Hubler, Lani Czarniecki, Ed Simcox, Pastor Charles Lake, Ed Feigenbaum, Matt Brooks, Andrew Murray, Dan Murphy, Mike Stevens, Dr. Sue Ellsperman, and Jennifer L. Ping.

His lord said unto him, Well done, good and faithful servant; thou hast been faithful over a few things, I will make thee ruler over many things: enter thou into the joy of thy lord.

(Matthew 25:23 KJV)

CONTENTS

FOREWORD

I have known Mike Pence for almost 25 years. We share the same passion and values for faith, family, conservative causes, and servanthood for our nation. We have a lot in common. While I served the body of Christ as a pastor, Mike Pence was considering the priesthood. When I became a servant for our country as Lt. Governor, then as Governor of Arkansas, Mike Pence was a member of the U.S. House of Representatives in Indiana. We both have three children and wives who have stood the test of time as faithful companions and prayer warriors. Most importantly, when we've both faced what seemed at the time as insurmountable circumstances in our lives, we've both turned to God for His support, encouragement, and strength, and matured in our faith as a result.

Mike Pence is not a politician who wears his faith on his sleeve. He wears it in his heart and soul. He is a man who seeks and desires to do God's will in every area of his life. While many politicians claim faith as a badge to sway votes or to impress a group of pastors or evangelicals, Mike Pence stands out as the real deal, a man who says what he means and means what he says. His heart for God is evident in his pro-life stance, in his advocacy for Israel, and other policies he boldly fights for. You never have to question where he stands on an issue because it's always from a biblical worldview. I am proud to call him our nation's vice president, a friend, and my brother in Christ.

Within these pages, Leslie Montgomery has painted an exquisite picture of the real Mike Pence that is seldom if ever reported upon by media. In interviews with his family, friends, colleagues, and even those who are on the other side of the aisle, Montgomery has shown us his proud Roman Catholic roots, the young dreamer he grew up to be in a loving home, the struggling young man seeking to find himself in college, the fallible man seeking redemption through faith, the ambitious side of politics, and the spiritual journey that ultimately led him to be our vice president. There is no other book out there that captures the truth behind all of these moments in time in the life of Vice President Mike Pence.

—*Mike Huckabee*

INTRODUCTION

Have you struggled with your faith?

Have you wondered about your purpose in life?

Has your life been forever changed because someone took the time to care?

Leslie Montgomery's new book, *The Faith of Mike Pence*, explores how this grandson of Irish immigrants found his inner spiritual light, was held up by loving brothers and sisters in Christ, and rose to become vice president of the United States.

Many are faith-filled, but Leslie's book celebrates the joy of becoming Christ-centered, by sharing Mike Pence's deeply personal walk of faith. Here, we read about a faith that wasn't full, a faith that was abandoned—and then, out of the darkness, a faith that was joyfully reborn in Jesus Christ.

You'll also meet the real Karen Pence, who shares her gift of faith with the husband and father she loves. Karen Pence is not only a gift to Mike Pence, but a gift to our nation, because she has a devoted faith and calming spirit that calls us to stop, listen, and learn.

Mike Pence is a prayerful leader who trusts in the Lord, gives thanks for his family, and celebrates our God-given liberty every day. That's the Mike Pence we see in *The Faith of Mike Pence*.

I've known Mike Pence for nearly twenty years and have never seen a leader so devoted to God and country. He has a servant's heart and a compassionate soul that lifts people up. He reminds me of America's founders and he also shares Ronald Reagan's optimistic spirit and love of country.

This book is a must-read for anyone who wants to know the real story about Mike Pence. Leslie's in-depth study, full of engaging, personal stories, introduces us to a prayerful and humble-hearted leader who is restoring hope to the America we love.

—*Rex Elsass*
CEO, The Strategy Group Company

1

THE BLESSING

After removing Saul, he made David their king. God testified concerning him: "I have found David son of Jesse, a man after my own heart; he will do everything I want him to do."
—Acts 13:22

Mike Pence stood in the sanctuary of the historic, 200-year-old St. John's Episcopal Church, surrounded by stained-glass windows and a small group of friends and family for an intimate, private prayer service.

Dr. James Dobson, founder of Focus on the Family and *Dr. James Dobson's Family Talk*, stood next to Mike, holding a copy of a prayer and blessing he'd written specifically for the vice president-elect. It was 8:30 a.m. With the inauguration only hours away, Dobson wanted to speak a personal blessing over Mike before he embarked on his new role. In his humble, Midwestern manner, Mike clasped his hands before him and bowed his head as Dobson began to speak:

> To commemorate this historic day, I would like to take us back to a passage in the Holy Scriptures, found in 2 Chronicles, chapter 1, verses 1–12, when Solomon, son of David, had been chosen as king over the house of Israel. We read, *that night God appeared to Solomon and said, "Ask for whatever you want me to give to you."*

Solomon answered God, "You have shown great kindness to David my father and have made me king in his place. Now, LORD God, let your promise to my father David be confirmed, for you have made me king over a people who are as numerous as the dust of the earth. Give me wisdom and knowledge that I might lead this people, for who is able to govern this great people of yours?"

God answered Solomon, "Since this is your heart's desire, and you have not asked for wealth, riches, or honor, nor the death of your enemies, and you have not asked for long life, but for wisdom and knowledge to govern my people over whom I have made you king, wisdom and knowledge will be given to you."

As we know, Solomon became one of the wisest men who ever lived.

The Scriptures teach us that wisdom is being able to perceive things from God's point of view. No greater blessing can be given to a leader than the ability to grasp eternal truths and put them to use. After all, these biblical concepts come from the Creator Himself.

Mike Pence has demonstrated that his values are in the right place. I have known him for twenty-five years and watched as he was given increasing responsibility for government. Humility and integrity have been his way of life. When he introduced himself to the American people last year, he wasn't embarrassed to say simply, "I am a Christian." Let me close this historic moment with a prayer:

Heavenly Father, I ask You to lay Your hands on Mike Pence and the new president of the United States, Donald J. Trump, as they assume the burdens of national leadership. May they be keenly aware of Your presence when the challenges are too heavy to bear. May they lead the nation with righteousness. Protect them from those who would try to cause them harm, and preserve this great country from international intrigue. May You grant them wisdom and knowledge in the measure of Solomon in days of old. When their terms of office are complete and life moves on, may they hear You say those beautiful words, "Well done, thou good and faithful servants." In the name of the Father, the Son, and the Holy Spirit. Amen.[1]

ENDNOTES

1. From James C. Dobson's personal correspondence with author, August 17, 2018.

2

IRISH ROMAN CATHOLIC
TO THE CORE

The LORD had said to Abram,
"Leave your country, your people and your father's household
and go to the land I will show you."
—Genesis 12:1

Twenty-year-old Richard Michael Cawley climbed aboard the S.S. Andania in Liverpool, England, on March 14, 1923. It was a cold, rainy day and he had the equivalent of $23—equal to about $335 today. Not a lot to start life in a new land.

As he prepared for the twenty-nine-day journey to New York in his third-class cabin, the young, gray-eyed Irishman longed for the promises of America that assured him of success and prosperity through hard work, determination, and initiative. Fleeing poverty and the Irish civil war, where he had served in the Irish Free State's Army, Cawley yearned for peace and financial stability. His courageous mother had given him a one-way ticket to the land of the free.

"The legend in our family was my great-grandmother had stood outside that little house and looked over at the Ox Mountains and looked off to the west, and told him that he needed to go because she said, 'There's a future there for you,'" Mike Pence says.[1]

The son of a tailor from the rural village of Tubbercurry in County Sligo, Ireland, Cawley was the third of eight children who had been raised in a two-room house. Born on February 7, 1903, he worked on the family's farm and quit school in eighth grade so that he could work as a coal miner to help to support his family. An older brother, James, and an uncle had proceeded him in making the trip to America.

As the S.S. Andania pulled into New York Harbor on April 11, the breathtaking and towering Statue of Liberty was a welcome sight for Cawley and the other immigrants. His first step off of the boat and on to American soil would prove to be the beginning of something he couldn't have even imagined at that time, the fruition of a promise that was ordained by God: that He would bless the young man's life and that of his children and grandchildren, if he clung to Him in faith.

The immigration inspection process on Ellis Island took several hours. Afterward, Cawley spent some time with his brother, who lived in New York, then headed for Chicago, where he found an established city of Roman Catholic churches, schools, and a heavily Irish Democratic political community.

Cawley worked odd jobs to support himself in the suburbs of Chicago until 1927, when he landed a job as a streetcar driver for Chicago Surface Lines. He eventually became a bus driver and worked for the company for more than forty years. During his first few years of driving, Cawley met and married Mary Elizabeth Maloney, a schoolteacher and first-generation American whose family hailed from Doonbeg, County Clare, 225 miles south of Cawley's birthplace. The couple moved into a small flat on the South Side of Chicago. Over the next three years, Mary Elizabeth gave birth to two daughters: Mary Ellen, born in 1931, and Anne Jane, born in 1933. The latter, Mike Pence's mother, went by the name Nancy.

Shortly after Nancy's birth, Cawley left his wife and two young daughters to travel to Ireland to be with his dying mother.

"He was gone so long," Nancy recalls, "my mother worried he wouldn't come back."[2]

AN AMERICAN WITH ROOTS IN IRISH SOD

But he did return and Cawley became an American citizen in 1941. Yet he never forgot his roots, marching in St. Patrick's Day parades and playing the piano and singing Irish tunes with his wife and daughters every Saturday night.

Mike Pence's paternal grandfather, Edward Joseph Pence Sr., was born in 1902 to a German and Irish Catholic family and raised in the working-class neighborhoods of Chicago. He quit high school after his freshman year to work at the stockyards as a cattle handler and later a hog salesman. Edward married Geraldine Kathleen Kuhn, the daughter of Irish and Prussian immigrants, Mary Anna and Philip Blaze Kuhn. Edward and Geraldine lived near the historic Union Stock Yard Gate and were parents to a daughter and two sons. The eldest was Mike Pence's father, Edward Pence Jr., born in 1929.

Edward Sr. was known to be a "very hard man," according to Gregory, Mike's older brother.[3] He refused to provide any financial support to his oldest son, Ed, after he graduated from high school in 1947. Edward Sr. believed his children should learn the value of hard work, especially to accomplish their dreams. He practiced what he preached, eventually attaining a seat on the coveted Chicago Stock Exchange, a very challenging and expensive task.

Raised to believe that hard work, faith, and family were the three most important aspects of life, Edward Joseph Pence Jr. nurtured all three successfully. Receiving a loan for college from an aunt, he studied law at Jesuit Loyola University, a private Catholic research university in Chicago. It didn't take long before Ed realized that it would take more money than both he and his aunt had to earn a degree. He quit college.

Ed enlisted in the U.S. Army in 1950 after North Korea invaded South Korea following a series of clashes along the border. Rising to the rank of lieutenant, he served in the 45th Infantry Division, which remained on the front lines in such engagements as the Battle of Old Baldy. Ed earned a Bronze Star in 1953 for his courage under fire after he led his platoon across a minefield, walking ahead of them to make sure it was safe.

To his friends, Ed was "an affable, light-up-the-room" kind of guy with a gift for wisdom, communication, and leadership, says Jay C. Steger, a family friend who was raised in neighboring Warsaw, Indiana.

After his Army service, Ed worked in the oil industry, making it his life's career.

Mike Pence's mother, the former "Nancy" Jane Cowley, was known by family and friends to be outspoken, quick-witted, and engaging. She made friends easily and did well academically. After graduating from high school, she attended secretarial school.

One evening, out with friends in downtown Chicago, Nancy spotted Ed in uniform at a local tavern. They started talking and Ed instantly fell for the vibrant redhead with crystal blue eyes. They were engaged within months and married shortly after the 1956 New Year.

Nancy gave birth to their first son, Gregory, on November 14. A second son, Edward Phillip, soon followed. The young family of four lived in a modest home while Ed worked for both Pure Oil Company and Marathon Oil Company.

Shortly after Nancy learned she was expecting again, Ed accepted an executive position with Kiel Brothers Oil Company in Columbus, Indiana, 227 miles south of Chicago. The growing family left the Windy City, with its population of more than three million, and moved to small-town Columbus, with a population of less than 21,000. They found a three-bedroom, brick ranch home in the quiet, northern suburb of Everroad Park West. It was a time in history when the average cost of a new home was $12,400, the average yearly wage $5,010, and a gallon of gas cost twenty-five cents.

"I guess you could describe [the home] as modest at the time, although we never thought in those terms," says Mike's brother, Edward. "It was just our home."[4]

While Nancy stayed home with the boys, Ed helped Kiel Brothers grow into a Midwestern empire of more than two hundred gas stations throughout Indiana, Kentucky, and Illinois. He eventually became a part owner of the company.

"This was a time, if you roll the clock back, when there were lots of service stations all over the place," recalls Jay Steger. "Every couple of corners had a gas station and you'd never think of buying milk or food [there]. Almost all of them would have auto mechanic repair shops. So, the stores basically pumped gas, you fix your car there, and you bought cigarettes."

It was the time of the civil rights movement and some landlords refused to rent or sell homes to African-Americans. Catholics faced prejudice as well, according to Gregory, who recalls Protestant kids throwing stones at him.

NAMED FOR MATERNAL GRANDFATHER

Less than six months after his family moved to Columbus, Michael Richard Pence, named after his maternal grandfather, was born on a warm Sunday afternoon on June 7, 1959. Within the first months after his birth, Mike was baptized and his parents willingly took on the commitment to raise their newborn son under the guidance of God and the Catholic Church.

"The parents, who are the primary catechists or teachers of the child in the ways of faith, make a promise to do that when a child is baptized," explains Father Clement T. Davis of St. Bartholomew Catholic Church on the south side of Columbus, which the family attended when Mike was a baby. Mike's mother and siblings still worship at St. Bartholomew to this day.

Partial to his namesake, Cawley, now in his fifties, went out of his way to spend time with his third grandson. Gregory says Mike inherited his grandfather's sense of humor and easy manner, strengthening their bond.

The Irish culture that Nancy had grown up with in Chicago was all but missing from the small town where they were living in Indiana. She longed for her friends and family who she'd left behind.

"I hated it," Nancy recalls. "I always looked forward to going back to Chicago."[5]

When Ed and Nancy's fourth son, Thomas, was born, they had their hands full with four boys under the age of seven. The family eventually moved into an upper-middle class neighborhood and vacationed in Chicago to visit family and friends.

Although Mike met all of his developmental milestones with ease, Nancy says he refrained from talking until he was three years old. Around that age, his grandfather taught him how to say some words in Gaelic, including the nursery rhyme "Humpty Dumpty." After that, Mike was "very talkative," Nancy says.[6]

Although the Pence home wasn't politically charged, they openly identified with the Democratic Party and cultivated a healthy admiration and respect for President John F. Kennedy. Mike's maternal grandparents emigrated from the same area in Ireland as the Kennedys, and the Kennedy name appeared down a branch in the Pence family tree. With their shared Irish roots and Catholic faith, Mike's parents had framed photos of JFK and Pope John XXIII atop their television set.

"My grandparents were so proud of the first Irish Catholic president," Mike says.[7]

One of his earliest memories, from age four, is watching President Kennedy's funeral on November 25, 1963. "I actually remember sitting on the floor in the living room, looking at our black-and-white television, and watching the caisson roll by and hearing the clip-clop of the horses."[8]

The family also revered African-American civil rights leader Dr. Martin Luther King Jr., who had spent years traversing the country in a valiant, nonviolent effort to expunge racial prejudice in America. The same year President Kennedy was assassinated, Dr. King became the youngest recipient ever awarded the coveted Nobel Peace Prize for his work to bring racial equality to America.

When Mike was five, in a rare public expression of their political views, Ed and Nancy had their four boys ride in wagons in a parade that supported Republican presidential candidate Barry Goldwater, a five-term senator from Arizona. They admired Goldwater's strong conservative views. Goldwater lost the election, but the Pences continued to find modest ways to express their traditional beliefs.

When Mike turned six, the Pences began to attend St. Columba Roman Catholic Church, a daughter parish to St. Bartholomew. The new parish was formed to accommodate the growing population of Catholics on the north side of town, where the Pences lived.

The following August, Mike began attending kindergarten at a new parochial school adjacent to St. Columba. Formed in 1964 for kindergarten through grade eight, the school reinforced the values of his heritage found in *The Catechism of the Catholic Church*, which gives instructions about following a spiritually and morally correct life, covering spiritual devotion, dedication to the family and the church, charity work, and respect for and promotion of human dignity.

While attending this school, Mike, an avid reader, first fell in love with the Christian-fantasy series *The Chronicles of Narnia* by author C. S. Lewis. He reread the books several times.

The school was taught by black-habited Benedictine nuns, who had committed themselves to a consecrated life of purity and service to God. The nuns were known to be strict, expecting their students to exceed high educational standards and maintain behavior that reflected the characteristics of Jesus.

"I did eight years of hard time at Catholic school—the name of Sister Rachel still sends a shiver down my spine," Mike would later joke before adding, "Honestly, I was the beneficiary of an extraordinary Catholic education," which "continues to serve and inform me every day."[9]

"THE BEST MAN I EVER KNEW"

As far back as he can remember, Mike looked up to his father with great admiration and respect, saying that among everyone he has known in life, his father had the greatest influence on him. He set positive examples for his children as a Korean War veteran, a successful small business owner, and a man devoted to his family and church.

"My dad was the best man I ever knew," Mike says. "He was a great father, a great husband."[10]

Ed had personal convictions about leadership that he diligently instilled in his children. He felt strongly that they should never perform for anyone else's approval or compete with others, but work their hardest and do their best for their own sakes. Ed often told his children, "Climb your own mountain," encouraging them to forge their own way in life.[11]

Raised to believe that "*from everyone who has been given much, much will be demanded*" (Luke 12:48), the Pence boys worked hard in school and faithfully helped out at their church as altar servers.[12]

"I was raised in a family where faith was important—church on Sunday, grace before dinner," Mike remembers.[13]

Mike's brother Gregory says, "Our life revolved around the church."[14] The Pence siblings "all grew up with a strong sense of doing what was right. Mike manifested that" in his public life, Gregory says.[15]

The boys were all altar servers and helped out at church services six days a week—weekdays and Sundays—and sometimes seven days if they were also serving at Saturday evening Mass. They performed such tasks as holding the Bible for the priest to read, lighting candles, and ringing the altar bells. Mike became an altar server around the time he turned ten and was in the fourth grade, when the Catholic Church believes a child is old enough to commit to living a moral and faithful life.

"Being one of four boys was very convenient for Father Gleeson," Mike jokes. The priest could call up his father at any time and "have a full team of altar boys ready for any Mass."[16]

Father Davis says Catholic parents take on the responsibility to raise their children unto God seriously.

Mike "would have received the holy confirmation and confession in the second grade, which is one where we emphasize the gift of the

Holy Spirit [that] helps us to be of service to others," he explains. "The Holy Spirit is to guide us into a life in which we use the gifts we have to benefit the whole community and others."

Even after his death, Mike found John F. Kennedy and his life of service to be a continual source of inspiration. He kept news articles about JFK, along with photos and banners, stored in a box in his bedroom closet. For a class assignment, he made a time capsule that contained photos and newspaper clippings of the former president.

Just two months before his ninth birthday, another hero of Mike's, Dr. Martin Luther King Jr., was assassinated in Memphis, Tennessee. King had taught Americans that violence and murder could not stop the struggle for equal rights. Mike took those words to heart and would carry them as a beacon throughout the coming years.

As the young Mike struggled to come to grips with the turbulent events of 1968—the assassinations of Dr. King in April and then JFK's brother, Robert F. Kennedy, just two months later—life in the Pence household, always full of faith and love, was about to change for the better.

Ed was rising through the ranks of Kiel Brothers and was well on his way to becoming partial owner and company vice president. The Pences moved from their modest, middle-class, three-bedroom home to a larger, split-level house in Parkside, an upper-middle class area of town that would accommodate their growing family.

For fun, Mike and his brothers would play football in a nearby field, ride their bikes to town to buy candy, build model airplanes, and play in a neighborhood creek. In the wintertime, they built snow forts in their yard.

DECIDED ON COLLEGE AT AGE 11

During the summer he turned eleven, Mike participated in basketball camp at Hanover College southeast of Columbus. He lived in a dorm, ate meals on campus, and toured the college in his spare time. Mike was so impressed by the college, he decided—at that age—that he would like to attend Hanover once he graduated from high school.

As a homemaker, Nancy poured her love into her children and their friends.

"She's very warm and if you're important in the life of one of her kids, you're important to her and you know it," says Steger. "She makes you very aware of it."

Nancy juggled the four rowdy boys with a firm, but loving hand.

"You can just imagine the short little Irish mom with four boys right in a row," says Steger. "There were no daughters [yet] to soften the edges of the boys. It's just non-stop boys wrestling and clowning around, knocking things over, and then you've got this tiny Mom who's making that all work out."

Before Mike entered his teens, Nancy gave birth to her first daughter, Annie, who was followed by Mary a year later.

"In a way, it was like our parents had two families," says Mike's brother, Edward, in describing the age differences in the two sets of siblings. "We had an unwritten rule to defer to your older brother, but it wasn't always followed."[17]

Nancy worked hard in the home, raising six kids, yet she somehow found the time to write a chatty column entitled "Memories Blossom with Arrival of Spring" for the local newspaper, *The Republic*. Both Nancy and Ed's commitment to family and work ethic served as an inspiration to their children.

"When I was young," Mike would say, "I watched my mom and dad build everything that matters: a family, a business, and a good name."[18]

When Mike was in seventh and eighth grades, Sister Sharon Bierman, a Benedictine sister from Our Lady of Grace Monastery in Beech Grove, Indiana, taught him math, science, and religion. She remembers him as being open and welcoming, going out of his way to befriend students who were struggling to fit in, such as those whose families were migrant workers.

"I believe he accepts every person for who they are. That's the way he was in school," Sister Bierman says.[19]

She also praised Mike's hard work and dedication in school. "He was always very thorough on every assignment," she says. "In religion, he excelled."[20] Mike was "polite, diligent, outgoing, and very smart," Sister Bierman adds.[21] She hoped he'd become a priest one day.

Mike distinguished himself by memorizing the principles of his faith; the seven sacraments (Baptism, Reconciliation, Eucharist, Confirmation, Marriage, Anointing of the Sick, and Holy Orders, which creates the hierarchy of deacons, priests, and bishops in order to serve the spiritual needs of others); the corporal works of mercy (actions performed that extend God's compassion and mercy to those in need, such as feeding the hungry and giving alms to the poor); and the mysteries of the rosary (meditations on episodes in the life and death of Jesus, from the annunciation to the ascension).

For his confirmation name, Mike chose "Christopher," which means "Christ-bearer." Christopher is also the patron saint of travelers.

PRIESTHOOD VS. POLITICS

As Mike memorized and meditated on the principles of his faith, a seed was planted in his heart about someday fulfilling Sister Bierman's dream for him to become a priest or vicar. At the same time, he had begun to verbally articulate his political interests and beliefs and became a stand-out amongst his peers as a leader.

"When I did a book for their eighth-grade graduation, so many of his classmates predicted he'd be the president of the United States," recalls Sister Bierman.[22]

Steger says Mike learned many of his leadership skills from his father because Ed was deliberate in teaching his sons lessons he thought would be instrumental for their futures.

"Mike told me one story about how his dad would teach the four boys," says Steger. "Something around the house would need to be fixed. Ed would go get the tools and bring all four boys, saying, 'Come on, I'm gonna show you how to fix this pipe' or this thing in the house. And so, the way he'd do it is, he'd have the tools down there and he'd start working and then Ed would start fumbling around and before you know it one of the four boys would jump in and say, 'Dad, get out of the way, I can do this.' And then Ed would just sit back and say, 'Oh, yeah, you're doing a good job,' or if they were messing up, it would be, 'Wait a minute, what are you doing there?'

"It wasn't learning by watching [their father] passively. It was, 'I'm going to get this started and you guys are going to figure this out for yourselves and I'm gonna be there to make sure no one cuts off a finger.'"

There wasn't much to keep kids entertained in Columbus back then, recalls Mike's brother, Gregory. "We sometimes got in the car with our parents on Friday nights and followed after the fire truck."[23] Although Ed and Nancy preferred that their children use their formal names, they didn't prevent their use of some light-hearted nicknames. "My name was General Harassment," remembers Gregory. "Michael's was Bubbles, because he was chubby and funny."[24]

Mike would come to be known for his wit and impersonations from an early age. He'd spend hours perfecting his ability to impersonate friends, teachers, and relatives, generating much laughter among family members when he imitated his grandfather's Irish brogue.

"Michael's hilarious," his mother says. "I attribute it to the Irish. We're faith-filled and have a good sense of humor."[25]

Steger says Mike is a lot like his father, Ed.

"Mike is just a good-natured guy and Ed was, too," says Steger. "If you're at a gathering, the part of the house or room that's laughing the most, you're going to find Mike Pence in the middle of that and you would have found Ed Pence in the same way, just able to go into a group of people and connect in a really good-natured way."

Steger says Mike often sought out his father's advice on everyday issues. "Mike revered his father and actively and constantly went to his dad for advice."

One of Mike's most cherished memories is riding along with his father as he went on errands in town.

According to Gregory, Ed Pence was a no-nonsense, strict disciplinarian.

"If you lied to him, you'd be taken upstairs, have a conversation, and then he'd whack you with a belt," Gregory says.[26]

Their father also expected the children to exhibit good manners. When an adult entered the room, the kids were expected to stand up and show respect. Ed also went out of his way to emphasize the meaning of hard work.

Mike's grandfather Cawley further emphasized that point, going out of his way to impress upon the young man that his dreams were not limited.

Mike says his grandfather taught him, "If you work hard, play by the rules, look after your family, you look after your neighbors, and you keep working hard, anybody can be anybody in America."[27] Mike took those words of advice to heart and began to dream about serving in Congress someday, like his childhood hero, JFK.

This dream wasn't something that his father necessarily favored. While Mike was growing up, his dad made it clear that he "didn't like politicians or lawyers."[28]

"We didn't talk politics a whole lot in partisan terms when I was growing [up], although [I] never remember too many dinner tables where we weren't talking about issues," Mike says, adding his parents and siblings were "all opinionated Hoosiers."[29]

When he was seventeen, Mike volunteered as a youth coordinator for the Bartholomew County Democrat Party. Walking throughout the streets of Columbus, he recruited members, rang doorbells, and handed out flyers.

A NATURAL ORATOR

For a kid who was a late talker, Mike was a natural at giving speeches...or so it seemed. In fact, he worked hard at it. He entered his first oratorical contest in the fifth grade and sailed past the competition—all older students in sixth, seventh and eighth grades.

"It shouldn't have come as a surprise," says Nancy. "He was always talking. What surprised me was how well he could talk in front of large crowds. When it came his turn, his voice just boomed out over the audience. He just blew everybody away. I had a hard time associating the boy up there speaking with our son."[30]

Mike continued to enjoy speech contests throughout his school years. He learned to listen carefully, probe deeply, and ask intelligent questions.

In the summer months, when not vacationing in Chicago with his family, Mike earned spending money by pumping gas at Ray's Marathon, one of the gas stations owned by his father. Being the owner's son didn't earn him any brownie points with the other employees. They didn't cause problems for him, but they didn't go out of their way to be friendly either. After several attempts at befriending them, Mike became frustrated and went to his dad for advice.

"Just outwork them," Ed said. "That's how you prove yourself. Be the hardest worker there."[31]

That's exactly what Mike did, which earned him some friends as well as his co-workers' respect.

Mike diligently saved up his wages to buy something he'd had his eye on at Tom Pickett's Music Center: an Epiphone guitar. When he finally had enough money, he walked into the music store, bought the coveted guitar, and signed up for guitar lessons.

Despite playing sports—football, basketball, and wrestling—Mike struggled with excessive weight throughout his childhood. He described himself as "a fat little kid...the real pumpkin in the pickle patch."[32] As a teen, he still carried the extra weight and it hindered his extracurricular activities and his self-esteem.

"The physiques on his three brothers, especially when they were young, were pretty chiseled, pretty well-developed, and Mike was not, carrying a few extra pounds," says Jay Steger.

Mike was frequently compared to his brothers, which didn't help his self-identity.

"Some of his brothers are rather well-built and kind of attractive guys, but as a young guy, nothing stood out about Mike," Steger says. "Now, when you met him, he had a lot of energy, a lot of charisma, a light-up-the-room kind of guy, but not because he was a dashing, handsome fellow. It was all personality and affability—and the fact that he loved people."

With his build and smaller stature, Mike was often the target of his brothers' roughhousing, Steger recalls. "Mike took a pounding from them. And part of that is where he came to understand that I can struggle against you, but we still love each other at the end of the day."

At fourteen, Mike was confirmed in the Catholic Church. Through this sacrament, young adults are invited to ratify the promises made by their parents on their behalf at their baptism.

In ninth grade, following in the footsteps of his two older brothers, Mike left parochial school and began attending Columbus North High School, which has the motto, "Respect. Responsibility. Relationships."

STRAYING FROM CATHOLICISM

Although he went through the motions of being Catholic during his teenage years, Mike slowly began to stray from the convictions he'd been raised under and began to question whether his faith was his own or a result of his upbringing.

"I grew up in a wonderful church family," Mike says. "But I walked away from that when I was in high school. I had no interest in faith. I thought it was for other people."[33]

Mike's parents were worried about his excessive weight, so after his sophomore year of high school, a doctor put him on a strict weight-loss program. Diligently focused on his goal, Mike lost fifty-five pounds that summer. When he returned to school in the fall for his junior year, some of his classmates thought he was a new student.

Mike's self-esteem skyrocketed. He ran for class vice president, but lost to a friend who lived down the street. The next year, he ran for senior class president and won, finally given a platform to use his gifts and talents.

Adamant to lead by example, Mike sought to improve his speaking skills. He spent hours watching videotapes of himself emceeing events such as talent shows and practicing for upcoming contests with his high school speech team, the Bull Tongues. During his senior year, the team ranked twenty-first out of 450 member schools and Mike finished second in the National Forensic League's boys' extemporaneous competition in Seattle. At the team's banquet, coach Debbie Shoultz presented Mike with the "Speaker of the Year" award.

Mike's Catholic faith and the servant-leadership foundation upon which he was raised at home both instilled in him the belief that he should find ways to serve others in the community. He first found an avenue to be a selfless servant by following in the footsteps of his brother, Gregory.

The Pence brothers were among several high school students who volunteered their time to help Mike and Mark Reardon, two brothers born four years apart who had muscular dystrophy. The progressive, neuromuscular disease attacks the respiratory system and restricts the person's ability to move. The Reardons were in wheelchairs and needed help with daily tasks such as getting dressed. Their parents, John and Ellen Reardon, had two other children and worked hard to meet everyone's needs.

Maynard Noll, a local automobile dealer and longtime volunteer with the Easter Seal Society, recruited a team of high school students to help the family on a rotating basis. Each morning before school, one or two students would go to the Reardon home and help Mark and Mike Reardon get ready for school.

Gregory Pence helped the Reardon family faithfully until he graduated from high school and went off to college. Mike voluntarily took his brother's place and served with joy, bonding with both teens and ending this volunteer work only when he, too, entered college.

The Reardon brothers passed away before they had the opportunity to do likewise—Mark at age fifteen and Mike at age eighteen. Mike Pence served as a pallbearer at both funerals. He remained close to the family and later delivered the eulogy at their mother's funeral.

In the fall of 1976, Mike applied for and was accepted to attend Hanover College—the private, co-ed, liberal arts college in Hanover, Indiana, where he'd once attended basketball camp. He graduated from Columbus North High School the following summer with A's and B's.

ENDNOTES

1. "Remarks by Vice President Pence to the American Ireland Fund National Gala," March 15, 2017 (Whitehouse.gov).
2. Sheryl Gay Stolberg, "I Am an American Because of Him," *The New York Times*, March 16, 2017.
3. Jane Mayer, "The Danger of President Pence," *The New Yorker*, October 23, 2017.
4. Harry McCawley, "The Mike Pence Story: From a youth in Columbus to candidate for vice president," *The Republic* (Columbus, IN), July 17, 2016 (originally published January 13, 2013).
5. Mayer.
6. Zack Peterson, "Vice President's Mother Discusses Young Mike Pence," *Chattanooga Times Free Press*, Chattanooga, TN, May 20, 2017.
7. Jennifer Wishon, "Rep. Mike Pence: 'It All Begins with Faith,'" Christian Broadcasting Network News, February 10, 2010.
8. Staff reports, "Pence, Trump share 'belief in the American dream,'" *Daily Reporter*, Greenfield, IN, January 17, 2017.
9. Bob Eschliman, "Vice President Pence Explains How Catholicism Impacted His Own Faith," *Charisma News*, June 6, 2017.
10. Mike Pence campaign speech.
11. Charlotte Pence, *Where You Go: Life Lessons from My Father* (New York, NY: Hachette Book Group, 2018).
12. Kirk Johannesen, "Exclusive interview: Pence, Trump share 'belief in the American dream,'" *The Republic*, January 18, 2017.
13. "Vice President Pence shares his testimony of Jesus Christ," Media Strategy Group, January 30, 2017.
14. Jonathan Mahler and Dirk Johnson, "Mike Pence's Journey: Catholic Democrat to Evangelical Republican," *The New York Times*, July 20, 2016.
15. Steve Kukolla, "Penance, Redemption Punctuate Life of Mike," *Indianapolis Business Journal*, January 31, 1994.
16. Tyler O'Neil, "Mike Pence Says Catholicism Is 'An Eternal Foundation in My Life,'" *PJ Media*, June 6, 2017.
17. McCawley
18. Mike Pence's acceptance speech for vice president at the Republican National

Convention, July 21, 2016.

19. Judith Valente, "Catholic Sister Recalls Her Pupil, Gov. Mike Pence," *NPR from Illinois State University*, August 1, 2016.

20. Ibid.

21. Ibid.

22. Ibid.

23. Jane Mayer, "The Danger of President Pence," *The New Yorker*, October 23, 2017.

24. Ibid.

25. Ibid.

26. Ibid.

27. Remarks by the Vice President to the Latino Coalition Policy Summit, Issued on March 10, 2017 (www.whitehouse.gov/briefings-statements).

28. Kukolla.

29. C-SPAN with host Brian Lamb, "Q&A with Mike Pence," January 19, 2006 (www.c-span.org/video/?190800-1/qa-mike-pence).

30. McCawley.

31. Charlotte Pence, *Where You Go*.

32. McKay Coppins, "God's Plan for Mike Pence: Will the vice president—and the religious right—be rewarded for their embrace of Donald Trump?," *The Atlantic*, January/February 2018.

33. "VP Mike Pence Shares Testimony at Church by the Glades," VFNtv (Vine Fellowship Network), April 8, 2017; "On Sunday Vice President Mike Pence shared his story of becoming a Christian during a visit to Church by the Glades in South Florida," TruNews, March 20, 2017; service was March 19, 2017.

3

THE WINDS OF CHANGE

Jesus answered him, "Truly, truly, I say to you, unless one is born again he cannot see the kingdom of God."
—John 3:3 ESV

A week before Labor Day in 1977, Mike's parents took him to Hanover College, dropped him off at Crowe Hall, and drove away. He was briefly overcome by a wave of fear and a lack of self-confidence.

Delivering the commencement address at his alma mater on May 24, 2008, he recalled:

"I was scared. A small town boy, ninety miles from home, with just one pay phone in the lobby. I was homesick by the dinner. And then I met my roommate, attended my first class, went to my first fraternity...'social gathering,' and I never looked back."[1]

Looking to make new friends, Mike began to visit several fraternities, looking for one where he felt comfortable to pledge. At Hanover, pledges were made during the second semester after Christmas break, so he had time to shop around. One day, Mike Pence met Mike Stevens, who was two years older, at the Phi Gamma Delta fraternity house. The two instantly hit it off and Mike found himself visiting the house often. The fraternity is nicknamed "FIJI" due to Phi Gamma Delta bylaws that limit the use of the Greek letters. Although it's a social organization, scholarship achievement is its members' top priority and its five core values are friendship, knowledge, service, morality, and excellence.

"Mike visited our fraternity house pretty regularly and it was clear before Christmas [that] he was going to pledge Phi Gamma Delta," says Stevens. "He developed a pretty quick friendship with a lot of the guys in the fraternity and there were several guys in his class who joined the Phi Gamma Delta fraternity at the same time."

JOINING BAND OF BROTHERS

The fraternity was full of young men who had also been raised Catholic. Mike pledged Phi Gamma Delta in January 1978.

"There were exceedingly bright guys" in the fraternity house, recalls Steger, who also pledged with Mike that year. "We had the highest GPA in the nation of all Phi Gamma houses. We had the highest GPA on campus, too. I think our average on a four-point scale was 3.6. So, you had to be a dean's list guy or better. I was always bringing our average down. I'd be at home and get my report card and I'd be on the dean's list and I'd be like, 'This is so great! I got a 3.5!' and I'd go back to Hanover and they'd say, 'You're bringing down our average, pal.' It's like, 'You've got to be kidding me!'"

Daniel Murphy, another close friend and former fraternity brother, says the fraternity included a diverse group of men.

"You had in that fraternity house everything from the sort of evangelical Christian crowd to some fairly hard-core drug users," Murphy says. "Michael was known to be friendly and accepting to all of them, regardless of which end of the spectrum they swayed."

Murphy says Mike quickly became known in the fraternity as a skilled cartoonist and someone who was always willing to be included on a prank—that is, if he wasn't the one to pull the prank in the first place. One particular prank included the fraternity mascot, a goat.

"We sewed two sheets together in a semi-abandoned dorm room, and in blue spray paint, Mike drew a caricature of a goat and wrote on it, 'Goat Power 1978!'" recalls Murphy. "We hung this huge banner over Parker Auditorium."

For three years, Mike and Murphy lived next door to each other in the fraternity house. "He lived in what we called the 'Wood Room' because students had lined it with old barn wood some years earlier," Murphy says. "It looked like a pirate ship cabin."

Mike and Murphy bonded over history, taking multiple classes together, and their shared Catholic faith. They occasionally went to Sunday church services together and as they walked back to the house afterward, they often shared their dreams for the future. Murphy was impressed with Mike's strong desire to serve the world and touch the lives of others in some capacity. He recalls Mike agonized over his "calling," not knowing whether to become a priest or go into politics.

During a visit home, Mike shared his indecision with his father. He didn't know if he should become a priest or go to law school after he graduated from Hanover. Ed suggested Mike start with law school, saying he could always become a priest at a later time.

Among his friends, Mike came to be known for his wit. It often got him in hot water.

"I remember he was witty and sometimes that wit would get him into trouble," says friend and fraternity brother Andrew Murray. "There was a lot of picking on Mike because he was good with words. You could not win with words with him, so you had to win by picking on him physically, jokingly beating up Mike. He'd get people chasing him because he'd get people mad at him because he was so good with wit and words."

With his easy-going nature, Mike had no problem making friends and it wasn't long before he was well-known across campus. He played his acoustic guitar frequently at college social activities and co-eds surrounded him. He kept busy studying, socializing, and attending church.

Stevens says Mike was a leader from the beginning, the "Pied Piper in college."

Although Mike continued to attend Mass and thought about becoming a priest, he admits he was struggling within. He yearned for something more; he just didn't know what.

"My own walk is I was blessed to grow up in a family that was in church every Sunday," Mike says. "Mom and Dad had strong faith, but for me, I found that something was missing as I came up and I went off to college and had largely walked away from the faith that I was raised to believe in."[2]

During this time, Mike began to meet other young adults who seemed to have a different kind of faith than he'd experienced while growing up.

PERSONAL RELATIONSHIP WITH JESUS

"I began to meet young men and women who talked about having a personal relationship with Jesus Christ," Mike says. "While I cherish my Catholic upbringing and the foundation that it poured into my faith, that had not been a part of my experience."[3]

Stevens, who was also raised Roman Catholic, knew exactly how Mike felt. He personally gave his life to Jesus Christ as his Lord and Savior in high school at a Fellowship for Christian Athletes event.

"Mike and I drew that parallel very quickly," Stevens says. "We had a lot of talks about growing up in the Catholic Church. For me, there was an institutional faith verses a personal faith and we talked a lot about that. A personal relationship with Jesus was just something that he hadn't talked about or experienced, so he was very much intrigued by that [and] I think he saw in me that I was able to make that switch and be relatively comfortable with it."

CHALLENGED BY EVANGELISM

"My reason for worshiping in an evangelical church has more to do with what challenges me more than any quarrel with the theology of the faith of my upbringing," Mike says today. "I have great admiration for the Catholic Church and great respect for the theology represented there."[4]

Mike's faith transformation began in college when another fraternity brother, John Gable, invited him to attend a Tuesday evening Christian fellowship group called Vespers. The group, formerly known as the Hanover Christian Fellowship, met in Brown Memorial Chapel on campus. Student-led sessions included prayer, worship music, and Bible readings. Mike initially attended out of curiosity, but kept going back after that first meeting because he saw a cute girl there.

"So, I kept going in hope of seeing her again," Mike says. "I can see now that God used that motivation to bring me back to the fellowship that [would play a] big part in bringing me to Christ."[5]

Vespers sponsored various activities that emphasized community service and growing in Christ, including trips to nursing homes, Bible studies, and retreats.

Mike felt encouraged by the group, not yet realizing that God's Spirit was drawing Mike into a personal relationship with Him.

"He started asking a lot more questions and he started reading the Bible a little bit," recalls Stevens. "I don't think he'd read the Bible very much prior to coming to college. He started digging into the Scriptures and it started becoming more real to him. It was a different approach to the Christian faith than he had growing up."

Several of Mike's fraternity brothers began to pray for his salvation and talked to him about their own faith journeys.

"There were quite a few Christian guys in the fraternity," says Stevens. Mike "saw their faith was real [and] he was intrigued because they were authentic, very decent folks."

Gable began talking to Mike one-on-one about God and His Word, the Bible, and the freedom associated with both when you take the step to accept Jesus's sacrifice on the cross for your sins and develop a personal relationship with Him.

"I said, 'John, I've decided I'm going to go ahead and be a Christian,'" recalls Mike. "He had this cross he wore around his neck and this was before everyone could order anything on their phones. I said, 'Where'd you get that good cross? Because I want to go ahead and be Christian now.'"6

When Mike learned Gable ordered the cross from a catalogue, he kept asking Gable to share his copy with him so Mike could order a cross, too.

However, Gable didn't give the catalogue to Mike. When the latter went home during a semester break, he bought a cross for himself at a local jewelry store. The next time Mike saw Gable, he was eager to show him his purchase.

"Mike said, 'John, look what I got on break,' and he pointed to his chest and he's got a cross on," recalls Steger.

And Gable told Mike, "You know you've gotta wear it in your heart before you wear it around your neck."7

Mike was under the false impression that wearing a cross around his neck would make him a Christian. He didn't yet understand that he needed to recognize that he was a sinner, that Jesus had paid for his sins on the cross, and he needed to ask Jesus to come into his heart to be his Lord and Savior.

"It just hit me," Mike recalls. "I think I stood there for ten minutes because I felt like he just kind of pulled the curtain aside and he looked right at me and said, 'I see ya. I see ya for where you really are.'"8

Gable said this gently, but "it hit Mike like a ton of bricks," says Steger. "Michael is saying to himself, 'What are you talking about, wearing it in my heart before I can wear it around my neck?'... So, John went on to explain to Mike that he felt he needed to make an adult decision to dedicate his life to Christ."

AT THE ICHTHUS FESTIVAL...

A few weeks later, Stevens invited Mike to attend the annual Ichthus Christian music festival in Wilmore, Kentucky, scheduled for the last weekend in April. Ichthus was a type of retreat for Christian students, organized by students at Asbury Theological Seminary.

Stevens told Mike they would camp out from Friday afternoon through Sunday afternoon and listen to contemporary Christian music and some preaching. Mike eagerly agreed to go.

"I had attended the festival the year earlier and was really into the contemporary music scene," recalls Stevens. "I shared what a good time it was. There were probably fifteen of us from Vespers who decided to go and Mike was one of them. We had four or five cars loaded to go down there. We pitched a tent and the college provided hamburgers and hotdogs."

The young men got there at noon on Friday and jumped right into the festival, listening to bands and various speakers as they preached.

Murray describes it as a "Christian Woodstock" of sorts, minus the drugs and sex.

Popular contemporary Christian artists Phil Keaggy, DeGarmo & Key, Sweet Comfort Band, and Andraé Crouch were all billed to play over the weekend, along with other performers.

"In addition to the bands playing at the main stage, they had several seminars that were set up," recalls Stevens. "They gave out flyers that had what professor was going to talk on what biblical topic."

The Phi Gamma Delta brothers split up, attended different seminars, and then regrouped to discuss what they had learned.

"I heard one preacher after another not talk to me so much about what Jesus has done to save the world, but what Jesus had done, He'd done for me," Mike recalls.[9]

He had a revelation during the festival.

"I heard lots of great singing," Mike says, "and I heard lots of wonderful preaching. And Saturday night [while] sitting in a light rain… my heart really finally broke with a deep realization [that] what had happened on the cross, in some infinitesimal way, had happened for me. And I gave my life and made a personal decision to trust Jesus Christ as my Savior."[10]

Stevens recalls the moments after Mike made that decision. "He came back from a seminar and said there was an invitation to accept Christ and he did it. We all kind of hugged him and were excited for him."

For Mike—making the decision after several months of being witnessed to by numerous friends—it was a commitment to live a righteous life as an example to others and to love others sacrificially, as he came to know that Christ loved him.

"I will tell you that it was very significant for Mike," Steger says. "It wasn't a step—it was a leap. But it fit him well. It fit the way he thought about things and as he began to live into it, it unleashed a deep passion in him."

When they returned to college after that weekend, Mike was visibly a changed man.

"There was a peace you could see on his face," says Stevens. "He was always sort of a jokester, but there was calmness about him."

Mike was feeling God's love, grace, and *"the peace of God, which surpasses all understanding"* (Philippians 4:7 esv).

Mike began to read the Bible and pray every day. He continued to attend Vespers and looked to his fraternity brothers for spiritual guidance.

"It wasn't uncommon to go back to the fraternity house and talk about whatever the topic was [shared] at Vespers that night," recalls Stevens. "We prayed together in our rooms and would go through Scripture, what it meant and how it applied to our lives. Mike would bring his guitar and play."

Before long, Mike was playing his guitar along with the worship team at Vespers, finding a solid niche where he belonged and could mature in his faith.

"Mike was a big deal there," recalls Murphy. "He played the guitar and there was always a gaggle of girls around him."

SHARED SPIRITUAL EXPERIENCE

As Mike's faith grew, the way he lived his life spoke to other men in the fraternity and he looked for ways to share his spiritual experience with them.

When Mike returned from the Ichthus Christian music festival, his friendship with Steger continued to grow.

"Mike is articulate and there's a big evangelistic piece to him," Steger says. Mike became a spiritual mentor to him.

"At some point, he says, 'Have you made a decision? Have you made an adult decision [for Christ]?'" Steger recalls. "And I kind of went, 'No.' I mean, because I thought that was all taken care of because we were Catholics, so I began probing Mike the way Mike had probed John Gable and Mike Stevens, [wondering] *what is this? How does this born-again thing work?* Almost like Nicodemus in the Bible, who basically said, 'How can a man be born-again? How does it work?'" (See John 3:3.)

Mike patiently and consistently took Steger through the Bible to show him the answers to his questions.

"So, Mike and I just work together—this is all very informal, just little bits here and there," recalls Steger. "We would be up late lots of nights, just talking philosophy. I mean, you're picturing most fraternity houses, most guys are up drinking beer, [and] we're talking philosophy and theology all the time. College nerds. Through the conversations over a period of months, I made my own adult decision for Christ."

Although Steger knows it was the Holy Spirit drawing him into a personal relationship with Jesus, he gives Mike the credit for being a conduit to his becoming a born-again Christian.

"I will say, without question, that it was largely because of Mike's passion, guidance, and clarity, and where he was in his walk," says Steger. "And frankly, in all earnestness, wanting me to come along on that walk as a friend. He did it beautifully, did it with kindness and tenderness and earnestness, and I'm a little hard-headed, so he did a good job getting through that."

Steger wasn't the only friend and fraternity brother Mike would witness to and lead to Christ. Murray says Mike invited him to the Ichthus retreat two years later and he experienced the same type of revelation that Mike had.

"He was the one who ultimately said, 'Hey, there's this Ichthus thing, why don't you come?'" recalls Murray. "He was open about his faith. I remember him reaching out to a lot of people in the fraternity, catching some flak for it obviously, but after that commitment he made, he was pretty open and vocal about his faith."

A HURDLE FOR CATHOLIC PARENTS

Not everyone was supportive of Mike's conversion to evangelical Christianity. His family, especially his mother, found it disheartening.

His mother's disapproval ate at Mike and made him question his decision, Stevens recalls. "Initially, he had a hard time. He was pretty sold-out to the Catholic Church and I think that was primarily from the strong family influence he came from."

During a visit to the Hanover campus, Stevens' parents asked him if he was going to Mass every week. When he told them he was attending a Methodist church, the look on his mother's face was utter shock and disapproval. He knew then exactly what Mike was going through.

"I had a similar thing," Stevens says. "I remember talking to Mike. I said, 'I understand where you're coming from and the pressure from your parents is making this really difficult for you. That's going to be a big hurdle you're going to have to overcome.'"

Steger, who was also raised as a Catholic, also understood Mike's situation.

"This is a really strong, Irish, Catholic family," says Steger. "The family had a really rough time with that. You have to put it in the context of the time. [They believed] you don't need to be born-again because all of Catholic catechism says that happens when you go through confirmation. So I think there were emotions all over the place within the family of going against Catholic teachings."

Stevens agrees, saying going from Catholicism to born-again Christianity is detrimental from a parent's perspective.

"Part of the deal with the Catholic [Church] is you've got to observe all the Catholic doctrine," Stevens says. "You have to go to church every Sunday and you have to go to confession" to walk righteously.

Of course, Mike's family still loved him, but friends say his conversion as a born-again Christian would prove to be a trial that would take some time for them all to work through. Mike matured fast in his faith and his friends watched God transform his life.

"He's a voracious reader and he got through the Scriptures rather quickly," says Stevens. "He threw a lot of questions back at me in his own study of Scriptures. We would challenge each other to live it out every day. The ultimate challenge is not to waffle or compromise." As a result, Mike "started applying all the biblical principles to every aspect of his life pretty quickly. I remember him talking about dating girls and he pretty quickly developed an approach that, 'I'm going to treat women appropriately as a Christian man should.'"

Mike wanted others, specifically his friends and fellow fraternity brothers, to experience the freedom he had found in Christ. Instead of just sitting them down and preaching to them, serving in a leadership role, he took several under his wing as a spiritual mentor to disciple them in Christ. In this endeavor, a new Christian is given care and instruction from a more mature believer on how to live a life dedicated to God, grow spiritually by nurturing a personal relationship with Christ, study and understand the Bible and prayer, and allow God to transform and redeem one's life for His will.

"At the end of my junior year, I didn't get much discipleship," says Murray. "My life didn't change a whole lot because I was not discipled a whole lot. I knew I had made that decision and I knew it was real, but Mike was pretty open about discipling me."

Murray credits Mike with helping him grow and mature in his faith, helping him to become the man he is today.

Not everyone Mike mentored would retain their faith.

While attending various church-related activities, Mike found an unlikely comrade: future Oscar-nominated actor Woody Harrelson, who was attending Hanover on a Presbyterian scholarship. Harrelson had made a profession of faith when he was young and was studying ministry. He and Mike were involved in church activities together and shared similar convictions. They spent some time encouraging one another in their faith on a regular basis, but Harrelson eventually turned away from his Christian roots.

"I actually considered being a minister, then I kinda went a different way," Harrelson says. Asked about Mike, he says, "I actually quite liked him. I thought he was a pretty good guy. You know, he's very religious, very committed. Seeing as how I'm not quite in that ballpark now, I don't know how we'd get along." Harrelson says he started questioning the Bible and put his faith "on hold" so he could live his twenties and thirties "in extreme hedonism."[11]

ENDNOTES

1. https://history.hanover.edu/texts/HC/2008pence-graduation.html.
2. First Baptist Church of Jacksonville, "The Man of God, The Man of Government," September 18, 2016 (www.youtube.com/watch?v=mlX9JH90eDg).
3. Jennifer Wishon, "Rep. Mike Pence: 'It All Begins with Faith,'" Christian Broadcasting Network News, February 10, 2010.
4. C-SPAN, "Q&A with Mike Pence," January 19, 2006.
5. Anne Klouman, "Vespers Looking Up," Hanover College Triangle, September 27, 1980, Vol. 73, No. 1.
6. "VP Mike Pence Shares Testimony at Church by the Glades," VFNtv.
7. Ibid.
8. Ibid.
9. First Baptist Church of Jacksonville, September 18, 2016.
10. "VP Mike Pence Shares Testimony at Church by the Glades," VFNtv.
11. Woody Harrelson on Jimmy Kimmel Live, ABC, May 9, 2018.

4

MATURING IN FAITH
AND POLITICS

And the boy Samuel continued to grow in stature and in favor
with the LORD and with men.
—1 Samuel 2:26

As Mike began intense studies of the Bible and grew in his new-found faith, he went through a time of spiritual introspection and grappled with reconciling his Catholic upbringing with being a born-again Christian. At that time, friends say, he referred to himself as a "born-again, evangelical Catholic," continued to attend Mass, and worked as a youth pastor at a Catholic parish.

"I think Mike back then saw it as more of a progressive journey," says Steger. "He didn't really see his committing his life to Christ in any way as divorcing himself from the Catholic Church. He just saw it as the next step in the journey, an enrichment and an enhancement and flourishing of the Spirit within him."

Another friend, Patricia Bailey, says Mike "was part of a move-ment of people, I'll call it, who had grown up Catholic and still loved many things about the Catholic Church, but also really loved the con-cept of having a very personal relationship with Christ."[1]

A SOPHOMORE PRESIDENT

During his sophomore year at Hanover, Mike had a strong desire to further hone his leadership skills for the future. So in the fall of 1978, he ran for president of his fraternity…and won.

"It was a big deal," says Murphy. "You didn't often have a sophomore president."

Stevens agrees. "That never happens. It's usually a senior."

Mike and Steger often talked of his leadership ambitions.

"Now if you asked me about his ambitions as a young man, [as] a sophomore at Hanover, did Mike see himself in Washington? The answer is yes," Steger says. "I would say pretty strongly that Michael saw himself in a leadership role, in a helper's role in Washington of some sort."

Mike's leadership skills at Phi Gamma Delta were put to the test not long after he was elected president.

"Mike got off to a rough start as a sophomore president," says Steger. "Frankly, yours truly was organizing a party that got out of hand. Ultimately, the call came in that the dean of students, [Kenneth] Felt, was on his way over. I yelled out that he's coming over and then started telling guys to do everything from mopping the beer off the floor to getting the bunks back where they belonged. The kegs were thrown into the ravine. The guys did a phenomenal job, just getting the house all the way back where it needed to be."

Like many other colleges, Hanover was a "dry" campus, prohibiting possession of alcohol. When the dean showed up at the fraternity house and didn't find any evidence of a party, he asked specifically to talk to Mike.

"Mike was not a huge partier or drinker," says Murphy. "He'd have his cup and sip on it. He could nurse a cup for a long time just to be social, [but] I'm not even sure he was at the party. But because he was the president, when the college officials came over, he had to go and deal with them."

As Mike stood before Dean Felt, his fraternity brothers wondered what he would say.

When the dean "posed the question to him directly, 'Did you or did you not have a party here tonight, Mr. Pence?' Michael just said, 'Yes, we did, sir,'" recalls Steger.

The dean left after promising the fraternity would face consequences for their actions.

Mike "came to my room right after he'd done this and told me what he'd said and I said, 'Yeah, that was the right thing to do given the circumstances," says Murphy. "Up to that point, we'd been getting this line from the administration of, 'Oh, just work with us and we'll work with you.' So Mike, in the crisis of the moment, decided [to cooperate]. So, he led them to the keg. Instead of treating us better because Mike was trying to work with them, they decided to stick it to us."

Phi Gamma Delta paid dearly for Mike's honesty. The fraternity was put on social probation and their annual spring Fiji party, the highlight of their year, was cancelled. Mike's fraternity brothers were furious.

"We were all pretty discouraged after that," says Murphy. "As a future leader, Mike was learning how to deal with adversity and with people who lie to him."

Returning home to Columbus for the summer, Mike sought his father's counsel.

DAD: "WHAT IS YOUR MISSION?"

"Mike goes home saying to himself, 'I'm not cutting it as president. All the guys are mad at me,'" recalls Steger. "So, he had a series of discussions over the summer with his dad, just talking about leadership, just about, 'How do you do this? What mistakes am I making?' Ed said, 'I'm going to help you, but you're really going to figure this out for yourself.' He said, 'What is your mission? What is this fraternity about? I was never in one. Until you know what you want to accomplish, you're gonna be pretty bad at it.'

"Mike was all puffed up about, 'Well, we study, we do this and we do that,' but by the end of the summer Ed [said], 'You still don't have clarity on your mission.'"

The day he prepared to go return to Hanover for fall classes, Mike finally had a suitable answer for his father.

"He said, 'Dad, I think we're a social organization,'" says Steger. "His dad looked at him and said, 'Then go be the best damn social organization you can be.'"

Mike went back to Hanover with a renewed excitement and vision about leading the fraternity.

"He grew a lot, thought a lot over that summer, and came back and had a blast in every dimension imaginable," says Steger. "Whether it was academics or intermural sports or parties, we won it all, beat them all, and had a hell of a good time doing it."

Murphy agrees. "Mike didn't break. He ended very strongly."

Mike underwent a political transformation when he started taking history classes taught by Professor George M. Curtis III.

"Mike came back to the fraternity house for lunch and throws his stuff down on a chair and says to me, 'Steger, you gotta take this class on constitutional legal history with the new [professor], G. M. Curtis. I say to him, 'I saw the class on the listing and I thought it looks very interesting, but Mike, it just doesn't work in my schedule, I can't fit it in. It's just not going to happen.' Mike literally followed me around for a couple of days, dogging me to take the class. I finally gave in. So, we go to the class and it's utterly fantastic."

Steger credits Mike with not only pestering him to take a class that he thoroughly enjoyed, but also connecting him with his future wife.

"G. M. invites me to his home one Saturday," recalls Steger. "So I'm around there in the afternoon when in walks this lovely young lady who would become my wife of thirty-four years. So, I never would have met Annie had it not been Mike getting me into G. M.'s class our senior year."

Curtis would become a mentor to both Mike and Steger. His impact on them was life-changing.

"Mike grew up as a John Kennedy, Irish Catholic Democrat, and he'll credit [President] Ronald Reagan as moving him to be a conservative, and that's correct to a degree, but it was principally, in the beginning, G. M. Curtis who literally just explained the difference between liberal thought at the time and conservative thought," Steger recalls. "And there were not these kinds of dividing lines that there [are] today. Frankly, I was a political science major and I didn't know what conservative thought was. Our [professors] at Hanover just never even mentioned it. They just taught liberal thought and you thought that's how everything works."

Curtis took both Mike and Steger under his wing and sought to expand their view of the world of politics, but he went the extra mile with Mike and became a mentor to him after he graduated by including him in multiple, rather intense Liberty Fund conferences. The organization's mission is "to foster thought and encourage discourse on enduring issues pertaining to liberty."[2]

Conservatives believe in individual liberty, civil rights, a smaller role of government in the lives of citizens, lower taxes, separation of power at the federal government level, and moving power from the centralized federal government back to the individual states. Through Curtis's guidance, Mike sought out answers regarding conservative thought and how the United States should be led.

"Michael is a thoughtful, synthetic thinker," says Steger. "What I mean by that is he can analyze facts well enough, but he works hard to clearly understand how the details fit back into a unified whole. Michael took the academic route and understood how conservatism works. You may call him ideological, but the reason you have an ideology is because you think there's a way all of this works logically together. Mike is steeped in rigorous study of conservative thought. If you combine that with a guy who is a disciplined reader of the [Bible], add to that a deep passion for both, and the foundations of Michael's servant's heart begin to take shape."

Curtis remembers Mike as an extraordinary student.

"Mike, by nature, was an outgoing person," remembers the former professor. "But he was an extraordinarily good listener as well."[3]

BECOMING A REPUBLICAN

Mike also began to admire Ronald Reagan, who was campaigning for the presidency.

"I started to identify with that kind of common-sense conservatism of Ronald Reagan," Mike says. "Before I knew it, I decided I was a Republican."[4]

There was something about Reagan that he admired, Mike says. "His ideals inspired me to leave the party of my youth and become a Republican like he did.... I don't know if it was the fact that he was an unambiguous Irishman, [or] his Midwestern roots, but he inspired me. I started my career like he did, in radio.... I looked at Ronald Reagan's season as governor and I saw his commitment to pro-growth policies, to lower taxes, to education reform. And I saw him as a solutions conservative."[5]

In the fall of 1980, when Mike was just starting his senior year at Hanover, his parents and sisters moved to a bigger, more expensive home. Grandfather Cawley, newly widowed and ailing, joined them. To the first-generation American, the four-thousand-square-foot house seemed like something out of the movies. It was so big that it would come to be known by the family as the "white whale."

In October, Mike was home for a visit and found his grandfather sitting on the couch with tears in his eyes. He asked Cawley what was wrong. His grandfather, who had grown up in a two-room house in Ireland, shook his head.

"I just never thought a child of mine would live in a house like this," he replied.[6] He died just weeks later, on Christmas Eve.

As Mike's senior year came to a close, he continued to wrestle with what to do with his life—should he go into law and politics... or become a priest? Wavering in his decision, he talked to a Catholic bishop about the requirements for becoming a vicar and applied to the Catholic University in Washington, D.C.

"I think the motivation to be a priest was from his helper's heart," Steger says. "He's like, 'Well, how do you help people do meaningful things in their lives?' When you become a pastor, you're right in the thick of it. So, I think in the early days, it was a seeking, just kind of, 'Is this how I'm supposed to serve?' So, you had this young guy who is wrestling with, 'Should I be a theology major? What am I really doing here?'"

Steger says Mike also grappled with the role of a priest because he didn't feel the ceremonies and rituals of the church fit his gifts very well.

"Michael is a very engaging guy, and certainly pastors and priests can be that, but I think he saw a rub between the formalities of the Catholic Church, especially at that time," Steger adds. "This is when guitar Masses [were considered] controversial. I think he felt that the formalities of the Catholic Church did not mesh well with his personal talents. Michael is someone who connects with people instantly in a very charismatic and engaging way. He desires to bring good things to others. Somehow, he manages to do that gently, with ease and wit."

GIRLS...AND SPIRITUAL GIFTS

There was another significant issue preventing Mike from pursuing the priesthood.

"Girls," Steger says, laughing. "Priests remain celibate and unmarried and I think that had a lot to do with his decision. I don't think he saw his life as one of a single man in the priesthood. I don't think it fit for him. I think he kept saying to himself, 'No, I envision a life with a wife and children.'"

Mike also considered his spiritual gifts. "I looked at my gifts: to articulate, to advocate," he says. "I felt convicted to pursue a long-term goal" in the public eye.[7]

As college graduation drew near, Curtis served as Mike's senior thesis adviser. Mike presented an in-depth, scholarly study on *The Religious Expressions of Abraham Lincoln*, which traced the sixteenth president's religious evolution from a young man who trivialized faith and even wrote an essay arguing against Christianity to a bold believer who read his Bible, prayed, and thanked others for their prayers.

Mike's thesis includes thoughtful insights about Lincoln. For instance, he quoted from Lincoln's September 1864 letter to his friend, the Quaker minister Eliza P. Gurney: "The purposes of the Almighty are perfect, and must prevail, though we erring mortals may fail to accurately perceive them in advance."[8]

In his State of the Union Message to Congress in December 1864, Lincoln declared, "Again the blessings of health and abundant harvests claim our profoundest gratitude to Almighty God."[9]

In a sign of great respect, Mike's classmates voted for him to deliver the senior speech at commencement. He earned his Bachelor of Arts in History on May 24, 1981, with a 3.4 grade point average.

After graduation, Mike took the first of several trips to Ireland to visit his grandfather's hometown—a trip he was supposed to take with Cawley. Ed insisted that his son go, saying he owed it to his grandfather to see the place where he'd grown up and discover his family's origins.

So Mike visited the two-room house amid open, rolling hills where Richard Michael Cawley once lived. Later in Mike's life, his wife framed the photo he took of that home, along with the inscription, *"As for me and my household, we will serve the LORD"* (Joshua 24:15).

By the time he took that first trip to Ireland, Mike was deeply religious, but had decided not to attend Catholic University. Instead, he applied to Indiana University's Robert H. McKinney School of Law. While waiting to hear whether he was accepted, Mike and his fraternity brothers went on one last hurrah together out of town.

"We went to a house way out in the country in southern Indiana," says Murray. "We went there for a big gathering, a bunch of us celebrating seniors from the fraternity. To show our love for Mike, we all picked him up and we threw him in the pond."

The exuberant act caused Mike to become seriously ill with typhoid fever. He spent the rest of the summer recovering at home in Columbus.

TRAVELS ACROSS INDIANA

Mike's first application for acceptance to Indiana University was denied because of a low score on the Law School Admission Test (LSAT). As he pondered his future, Hanover offered him a job as an admissions counselor. Thus, Mike took a break from academics to crisscross the state of Indiana, visiting high schools and promoting his alma mater. Those travels would prove to be beneficial for him in his future endeavors.

Many of his fellow graduates and fraternity brothers stayed around campus, so Mike started a Bible study.

"He lived in a little house on campus," says Murray. "When he came back to work as an admissions counselor, he brought this (toy) bear back with him from being nursed back to health at home that summer. We named it Typhoid Teddy and as my fraternity brothers and I would visit him, we'd do all kinds of things with the bear—take it, steal it, and hang it from places on campus, put it in the freezer, and strap it over his toilet."

It was all done in fun, Murray says. The real reason everyone gathered at Mike's house was because of his spiritual leadership and influence on them.

"I was dating a gal who was still at college, so I'd come back from graduate school and stay with Mike," says Murray. "I'd visit on the weekends. The Word (Bible) in Mike's little living room was opened quite a bit. People were over. I remember a homecoming at his house. It was packed and the Word was open."

Mike's impact on Murray was immeasurable. "His influence on me was really one of being more vocal about my faith and being more of a risk-taker in being more vocal," says Murray.

After graduation, Mike and Steger went their separate ways, but kept in touch. Steger went home to Warsaw, Indiana.

In 1981, "Reagan was just taking off as [Jimmy] Carter was finishing up his term as president," Steger recalls. "We were stuck in stagflation. Jobs, especially for liberal arts under-grads, were tough to get at that time."

Steger couldn't find peace living in Warsaw and reached out to Mike for help. His job "was not what I was looking for," he explains. Besides, G. M. Curtis's daughter, Annie, was still at Hanover.

"So I called Mike and said, 'Look, Annie's down at Hanover. You're at Hanover. You're in a house with an extra bedroom. Can I just come down and stay with you for a while?'" Steger recalls.

Mike let his friend move in and the two young men began to have regular devotional time together, studying the Bible.

"We didn't call it a Bible study; we'd just work on reading the Bible," recalls Steger. "It's kind of like, we had been in this intensive educational program [to earn their bachelor's degrees and] now we had nobody telling us what to read, so we read the Bible. We'd been doing that [at Hanover] so it wasn't anything that was unusual, but it had more of an intellectual streak to it. He might be reading something and say, 'Steger, what do you think of this? What are they really saying here? Would you connect this passage with that passage?' It wasn't anything like every Wednesday at seven o'clock a Bible study." Instead, it was more "constant," a daily devotion to the Word of God.

Steger admired Mike's commitment to Christ and looked up to him as a spiritual mentor.

"He's highly disciplined in reading his Bible, so he gets up and he's at it," Steger says. "It's pretty much the first thing he does in the morning. I tended to read at night. Then we'd just bat it around. We'd talk it through. It was great. That was a wonderful year, where we were just young kids, asking a lot of questions and bouncing ideas off each other. We had a lot of good talks."

After working as an admissions counselor for two years, Mike reapplied to Indiana's University's Robert H. McKinney School of Law. This time, he scored in the eighty-fourth percentile on the LSAT. Mike packed up his things and moved almost a hundred miles north to Indianapolis. At the same time, Steger moved to Indianapolis to attend Butler University, where he became a dorm director for Ross Hall.

"ARE YOU GOING TO SEND ME A BOY?"

"Mike lived in a dingy apartment downtown," recalls Steger. "Back then, downtown Indy was pretty rough. And I knew he wasn't happy down there." Ross Hall was about four miles north of Mike's residence.

"Early on, in my first days, the phone rings and an elderly lady is on the other end," Steger relates. "I answer the phone, 'This is Jay Steger, dorm director for Ross Hall.' This elderly woman with a scratchy voice literally says, 'Are you going to send me a boy?' I just said, '*Excuse me?*' and she says again, 'Are you going to send me a boy?' I said, 'Ma'am, I think you have the wrong phone number.' She said, 'This is Ross Hall, isn't it?' I said, 'Yes.' She said, 'You're the dorm director?' And I said, 'Yes, I'm new here.' Then she just said, 'Oh, okay.'"

Steger says the woman, Zelda Metzger, "went on to explain that she had an agreement with the previous dorm director that he would keep his eyes out for a nice young man who was tight on funds and then she would make the second floor of her house available to him at no charge. She just liked having a man in the house for protection purposes. And so, I'm new in Indy, I don't know anyone, and all my guys at Ross Hall are contracted to have a room at Ross, so guess who I call? I call Michael.

"I said, 'I have no idea what this is about, but if you want to call Zelda, here's her number. The next thing I know, he's moving in about four blocks down the street from where I'm living. Zelda Metzger ends up being the great-great-granddaughter of Lou Wallace, who wrote *Ben Hur*. And we found that out because there was this painting over her mantle place and Mike just said, 'It's a beautiful painting,' and Zelda said, 'My great-great-grandfather painted that.' And Mike asked, 'Well, who was that?' and she said, 'Lou Wallace.'"

Steger and Mike learned later that Metzger was also the great-granddaughter of former Indiana governor David Wallace.

COMPETITORS BECOME FRIENDS

While in law school, Mike began attending meetings of the Christian Legal Society, a non-denominational group that provides law students with resources for faith-based issues. The group's goals include helping law students grow in their Christian faith and aiding them in integrating their faith with the study of law. Mike met Mark Bailey, a fellow law student, at the society. They didn't have any classes together, so the next time they met was during a moot court competition in which law school students argue a case in front of mock judges.

"My partner and I were in the semifinals and came up against Mike and his partner and they thrashed us soundly," Bailey recalls.

The two men quickly became friends and began to spend time together.

"Mike's an excellent speaker, he presents himself well, and he's just a bright guy," says Bailey. "When I got to talk to him outside of the competition, I realized that he's really more of a genuine guy, a guy who's interested in people. And that's not always the case with law students. He was an easy guy to talk to."

Besides their common interest in law, Bailey says they connected over their shared faith. Mike encouraged and challenged him as a born-again Christian, he says.

To this day, Mike "is very faithful to talk about his faith, and God and Jesus, and what they mean in his life," says Bailey. "I think that's a challenge to anybody who knows him, to be reminded that faith is not just something you put on when it's convenient, that if it's genuine, it's got to be a part of your whole life, and that includes sometimes [when] you may be criticized or ridiculed."

After she graduated from law school, Mark's wife, Patricia Bailey, taught legal writing for a year at the Robert H. McKinney School of Law. Although he was not in any of her classes, Mike came to her for advice, encouragement, and individual guidance on legal writing.

"He was very gregarious and very well-spoken and he seemed to just kind of love life," she recalls.

At the time, Mike's profession of faith and willingness to share it openly inspired her, Mrs. Bailey says.

"He was very overt about talking about his faith," she says. "Not in any kind of way that would make people uncomfortable, but he was very comfortable in his skin—and his faith is part of his skin, so he was very comfortable sharing his faith. He was very comfortable when the occasion arose to sharing his journey because his journey was very different than many others' journey. So his faith was part of who he was. They were absolutely not separable."

Mike's ease at sharing the gospel challenged her.

"I was always so impressed with the comfort level with which he shared his faith or shared the existence of his faith," she says. "He's much more comfortable with that than I am in similar settings and that's a constant challenge that he poses to me."

Law school is often very intense and stressful. One of Mike's outlets for relief was drawing a comic strip he created called *Law School Daze* for the student newspaper, *Dictum*. In it, he shared some of his humorous, sometimes sarcastic ideas about law school. In one, a smiling man says, "As your professor, I want you all to realize that your individual performances on the final will in no way effect my approach to you during the second semester..." In the second panel, the man glares and says, "You can rest assured that I will continue to treat each of you with the same conscious disregard for your self-esteem as I have all along."

ENDNOTES

1. Mahler and Johnson, *The New York Times*, July 20, 2016.
2. www.libertyfund.org/about-liberty-fund.
3. Craig Fehrman, "INcoming: Mike Pence. How the governor-elect found his conservative voice and a strategy for winning the race: keep it quiet," *Indianapolis Monthly*, January 2, 2013.
4. Brian Eason, "Trump's VP: 11 things to know about Mike Pence," *The Indianapolis Star*, February 24, 2018.
5. C-SPAN, "Mike Pence Remarks at the Ronald Reagan Presidential Library," September 8, 2016 (www.c-span.org/video/?414899-1/mike-pence-delivers-remarks-reagan-library).
6. Boris Ladwig, "Growing Up as Part of the American Dream," cover story for special commemorative section entitled "Gov. Mike Pence: A Political Journey," *The Republic*, January 3, 2013.
7. Kukolla.
8. Michael Richard Pence, *The Religious Expressions of Abraham Lincoln*, December 14, 1980.
9. Ibid.

5

LOVE & LAW

*He who finds a wife finds a good thing and
obtains favor from the* Lord.
—Proverbs 18:22 esv

Mike was happy for his friend Steger when he announced his
engagement to Curtis's daughter, Annie, yet at the same time, he longed
for a companion of his own. Mike dated occasionally while attending
law school, but didn't find anyone he really felt was wife material.

"Mike had a more mature understanding of what he was looking
for in a mate at a time when most guys don't," says Steger. As a "strong
and vibrant Christian," Mike "wanted a wife who really was on par
with him, somebody who could challenge him and stay up with him at
the same time," someone with "a vibrant faith" of her own.

MEETING KAREN

Mike had been attending a non-denominational Christian church,
but one Sunday morning in October 1983, he went to St. Thomas
Aquinas, the nearest Catholic church. A striking young woman with
dark hair and eyes played guitar and sang during the service. Taken by
her stunning beauty, Mike caught up with her afterward in the church
parking lot and tried to engage her in conversation. He mentioned he'd
also like to play guitar during services. She shrugged him off, saying

he'd have to talk to the person in charge of worship music. Realizing he was getting nowhere fast, Mike introduced himself.

Through their brief interaction, Mike learned her name was Karen Whitaker and her sister, Sheryl, was also attending McKinney law school.

They ended their conversation and went their separate ways. Mike was infatuated, but frustrated. He didn't ask Karen for her phone number. The way she was carrying her guitar hid her left hand, so he couldn't tell if she was single or married.

"He's enthralled with her. It really is love at first sight for Michael," says Steger. "After he talks to her, he beelines over to my office, which is only about three blocks away, and literally talks for an hour and a half, describing everything about her—her hair, her brown eyes, the way she played her guitar, the kind of guitar she played, and so forth. And after this went on for [so long], I said, 'Michael, how long did you talk with this girl?' He said, 'Two or three minutes.' I threw him out of my office at that time and said, 'I've got work to do, get out of here!'"

Mike couldn't get the brown-eyed beauty out of his mind, so he looked for a way to find out if she was married. The first thing he did was call the elementary school where Karen was teaching art. He told them he was working on a church directory and needed to know if he should put "Miss" or "Mrs." in front of Karen's name. They told him "Miss."

Then Mike went to the Indiana University registrar and asked for Sheryl's phone number. No, he was told, it's against the school's rules to give out students' personal information. He walked away... then went back and explained why he wanted the number. His honesty touched the registrar and she relented. Handing him the number on a slip of paper, she jokingly told Mike to make sure she was invited to the wedding.

Hanging out with a buddy later in the day, Mike built up the nerve to call Sheryl to ask for Karen's number. However, when he called,

Karen answered the phone. Flustered, Mike hung up on her. His buddy encouraged him to call her back...so he did.

As it turned out, Karen was babysitting her niece and nephew for the week while her sister and her husband were out of town. Karen remembered Mike from church and invited him over for a taco salad dinner. A few days later, on November 6, 1983, Karen asked Mike to join her and the kids for ice-skating. It became their first of many dates.

Karen's ten-year-old niece bet Mike a dollar that he would marry her aunt.

For her part, Karen says, "When I first met Mike Pence, it was love at first sight." During their first date, she says, "we skated around for a little while and then he reached over and took my hand. Of course, Mike was right there to catch me if I fell.... He has a servant's heart and he always puts others first."[1]

BORN ON AN AIR FORCE BASE

Karen Sue Batten was born on January 1, 1957, to Lillian (Hacker) and John Marshall Batten on an Air Force base. The family lived in Indianapolis, but Karen's parents divorced when she was just four years old. Karen and her mother moved to the middle-class area of Indianapolis called Broad Ripple. Karen found solace in books and became an avid reader. Among her favorite books was *Harriet the Spy* by Louise Fitzhugh. Karen says her second grade teacher, Laila Harman, further solidified her love of reading and being read to.

In 1967, when Karen was ten, her mother married Bernard Barcio, who taught at Karen's elementary, Park School. His love and joy in teaching rubbed off on Karen and she decided she, too, would become a teacher one day.

After finishing sixth grade, Karen transferred to St. Luke Catholic School for junior high. A straight-A student, Karen made the honor roll. When she turned fourteen, she began attending Bishop Chatard High School, a Catholic coeducational preparatory school. A few priests from the Archdiocese of Indianapolis and the Benedictine

Sisters of Beech Grove taught some classes, but the vast majority were taught by lay people.

A popular student, Karen was Speech Club president and a member of the French Club, Cheer Block, Student Council, and the National Honor Society. Karen was so active in the school's extracurricular activities and so accomplished academically that she was named senior class valedictorian. One of her classmates, Steve Whitaker, was her steady boyfriend.

After graduation in 1975, Karen attended Butler University, less than three miles from home, making it convenient and easy for her to stay connected to her mother and stepfather. She majored in elementary education and minored in art.

Karen's love of planes and flying led her to become a licensed pilot. "I haven't kept it current because it's expensive and dangerous," she says. Besides being born on an Air Force base, "my dad worked for United Airlines, I kind of grew up around planes, my godfather had his own plane, and when I was a teenager, I got to fly with him. And it just kind of got in my blood."[2]

Karen and Whitaker wed while he was still a medical student at Indiana University. But the many hours he spent at the hospital for his residency drove the couple apart and they decided to divorce. They later had the marriage annulled by the Catholic Church.

"We were kids," Whitaker says. "We probably didn't necessarily know what we were doing."[3]

Karen earned her bachelor's and master's degrees in elementary education and started her teaching career immediately after graduation. She taught at various elementary schools and was teaching shop at Orchard Country Day School by the time she met Mike.

Both Mike and Karen quickly realized they shared common beliefs in faith, family, and education. They continued to date and their mutual faith in God was the foundation of their relationship. Mike worked hard at being the spiritual leader of the union and guided

Karen into making a confession of faith and receiving Jesus as her personal Savior. Their relationship only strengthened.

GOD MUST BE NUMBER ONE

"When we first started dating," Karen says, "I remember saying something to Mike, something silly like, 'Oh you're my number one.' And he stopped right there and he said, 'You know what? I'm probably going to disappoint you if you make me number one in your life.' What he was talking about was you need to have God as number one. Jesus needs to be number one in your life. [Mike] doesn't mind being number two but he just said, 'You know, I'm human and I'm going to let you down.'"[4]

Six months after Mike and Karen started to date, they attended the wedding of Steger and Annie Curtis. Mike served as best man.

"Mike wrote one of the most beautiful toasts I've ever heard at any wedding," Steger says. "Of course, I'm only a little biased; he was my best friend and my best man, and it was my wedding. But he wrote a toast on 1 Corinthians 13 and he had the entire room both in stiches one minute and then crying the next."

Not long afterward, Mike started to consider the idea of marrying Karen, but it was important to him that she understood his future ambitions.

"When he first met Karen he [knew] he had a mind to play some kind of role in public service and before he proposed to her, he made it very clear that he had envisioned a life in public service," recalls Steger. Mike "wasn't just looking for a helpmate who would say, 'Okay, honey, well that means you're going to go do things at night, you know, social parties or fundraisers or stuff like that. You go do that and I'll take care of the kids.'"

Mike made it clear to Karen that he intended to serve his country in some capacity, as God led him, and wanted a wife who would be with him all the way as a partner.

"Before I married him, he told me, 'In my fifties, I'd like to run for Congress," Karen says. "It was fine with me. I didn't know much about politics."[5]

Mike's friends knew she was the one for him.

"Karen was a smart, highly talented young lady, valedictorian and pilot, who was ready to be side-by-side with him, evenly yoked for the journey they shaped together," Steger says.

ENGAGEMENT AFTER 9 MONTHS

During their nine months of dating, they frequently walked along a canal in Indianapolis to feed the ducks. On August 6, 1984, Mike brought along two loaves of bread. Inside one, he had concealed a small bottle of champagne. The other held an engagement ring for Karen to find as she tore off pieces of bread for the ducks. When she found it, he dropped to one knee and asked her to marry him.

Anticipating the proposal, Karen had the word "yes" engraved on a gold cross. When Mike proposed, she promptly took it out of her purse and presented it to him.

Ten months later, Mike and Karen wed at St. Christopher's Roman Catholic Church in Speedway, Indiana. The registrar who'd given out Karen's sister's phone number was invited and attended the wedding. After a reception at Midway Motor Lodge, the newlyweds left for their honeymoon trip to Nassau in the Bahamas. They soaked in the tropical climate and natural beauty as they spent time getting to know each other as a married couple.

The newlyweds returned to live in a small bungalow in the Broad Ripple neighborhood in Indianapolis. While Karen taught second grade at Acton Elementary School, Mike worked as a law clerk for the firm Dutton and Overman during his last year of law school. He earned his law degree in the summer of 1986 with a B average, grateful that it was behind him.

"No one I know likes law school," Mike jokes. "It was a bad experience. I wouldn't wish it on a dog I didn't like."[6]

Mike applied for positions at various law firms and became active in Marion County Republican politics. It wasn't long before he began practicing with Stark Doninger Mernitz & Smith of Indianapolis, which focused primarily on real estate, business, and commercial law. Mark Bailey had already been working there a month.

"Mike actually joined our firm in June of 1986, so he and I were new lawyers together for several years and had side-by-side offices, sharing all of the challenges of learning how to be a lawyer," recalls Bailey. "When he joined the firm, he and I had adjunct offices and we'd often start the morning in one of our offices or the other with a prayer time and sometimes a Scripture reading."

Rather than eating lunch, they ran three or four miles daily together.

"He talked on a number of occasions [about] how his faith influenced his position on various matters," Bailey says. "He thought he hit the jackpot with Karen."

Mrs. Bailey had already been working for the firm for a couple of years and welcomed Mike on their team, somewhat mentoring him in his new role.

"Philosophically, our firm kind of takes the approach that a young lawyer needs to do a little bit of everything, so he was in that doing-a-little-bit-of-everything period, but he was more interested in litigation and that kind of opportunity at that point," she says. "So whenever more opportunity for that came, he probably got more opportunities to do litigation than someone who wasn't interested in that."

DRAWN TO EVANGELICAL CHURCH

Shortly after Mike began working for Stark Doninger Mernitz & Smith, he and Karen started to attend evangelical churches, eventually settling on one south of Indianapolis.

"I met Karen at some point when he brought her to a Christmas party or firm event," recalls Mrs. Bailey. "She's one of those people I felt like I'd known forever." She praises Karen, calling her "a rock...

grounded [and] deep. She's a force to be reckoned with, but not in a scary kind of way. She's perceptive, a great combination of left brain and right brain. She's very genuine and caring."

Mike often raved about his wife and credited her with being the spiritual backbone of their marriage.

"Karen obviously was a big part of his faith journey," says Mark Bailey. "He's often talked over the years in various settings about her. He'll say she's the real prayer warrior of the family."

Patricia Bailey agrees. "He'd talk like he's the luckiest man in the world to have met her and for her to have fallen in love with him. He was always very, very grateful for Karen, and that she was by his side, and he was always very overt about that."

Mike worked at Stark Doninger for two years before he went to Steger to talk about his frustrations with the job.

"I remember it just so clearly," Steger says. "We were both early in our careers. He was at a downtown Indiana law firm and I was already independent in my own company. I remember him coming over and saying, 'I'm dying. I'm just dying. I spend my whole day reading briefs and then writing up little legal documents.' Here's a guy full of energy, loving people, articulate, and thoughtful, and he just found himself as a brand-new lawyer at the bottom of the totem pole, just reading and writing all day, chained to his desk. He wasn't in a courtroom litigating or defending somebody and he was just bored stiff. It wasn't for him."

Gregory agrees, saying, "Law really wasn't [Mike's] thing.... He's completely unmotivated by money. I don't think he would think for one second about it, if it weren't for Karen."[7]

Mike knew he couldn't just quit his job without something to replace it, so he considered politics, which had always been close to his heart.

"There was no aspiration at the time of, 'Oh, I want to run for Congress, so I'm not going to be an attorney.' He was nowhere close to that in that timeline," recalls Steger. "What he did do around that time was go to the Republican County Chairman, John Sweezy, to talk to him about how [he could] get involved in politics."

John William Sweezy served as Marion County Republican chairman for more than twenty-eight years and was well-known throughout Indiana for helping the party win many elections.

FORGET CAPTAIN; CONSIDER CONGRESS

"Mike was hoping like crazy that the county chairman would say, 'Hey, we can make you a precinct captain' or something along this line," says Steger. "Mike wasn't even clear necessarily how things were organized in the Republican Party, especially in Indianapolis. Mike was envisioning working the polls on Election Day, doing some door knocking, talking to people, and that kind of thing."

Mike met Sweezy and asked him, "What should I be doing now if I want to run for Congress in my fifties?" Sweezy told him, "You should run for Congress now."

Shocked, Mike hurried over to Steger's office to tell him about this conversation.

"Mike was just flabbergasted," says Steger. "He couldn't believe Sweezy was really serious, but Sweezy knew no one was running on the Republican ticket in the district Mike grew up in."

After leaving Steger's office, Mike went right to Karen with the idea of running for the congressional seat. She immediately supported her husband's aspirations and the opportunity that presented itself. Karen was sure that people would appreciate Mike's good qualities, just as she did.

"I just thought that's great," she says. "I think you always think you're going to win."[8]

Mike was twenty-nine at the time and committed to the idea, but was not sure how to run a campaign. So he invited a dozen friends from college and law school over to his house in Broad Ripple for an important announcement. After Karen put out snacks for the men in the living room of their small bungalow, Mike told them why he'd brought them all together.

"Mike says, 'I have something I want to talk to you all about,'" remembers Steger. "He said, 'I've decided I'm going to run for the House.' Then he starts talking about it. We're probably twenty minutes into it and I call a time-out. I said, 'Michael, it sounds like you're talking about Washington, not the State of Indiana House, but Congress,' and he goes, 'I *am* talking about Congress.'"

Although shocked that Mike would seek election to the U.S. House, with no prior experience in public office, his friends were still supportive. Mike announced his candidacy for the U.S. House of Representatives on February 23, 1988.

Mike kept his job at the law firm while simultaneously running for the seat in what was then Indiana's second congressional district. (It was renumbered the sixth district beginning in 2002.) His buddies from that first meeting in the Pences' home signed on to help, with Steger serving as treasurer.

While Mike had the support of Karen, his friends, and Sweezy, his father, Ed, was opposed to Mike running for Congress—or any political office. He made himself very clear on that score.

"Michael said, 'My dad despises attorneys and politicians!' First, Mike became an attorney [and] then he became a politician. So Ed was reluctant, really, when Michael wanted to run for Congress," recalls Steger.

"Ed was really upset about the decision," Nancy says. "At first, he was dead set against it and he really grilled Mike about why he would want to do such a thing."[9]

Furthermore, Ed didn't think Mike had the slightest chance of winning, so he asked Mike's older brother, Edward, to try to talk him out of running.

"It was over Christmas, and I got this call asking me to come over and help talk Mike out of his decision," Edward recalls. Both father and son "thought it was Don Quixote-ish and didn't think he had a prayer."[10]

DAD BECOMES SUPPORTER

But it may have been their father's own philosophy that helped to change his mind eventually. "One thing Dad always preached to us was that we had to climb our own mountain," Edward says.[11]

"In the end, Dad came around," Edward says. "In fact, he became a big supporter and was really helpful in coaching Mike on raising money for the campaign. He took Mike throughout the district and introduced him to all the acquaintances he had made in his business career. It was invaluable."[12]

In fact, Mike's father went beyond fundraising in his efforts to help his son. Less than a month before the primary election, he drove to his son Edward's house with his trunk loaded with Mike's campaign signs.

"He told me to get out in the district and put out those yard signs," Edward recalls. "He was really excited about how things were going for Mike."[13]

With Sweezy's backing, Mike was successful in attaining the support of ten of the eleven Republican county chairmen in Indiana's second congressional district. Thanks to their support, generous Republican donors jumped on board to support Mike. He felt sure he had the nomination in his pocket.

Steger wasn't so sure.

"In our first campaign, we had some good advisors, but we didn't have any major consultants helping us at all and no one had beaten a sitting congressman for ages," says Steger. "In 1988, Democrats had controlled the (U.S.) House since 1933, save four years where Republicans took control. Democratic congressmen didn't lose their seats; they retired in them."

On April 13, less than six weeks after Mike announced his candidacy, he received an unexpected and emotionally fatal blow. While in the office making calls to potential supporters, Mike received an urgent call from a family member. Ed Pence had been playing a round of golf at Harrison Lake Country Club when he suddenly slumped to the ground. He was taken to Bartholomew County Hospital, where doctors unsuccessfully worked to revive him. Mike's father died of acute cardiac arrest that afternoon at age fifty-eight.

Mike was devastated. He left his office and went straight to his mother's side. The Pences were beside themselves, wondering how they'd survive without the family patriarch. Mike put his congressional campaign on hold while the family made preparations for Ed's funeral.

Three days later, family and friends packed St. Columba Roman Catholic Church, where Ed was eulogized as a dedicated husband and father, a successful businessman, and a faithful church member. Mike credits his mother, Nancy, for holding the family together during this difficult time.

"I love my mom. She's my hero," Mike would say. When Ed died, "Mom held our little family together.... She's just the most courageous, amazing person that I know."[14]

Father Davis gives Nancy credit as well. "Nancy had a tragic loss of her husband, leaving her with these kids to continue to be raised," he says. "Her faith was a very important part of that process. She did it. She held it together. She was a single mom and [the] matriarch of the family." Mike's two sisters were still in their teens.

Two days after the funeral, Mike and Steger met for lunch at a local family-style restaurant.

"I look at him and he's just kind of pushing his food around his plate, not looking up, and just depressed," remembers Steger.

Steger understood that Mike was not only grieving, but was also the underdog in the congressional fight.

"DAD DIDN'T RAISE A QUITTER"

"We were kids anyway, it was his first shot at it, and he just lost his dad," says Steger. "The odds of beating an incumbent congressman in those days were very long. I said, 'Do you want me to just shut it down?'

meaning the campaign. Michael slowly raised his gaze at me and said with a clinched jaw, 'Dad didn't raise a quitter.'"

The idea of giving up ended there.

"He was effectively saying, a couple of days after he buried his dad, 'I'm going to get through this and we're charging forward and we're not easing up at all,'" Steger says.

Everyone involved with the race, including the opposition, wondered if Mike would be able to continue the hard-hitting schedule of campaigning and fund-raising he'd been doing before his father's death. But the next business day after his lunch with Steger, Mike was back in the office to call potential donors and out pounding the pavement to secure votes.

Mike won the Republican primary election on May 3 with 71 percent of the vote.

Wearing shorts, a T-shirt, and sneakers, Mike hit the campaign trail on a single-speed bicycle, with Karen biking by his side. A van decorated with "Pence for Congress" signs traveled behind them. Mike and Karen biked 261 miles across the second congressional district in east-central Indiana that hot summer, going twenty or twenty-five miles at a time. They kept their cool when passing motorists yelled at them to get out of the way.

Mike garnered both local and statewide attention. He stopped to talk any time he saw someone in their front yard, working in a field, or running a business. His personable demeanor, ability to relate to fellow Hoosiers, and talk about his vision for Congress and his values earned him support throughout Indiana.

"I think people respond well to someone who comes riding along down the street straddling a bicycle," Mike said during that campaign. "It's nothing more than one person relating to another, and I don't think you can get any more effective in campaigning than that." He hoped it would have "a ripple effect. I can make contact with a few people, then they'll make contact with a few more and it can go from there."[15]

Mike met Mike Murphy, a Republican with political dreams of his own who would eventually become a member of the Indiana House of Representatives.

"Mike's hard not to like," says Murphy. "He's sharp and affable and sincere all at the same time. He's self-depreciating and he's always struck me as a sincere guy who lives his faith. He's not a typical politician. He is what he says he is. This guy's the real deal."

Murphy was impressed by Mike's commitment to his family and his faith.

"You can't understand Mike Pence without understanding his faith," he says. "The more most politicians wear their religion on their sleeve, the more they're fooling around."

Murphy says Mike's walk with God challenged him in his own faith journey. "Just knowing there are people out there who can mix faith and politics is encouraging," he says. "There is room for people full of faith."

A ROCK-SOLID MARRIAGE

Murphy also admired Mike and Karen's marriage.

"They are solid as a rock, a piece of granite," he says. "I see them as a team, a true partnership. Karen is a very smart woman…an equal partner. I always believed what he said, that they make decisions together. She was never classed as just a political wife, but a partner to Mike."

During his first run for Congress, Mike had the chance to go to Washington, D.C., and meet Ronald Reagan, one of his heroes. He didn't know what he should say that might affect the president, so he asked his wife for advice.

"Just say what's on your heart," Karen encouraged him.[16]

"I walked in and I shook his hand. For all the world, it felt like I was talking to Mount Rushmore," Mike says. He told Reagan, "I want to thank you for everything you've done to inspire my generation to believe in this country again." It seemed as though the president blushed, Mike recalls, and Reagan said, "Well, Mike, that's a very nice thing of you to say." It was an "incredible moment" for Mike because Reagan displayed "real humility."[17]

Mike was confident about his chances in the general election against Phil Sharp, a popular incumbent Democrat. But Sharp was a seven-term congressman who had defeated his last three opponents with ease.

Sharp won the election, but it was the closest race in the district's history. Mike's faith-filled, personable campaigning style helped him capture 47 percent of the vote. State officials had told Mike that he had a good chance if he could raise $200,000; Mike ended up raising $350,000. He was far from a loser in the eyes of fellow Republicans.

"It's always hard to lose. Any time you lose, you think, what could you have done," Karen says. "I think I always thought he would win. I have such confidence in him."[18]

With the loss of the congressional race as well as Ed's passing still fresh in their hearts and minds, Mike and Karen decided to take a break and vacation on Sanibel Island, Florida. Located on the Gulf Coast, the island is known for being both relaxing and family-friendly. It was a perfect place for them to recuperate, rest, and reflect on what the future might hold. It was to become one of their favorite vacation spots.

Sharon Disinger, who co-owned WRCR-FM radio station in Rushville with her husband, Louis, called Mike to congratulate him on how well he performed in the race. She reminded him that Ronald Reagan had an early career in radio and offered him a thirty-minute weekly radio slot. They'd call his Saturday morning program *Washington Update with Mike Pence.*

"Our idea was just to keep his name out there," says Sharon Disinger. "It was pleasant radio, like a fireside-type chat."[19]

ENDNOTES

1. Pence4Indiana, "First TV Ad: Mike for Governor," May 15, 2012 (www.youtube. com/watch?v=xomOUS4mO9U).

2. Amos Brown, "Karen Pence Sits Down With Amos For In-Depth Revealing Interview On Her Role As Indiana's First Lady," *Afternoons with Amos*, *The Light & Radio One*, (praiseindy.com/2029883/karen-pence-sits-down-with-amos-for-in-depth-revealing-interview-on-her-role-as-indianas-first-lady).

3. Ashley Parker, "Karen Pence is the vice president's 'prayer warrior,' gut check and shield, *The Washington Post*, March 28, 2017.

4. Jenna Browder, "Indiana Nice vs. DC Vice – Karen Pence on Faith, Family and Her Heart for Healing," CBN News, April 10, 2017.

5. Shari Rudavsky, "Karen Pence is right at home," *The Indianapolis Star*, December 12, 2013.

6. Kukolla.

7. Mayer.

8. Rudavsky.

9. McCawley.

10. Ibid.

11. McCawley.

12. Ibid.

13. Ibid.

14. Kirk Johannesen, "Mom to Mike: Keep your day job," *The Republic*, January 29, 2015.

15. John Schorg, "Riding the 2nd District: Pence 'pedals' his candidacy for Congress," *The Republic*, July 10, 1988.

16. Charlotte Pence, *Where You Go*.

17. C-SPAN, "Mike Pence Remarks at the Ronald Reagan Presidential Library," September 8, 2016.

18. Rudavsky.

19. Michael Barbaro and Monica Davy, "Mike Pence: A Conservative Proudly Out of Synch With His Times," *The New York Times*, July 16, 2016.

6

ROUND TWO

Here is a trustworthy saying that deserves full acceptance:
Christ Jesus came into the world to save sinners—
of whom I am the worst.
—1 Timothy 1:15

The day after he lost the election, Mike and Karen drove through the second congressional district, thanking voters who had supported him. Many had faith he'd win if he ran again and urged him not to give up. Mike assured them that he would run again…if it was God's will.

It came as no surprise to anyone when, six months after his first campaign, Mike filed the necessary paperwork to make another run for Congress. This time, however, he quit his job at the law firm to campaign full-time.

As before, Mike invited his friends to join him for a preemptive meeting. Steger knew from the onset that this campaign would be nothing like the first one.

"First of all, it's in the Tea Room at the Columbia Club in the center of the city, and a pretty fancy place," recalls Steger. "I show up for the meeting a half hour early and no one's there. I wait a little while and I make a few phone calls and say, 'Is this meeting going to happen? Because there's nobody here.' Ultimately, I find out that there's fog in Washington and all the consultants are late for the meeting, which has been postponed for a couple of hours until all their jets landed. I thought, 'Consultants? This is going to be a different campaign.' And it was. Michael took direction from congressional consultants on how to win and he got really focused on [the goal] that he was going to be a congressman and was doing some pretty rough stuff to win that seat."

WASHINGTON INSIDERS

Mike was so focused on winning the election that he essentially put his faith aside. Instead of listening for God's *"still small voice"* (1 Kings 19:12 KJV) and receiving His guidance, Mike chose to listen to Washington insiders. They advised him to eliminate all one-on-one campaigning, focus on television and radio ads, and go hard after Phil Sharp this time around.

Mike's public persona of being a neighborly, approachable Hoosier went by the wayside.

Steger, who had committed to serving as a campaign advisor, knew the consultants weren't tapping into Mike's best qualities.

"I said to him, 'These guys are not playing to your strengths. You just need to be you and people will like you.'"

Mike wasn't convinced. One morning, Steger went to the gym where Mike worked out and followed him around, trying to convince his friend to reconsider his campaign strategy. Forty-five minutes later, Steger left, feeling certain that he'd convinced Mike to launch a grassroots effort like his first run for Congress. Steger began to craft a new game plan.

An hour passed and Steger found himself in a campaign meeting with Mike and the Washington consultants, who shut down his ideas. Steger pleaded his case, noting Mike's previous campaign had gone very well and he now had the name recognition. But his advice was ignored.

Steger stepped down from the campaign. From that point on, he stood on the sidelines and watched what was becoming the perfect storm.

Mike was forced to give up *Washington Update with Mike Pence* because Democrats were demanding equal airtime. "There's always somebody trying to put a bug in things," Sharon Disinger remarks.[1]

The late John Rumple, who served as Bartholomew County Democratic chairman from 1985 to 1989, had once coached Mike for speech contests and took a keen interest in the race. Sometimes, Rumple said, campaign advisers "get carried away. It gives you a very bad taste in your mouth."[2]

In the beginning, the race between Mike and Sharp was close. Mike quoted Scripture as proof of his future success: *"Ask, and it shall be given you; seek, and ye shall find"* (Matthew 7:7 KJV).

However, as Election Day approached, the campaign became uglier. A low point came when Sharp's staffers exposed Mike's campaign finance reports, showing he was using political donations to pay his personal expenses. The practice was legal at the time, but it further tarnished Mike's image and undermined his campaign. He ended up losing to Sharp by 19 points.

The race is remembered as one of the nastiest in Indiana's history. People who were acquainted with Mike were dumbfounded by his vicious attacks against Sharp. To them, the campaign didn't show the wholesome, godly man they knew.

"I wasn't involved with him at the time, but I was very involved with the party, which put me in a position to be a close observer of his campaign," says Ed Simcox, a former secretary of state for Indiana and friend of Mike's. "I remember how disappointed I was in him. And I know how these things can happen. I knew he was perhaps not in control of his campaign, but somebody was in control of it who was taking the low road. And the thing that bothered me most about it was that he was a man of faith and he had energized a lot of people in the Christian community who were excited about his campaign."

The Stegers picked Mike and Karen up after the polls closed and they knew he had lost the race. "We had a big Suburban; Mike and Karen sat in the back seat and we drove them home," recalls Steger.

"On the ride home, I don't think a word was spoken by anybody. It was just quiet. When we dropped them off, he said, 'Love you, man,' and other than hugs, nothing [else] was spoken."

A day or two afterward, the Stegers were getting ready for bed when he mentioned he was worried about Mike. Steger recalls, "I make a comment to her like, 'I hope he's okay. It was a rough loss.' My wife is a prophetic person and out of the blue she says, 'You watch, Karen will be pregnant in no time.'"

Mike admits he fell into a dark place emotionally and spiritually after the campaign.

"It was a terrible experience. A bloodbath," he says.[3] He took full responsibility for the campaign and expressed disappointment in himself for allowing it to get out of hand.

"We lost the race, and lost our mission—to honor God and love your neighbor as yourself," Mike says. "We scarcely did that."[4]

It was, he admits, a moral disaster.

A LIFE-ALTERING CONFRONTATION

Steger says Mike's confrontation with his campaign behavior in relation to his faith was life-altering. "It was a huge turning point in his life to say, 'What kind of leader do I want to be? What kind of person am I?' And effectively, he just realized, 'I just threw the whole spiritual side of me out the window because I wanted to be a congressman.'"

God convicted Mike for the way he handled the campaign and he was feeling it in his soul. More than a pang of conscience or anxiety at the thought of judgment day, Mike felt he was being reproved by the Holy Spirit for his behavior.

"He was in real pain during that time," recalls Steger. "There was very serious soul-searching as he worked his way through that loss and the behavior. He thought about what he should have done versus what he did, who he was listening to [and] who he should have been listening to. He was humbled."

Steger says after Mike's second run for a congressional seat, "he went from being a talented, articulate, hard-working, pretty aggressive young man to a humble adult and…a humble Christian." Mike went to God in prayer, saying, "Lord, what was I supposed to learn from this?"

Steger says this post-election reflection took some time.

"This wasn't something that took a week or two or three to figure out," he says. "This was a long, difficult—I'll use the word dark, in the way, 'I've lost my way, who am I?' Mike kind of said to himself, 'What do I really want?' and 'It matters how I go about getting that opposed to frankly listening to Washington insiders on negative campaign approaches and effectively saying, 'This is how the big boys do it in Washington and so I'm following the big boys.' It was a huge turning point."

Mike felt separated from God because he knew he'd sinned against Him and his opponent, Phil Sharp, in the way he led the campaign. He asked God for His forgiveness, and then felt compelled to seek forgiveness from Sharp. For support, Mike reached out to his friend, Bill Smith, who encouraged him to apologize "and backed him up."

Steger was proud of his friend for reaching out to Sharp and taking responsibility for his actions.

"One of the things I love about Michael is that he's courageous in that way," says Steger.

The effects of the negative campaign lingered.

On November 10, 1990, an editorial writer in the *Indianapolis Recorder* wrote:

"Most people must be breathing a sigh of relief now that elections are over—not because they do not like the electoral process, but few could stomach all the mudslinging that came into their living rooms each night. This year's election campaign has to take the cake for the most infantile, moronic, vicious media advertising in the history of the state, and, unfortunately, very few of the candidates rose above the muck and the slime. The result of this type of campaign is that the important issues are obscured and voters have very little to go on in choosing a candidate."[5]

Columnists and other politicians saw Mike as washed up, with no future in politics—and treated him as such. He spent the following weeks in an emotional funk, wandering around his home, desperately trying to find his way back to becoming the man of God he longed to be.

"He emerged from that a little battered, bloody and bruised, almost to a certain extent embarrassed," says Ed Feigenbaum, publisher of a trio of newsletters on Indiana politics, government, business, and education.

ANOTHER DISAPPOINTMENT

While dealing with this loss, Mike and Karen were grappling with another issue. Although they had been married for six years and tried to start a family, they were unable to conceive.

"An awful lot of [couples] struggle in that way and don't talk about it very much," Mike says. "We were one of them, month after month, hoping against hope that we'd have a family, only to be disappointed again and again."[6]

In her early thirties, Karen was distraught.

"We were ready to start our family, and it just didn't happen," she says. While all of her friends and relatives were getting pregnant, "I remember my little niece looked up at me one day and said, 'Auntie Karen, why don't *you* have any babies?' It can be a very heartbreaking experience."[7]

Even Ed had mentioned it, Karen says, telling them, "'You know, there's never a good time to have kids.'...So, we finally told him...'You know what, we've gone through several procedures, we don't know what's going on, but we can't seem to get pregnant."[8]

Mike and Karen took the matter to prayer, asking God to give them a child. They also wondered why He hadn't answered their request yet.

"All I ever wanted...was to be was a mom," recalls Karen. "I didn't care about fame or fortune, big house, fancy career, nice car—none of that has ever been important to me. I *just* wanted to be a mom. And so my main thing was, how could God put this desire in my heart and not bring me kids?… It made me question Him a lot. I kept thinking, we'd be these great parents; we're ready; we want kids; why don't You bring us kids?"[9]

Not being able to conceive was frustrating. Karen recalls, "We went through a lot of procedures, we went through a lot of struggles with it, and a lot of money, and our doctor just kept saying, 'I really don't know why you're not having kids. I *don't know* why you're not.'"[10] They also signed up with an adoption agency in the hopes of adopting a child.

In the end, they left the matter in God's hands. "We just had to wait until He was ready," Karen says.[11]

She has told friends who have struggled with their own fertility issues to "just hang in there" and trust in God. "You know, if it's going to happen, it's going to happen, and it's going to happen in God's time. You know, we were ready as well to just be a really great aunt and uncle and that would've been okay, too, if that was what God was calling us to," she recalls.[12]

SEEKING CAREER ADVICE

While struggling with the campaign loss and praying with Karen that God would look with favor on them and bless them with children, Mike still had to figure out his next career move. He didn't want to go back into law, but he wanted to do something that dealt with people, politics, and policies. He began to call and meet with people he knew would offer him some sound advice, among them Feigenbaum.

"Mike called me and asked me to go to lunch. We sat down and had a good time," recalls Feigenbaum. "He was not the ogre or demon that I had almost been led to believe he was from a lot of the mainstream media and Democrats back then, and even Republicans who felt he had essentially screwed up the ability to take that seat away from the Democrats. He said, 'I'd like to find a way to use my gifts and talents.'"

As they talked, Feigenbaum encouraged Mike to find a place to use the gifts God had given him, even if it meant pioneering his own way as Feigenbaum himself had done in his own career. Mike left their lunch meeting encouraged and inspired.

Shortly afterward, Mike was approached by friend Chuck Quilhot, who was putting together a project intended to feature the best in Indiana conservative thought. The Indiana Policy Review Foundation (IPR) had been incorporated the previous year and was already producing *Indiana Policy Review,* a journal featuring articles by free-market researchers and academics. Among the goals of the libertarian, free market think tank is to "exalt the truths of the Declaration of Independence, especially as they apply to the interrelated freedoms of religion, property and speech."[13] From Quilhot's point of view, it was time to expand. Mike's political views aligned with the foundation's, so Quilhot offered him the job as IPR's first president.

Mike had been involved with IPR from the beginning, as an advisor, so he was aware of the foundation's core beliefs, purpose, and goals. He took the job.

CONFESSIONS OF A NEGATIVE CAMPAIGNER

In October 1991, Mike published an essay entitled "Confessions of a Negative Campaigner" in *Indiana Policy Review.* It received national attention for its humility, transparency, and remorseful tone. Mike's essay began with a verse from the Bible:

"It is a trustworthy statement, deserving of full acceptance, that Christ Jesus came to save sinners, among whom I am foremost of all—1 Timothy 1:15."

In his mea culpa, Mike wrote:

"In the aftermath of the 1990 election cycle, witness to one of the most divisive and negative campaigns in Indiana's modern congressional history, the words of Saint Paul seem to provide an appropriate starting point for the confessions of a negative campaigner. Negative campaigning, I now know, is wrong," not because it's unfair, "works better for one side than the other, or because it breaks some tactical rule. It is a wrongness not of rule violated but of opportunity lost. It is wrong, quite simply, to squander a candidate's priceless moment in history, a moment in which he or she could have brought critical issues before the citizenry, on partisan bickering."

Winning should be the last "proposition" in a campaign, Mike says. First, "a campaign ought to demonstrate the basic human decency of the candidate. That means your First Amendment rights end at the tip of your opponent's nose—even in the matter of political rhetoric.

"Second, a campaign ought to be about the advancement of issues whose success or failure is more significant than that of the candidate. Whether on the left or the right, candidates ought to leave a legacy—a foundation of arguments—in favor of policies upon which their successors can build."

Mike had no plans to run for office again in the near future, but promised that if he did, he would not run a negative campaign.

"When he wrote the 'Confessions of a Negative Campaigner,' it didn't come anywhere near the grief that Mike felt at that time for the way he had conducted that campaign," says Steger.

"I was very thankful and relieved when Mike did his very public apology," says Simcox. "When he took stock of it after the dust settled, he saw it for what it was and it troubled him and clashed with his spirit. I never doubted his faith and I knew he was a sincere believer, but I also believe ambition at a certain point overrode moral constraints."

Friends say Mike was sincere in his contrite essay and matured as both a person and a Christian during this time.

"When it comes to faith and a deep understanding of it, Mike is just gifted in this way," says Steger. "Mike matured very rapidly as a Christian, in a way that, in many respects, he had to go it alone because very few people except Karen were there for him. He was just always reading more in the Word and made connections with the [Bible]. He's just able to quote chapter and verse. In pushing you if you're stating an opinion or asking questions, he'd say, 'Well, have you thought about this verse?' He spends a lot of time in the Word. I think it is a love of his, but also a real discipline. He [says], 'I've got a couple of minutes, what can I do?' A lot of guys would be watching a ball game and Michael would grab a Bible [with] a longing of, 'Let me get in the Word to better understand some things.'"

HAPPY FATHER'S DAY!

One day while on the road for his IPR position, Mike stopped at a pay phone to call Karen. "Happy Father's Day!" she told him. They were finally going to become parents.

Soon afterward, they received a call from an adoption agency they had registered with, letting them know that they could adopt a boy who was due in July. Karen was due to deliver their first child, Michael Joseph Pence, in November.

"We just felt like it wasn't right for us to still be on that list of parents who wanted to be considered by the birth parents, and so we withdrew our name," Karen says. "Of course, our son has never forgiven us. He goes, "Really Mom, I could've had a brother! Really? What were you thinking?!" But we just felt like God had shown us He was going to bring us a family, and we needed to pull our name off."[14]

Anyone struggling with infertility should consider adoption because it's "a real, viable alternative," Karen says. "Start looking into it, because it was something you know, once we prayed through it...we were 100 percent in. And however God was going to bring us a family, it was going to be fine with us."[15]

Mike and Karen were ecstatic about her pregnancy and repeatedly thanked God for answering their prayers.

Not long after their son was born, Karen decided to expand her education in art and take a class in watercolors. "I told Mike, 'I need a night when you're in charge and I just go have fun,'" she recalls.[16]

Karen's artistic talents blossomed. Mike's mother, Nancy, asked her to paint a picture of her lake house. Karen's sister, Sheryl, commissioned her to paint a portrait of her house. Karen realized she could bring in some extra money for the household by selling her watercolors, both on commission and at art fairs.

Watercolors dry quickly, so it was the perfect job for the mother of a toddler, Karen says, because "you can paint while they're napping."[17]

Karen would end up doing up to thirty-five paintings a year, often selling her work at the Broad Ripple and Penrod Art fairs.

Their prayers for a child answered, the Pences were content and feeling strongly that they were walking in God's grace and blessing. What more could they hope for?

ENDNOTES

1. Darren Samuelsohn, "The old cassettes that explain Mike Pence," *Politico*, July 20, 2016.
2. Kukolla.
3. Kukolla.
4. Ibid.
5. Hoosier State Chronicles, https://newspapers.library.in.gov.
6. Mike Pence, 2016 Indiana Leadership Prayer Breakfast (www.youtube.com/watch?v=jTNmA2A6dvM).
7. Melissa Langsam Braunstein, "Second Lady Karen Pence Opens Up About Her Struggles With Infertility," *The Federalist*, April 25, 2017.
8. Ibid.
9. Braunstein.
10. Ibid.
11. Ibid.
12. Ibid.
13. https://inpolicy.org.
14. Braunstein.
15. Braunstein.
16. Rudavsky.
17. Rudavsky.

7

LIFE ON THE AIR OVER AMBER
WAVES OF GRAIN

May my lips overflow with praise, for you teach me your decrees.
May my tongue sing of your word, for all your
commands are righteous. May your hand be ready to help me,
for I have chosen your precepts.
—Psalm 119:171–173

Mike led the Indiana Policy Review Foundation with great success. While tripling the think tank's fundraising efforts, he brought national attention to its purpose and helped it become a credible voice on Indiana policy and governance. In exchange, IPR provided a kind of refuge for Mike to overcome the lack of confidence and dejection that followed his 1990 electoral loss.

Working for IPR also enabled Mike to pick the brains of the prestigious politicos who surrounded him and consumed its research, increasing his knowledge of other Republicans' ideas and policies. He also began to build a strong foundation of financial backers who would support him for years to come. One of them was Howard Hubler of Hubler Automotive Group, who had a handful of dealerships sprinkled across Indiana.

As president of IPR, Hubler says, Mike "had two jobs: one was to raise money and keep the thing going; and two, his job was to write and be dialed into [what] Indiana wanted for their politics. And Mike said, 'The way I can impact politics or public discourse in Indiana is one, run for office, or two, I can be on the sidelines writing editorials, holding meetings, bringing in famous names, and having events around the city.' I supported Mike financially, attended the seminars, and we'd have lunch all the time."

Spiritually, Mike began to further embrace evangelical Christianity and promote "traditional family" principles and strategies in earnest. He also stopped referring to himself as a "born-again Catholic," instead identifying himself an evangelical, born-again Christian.

During this time, Mike met and got to know Cecil Bohanon, an economics professor at Ball State University.

Bohanon had initial reservations about Mike.

"I thought he was a friendly guy, but I was a little skeptical because I was more libertarian than conservative and I knew he'd been through two rather dicey congressional campaigns," says Bohanon. "I was a little suspicious. But when we started talking policy and talking about writing up commentaries and trying to influence public discussion, I knew we might not see eye-to-eye on everything, but we had a lot of common ground and I grew to really respect and admire him a lot."

Bohanon says Mike was an entrepreneur and a pioneer for organizations like IPR.

"In that time, public policy think tanks were just sort of popping up at a state level," Bohanon recalls. "I remember in Indianapolis, there was a national meeting of public policy think tanks at a state level and Mike was instrumental in getting it put together. Now, that's the State Policy Network, and that's rather instrumental in conservative, libertarian circles. So, he was the father and founder of all of that."

In the meantime, Mike and Karen were blessed with their second child, Charlotte Rose Pence, in June 1993.

"For us," Karen says, "it was really a matter of just letting God bring us kids when He was ready to bring us kids, and that's where they come from."[1]

STARTING A NEW RADIO SHOW

While Mike's career with IPR was going well, he wanted to reach more people. He had a one-hour public affairs show that aired Friday afternoons on a small Christian radio station in Plainfield, as well as Saturday mornings on a nearby AM station. Mike thought he could do more.

"I'm not sure he felt like he had the kind of impact he wanted to have or the reach he wanted to have," says Feigenbaum. "He got the bug in his ear to start a [new] radio program."

Friends say Karen encouraged Mike in this endeavor.

"We were both entrepreneurs at that time," says Steger. "Getting going in radio was particularly difficult. One day, we met at a little restaurant just up the road from the state capitol in Indiana," Acapulco Joe's. Touted as the first Mexican restaurant in Indianapolis, it was a place "political people" went to hang out.

"So we met there and he had an outline for this radio show," says Steger. "By that time, Rush Limbaugh had not only been on the radio, but was an awfully big name. So we talked about the format for the show, some things [Mike] thought would be entertaining for an audience."

Hubler recalls the time well, saying Mike also consulted with him about having a radio program.

"One day, Mike came to me and he said, 'Hey, I've got a job and maybe you can help me with it,'" says Hubler. "He said, 'WIBC has got this talk thing they're working on the local radio station. They want to know if I want to do *The Mike Pence Show*.' I said, 'That sounds great, but what's *The Mike Pence Show* going to be about?'" Mike said the show would be "'what the Indiana Policy Review is about, but I get to talk about it every day for two-and-a-half hours.' I said, 'Great, how can I help?' So, he invited me on the show."

As a successful businessman and fellow believer in Christ, Hubler gave Mike some insights into the state economic climate and industry. Mike ended up having Hubler on the show several times over the years.

Hubler also supported *The Mike Pence Show* financially by advertising his car dealerships.

"Mike knew exactly what he wanted his brand to be and who his audience was," says Feigenbaum. "Retirees and conservative housewives" made up the majority of his listeners and Mike catered to them.

Mike resigned as president of the IPR in December 1993, but continued to write for its newsletter, the *Review*. Mike was "getting too busy in public issues" for his role at the foundation, according to Quilhot.[2]

"It just seemed best for everyone, with my views, to make a clean break," Mike says.[3]

The career change to full-time radio would directly impact the Pence family income, especially now that Karen was home full-time with two toddlers. Things were a little rough financially, but Mike and Karen were committed to doing whatever it took to make it work out.

Mike said, "We just had to tighten our belts to get by," recalls Craig Fehrman, a journalist with the *Indianapolis Monthly* who interviewed Mike continually throughout his career.

Mike approached the Network Indiana broadcast news agency with the idea of going statewide with his radio show. Scott Uecker, creator of the Network Indiana Wire Service and the director of news, operations, and programming, agreed to give Mike a chance.

"There's got to be a certain style or personality there that the audience is going to accept and Mike truly presented himself as, 'I'm just a good Hoosier guy,'" says Uecker. "We had conversations early on about his show, about if you're going to be successful, people need to invite you into their homes on a daily basis to listen. I said, 'If you knock on the door and they slam the door in your face, we've lost. But if you knock on the door and they say they don't agree with your politics, Mike, or agree with you on this issue or agree with you on that issue, but you seem like a decent fellow and want to sit down and make some coffee and [say] we can talk at that point, we've won.'"

Uecker says Mike was the perfect person to head up the show because he was so versatile and affable. With the support of Karen and his friends, Mike jumped into radio full-time.

The Mike Pence Show debuted on Monday, April 11, 1994. It was broadcast from 9:00 a.m. to noon Monday through Friday and eventually aired on eighteen stations across the state, including WIBC in Indianapolis, Indiana's leading talk radio station. Mike also continued to host his weekend political talk show.

Not unlike other radio programs of the time, *The Mike Pence Show* followed a traditional format that included daily news, taking calls from listeners, interviewing guests, promoting non-profits across Indiana, making political points based on his beliefs, and a bit of sports news, such as talk about the Indianapolis 500. With Mike's sense of humor thrown into the mix, the show was a hit.

CLICKING WITH HOOSIERS

To ensure the show's success, Mike worked seventy hours a week and commuted from his home in southern Indianapolis to the Network Indiana studio on the north side.

Mike's daily radio show "seemed to click with mainstream Indiana," says Feigenbaum. "The folks who listened to *The Mike Pence Show* from nine to noon were the folks who were homebound—seniors, a lot of housewives, and, really, the Republican base. And they were Mike's people. Mike was just a natural for the radio broadcast medium. He had this shtick at the beginning, 'Greetings across the amber waves of grain' and he had this habit of shaking the paper he had his notes on or shaking the newspaper. He always had the [*Indianapolis*] *Star* and *The Wall Street Journal* in the studio with him and it was always opened to the editorial pages in both."

During a time in which angry, one-sided tirades were blasted across the airwaves in an attempt to bully listeners into accepting their opinions and points-of-view, Mike's program was refreshingly different. Referring to himself as "Rush Limbaugh on decaf," Mike earned a reputation for being able to present his conservative views in amiable, non-threatening ways and being able to interview people whose policies and beliefs were on the other side of the spectrum. He was able to politely challenge their policies without attacking them personally.

"While Mike is a very devout conservative and Christian, he's open-minded to different perspectives," says Bohanon. "He knows good and well that I am much more libertarian on social issues, yet we've always had good discussions on things. But clearly on issues of reproductive choice, on issues of gay marriage and things like that, he and I are going to see things differently and that's all right. I've always had productive discussions with him. He's a man who mutually respects other positions. Mike believes what he believes and he's probably not going to change that, but he's not a disrespectful person."

Indeed, "His Mikeness," as Mike came to be known, was far gentler and kinder than "Rush Limbaugh on decaf." He took particular care to treat everyone with courtesy.

"My obligation first as a Christian is to try to respect that person" who has a different point of view, Mike says. "There's a great misunderstanding out there about this. If you can't disagree and maintain some civility, then forget democracy."[4]

As a radio show host, Mike was never mean or angry, even when a guest was hostile. He was so likeable and pleasant that even guests who disagreed with his opinions enjoyed being on his show.

Uecker says Mike got along with everyone.

"Even Democrats in the state of Indiana didn't hate him and back then, even Democrats would do his show because they knew Mike would give them a fair chance," says Uecker. "Mike wasn't going to try to trick them in their own words. Mike was just going to ask some tough questions and at the end of the show, Mike would say, 'Well, we're just going to have to agree to disagree.' He wasn't threatening. He was just the nice guy."

THE BENEFITS OF LEGAL TRAINING

Simcox points out that Mike used the best of his legal training to his advantage.

"The mark of a good lawyer is you can fight an issue and you can represent your client and pull no punches and go toe-to-toe with another lawyer, but when it's over, you have no less respect for that lawyer if you beat him or her, or if he or she beats you, than you had before going in," says Simcox. "If you're a good lawyer, you have the ability to look at it dispassionately and understand it as not something you seek to destroy somebody, but something that you're doing for your advocacy and what the other person is doing for theirs. I've always admired people who could do that."

Steger agrees, saying Mike's personality suited his career in radio.

"Mike's public persona back then was much more light-hearted," says Steger. "He saw it as a way to use some gifts that he had to speak well, but I think just as importantly, he was able to appreciate people who disagreed with him and did so affably."

Mike's faith framed his show and listeners were often reassured that all of his convictions were biblically based.

"You knew Mike was a man of faith," says Uecker. "He was not going to run away from his faith, but he wasn't going to take a Bible and thump you over the head with it either. He respected you for who you were. He was a man of faith and he expected you to respect him for who he was. You could tell he had a certain set of Christian values and he was never going to stray from those. And I never saw him take a position that was counter to his faith. Whether you agree with him or disagree with him, I can respect a person for being that grounded in their values."

Although Uecker was Mike's boss, he says Mike's faith and the way he demonstrated it on a day-to-day basis caused him to look up to Mike as a spiritual mentor. He also admired the way Mike handled his personal life as a husband and a father.

"He talked about Karen a lot, and you could tell she was his love," Uecker recalls. "He did like to brag on his wife. A lot of people think Mike's joking when he says Karen's the boss, but she really is. My wife had a lot of respect for Karen and how she was raising their children and I had a lot of respect for Mike for the way he treated his wife. He was a good family man and a good husband. They were just starting to have kids back then and you could tell that fatherhood was something he was so very proud of. I [also] respected him a lot because I knew his faith was important to him and it wasn't just an act. I looked at him and thought, 'I want to be like that myself someday.'"

Steger says Mike would often use the catch-phrase, "I'm a conservative, but I'm not mad about it."

Mike "has a particularly strong talent, a gift if you will, for being able to stick to principle while making his political opponents or those who disagree with him feel like they are being heard and respected," says Ryan Streeter, a former aide who's now director of domestic policy studies at the American Enterprise Institute.[5]

When Mike knew he was going to be discussing highly charged topics, he used his sense of humor to ease any tensions.

Mike's brother Edward remembers the time Democratic Gov. Evan Bayh came on *The Mike Pence Show*.

"I remember that Mike had told him before they went on the air that he was going to be asking a lot of tough questions and probably put him on the spot," Edward says. "I'm sure that Bayh was expecting some pretty tough questions about political philosophy."[6]

Instead, Mike asked Bayh, a soon-to-be, first-time father of twin boys, to define "Binky" and "woobie"—names, respectively, for a pacifier and snuggly object such as a blanket.

In September 1995, Mike expanded his audience by taking over a Saturday morning television call-in show that debuted on WNDY-TV in Indianapolis, furthering his opportunities to share his conservative political views and his faith.

John Kenneth Blackwell, former secretary of state for Ohio and senior fellow at the Family Research Council, refers to Matthew 5:16 and how Jesus encouraged His disciples *"to let your light shine before others."* Mike does that, he says.

"While all of us have a candle, there are those who put it under a bush," Blackwell says. "They don't put it on a candlestick and pierce the darkness. Mike is one of those guys who has not hidden his light under a bushel; he's put it on a candlestick and he's threshed the darkness."

CARING FOR "THE LEAST OF THESE"

The Mike Pence Show did more than touch on political issues. Mike shared and fought for his core beliefs about supporting widows, orphans, veterans, and the elderly. Bohanon recalls a conversation about *"the least of these"* (Matthew 25:40) he had with Mike regarding Social Security.

"Mike said he thought of Social Security as being a sacred contract between the government and the people and that it was something that must be maintained," says Bohanon. "Mike would make sure it's fully funded, he'd want to make sure it's viable, and he wanted to make sure the thing didn't go bankrupt."

Mike's radio shows gave him great statewide name recognition and as his popularity soared, more and more Hoosiers tuned in every day.

Through his program, Mike garnered lists of conservative contacts and established an even larger national network of wealthy supporters who advertised on his show and saw him as someone worth investing in for the long haul.

Mike was given the freedom to share his faith on his show and did not shy away from using Scripture verses from the Bible to support the topics under discussion. He also frequently talked about his relationship with God and belief in the Ten Commandments.

In May 1997, Mike tackled the subject of Air Force Lt. Kelly Flinn, who was discharged for disobeying the regulation prohibiting relationships between officers and enlisted personnel and lying about her adultery with another man who was married. The media and some politicians expressed outrage that Flinn was prosecuted while the military has seemingly turned a blind eye for years on male officers who've done the same thing. Mike saw it differently.

"Is adultery no longer a big deal in Indiana and in America?" he asked. "I'd just love to know your thoughts because I, for one, believe that the seventh commandment contained in the Ten Commandments is still a big deal. I maintain that other than promises that we make of fidelity in our faith, the promises that we make to our spouses and to our children, the promises that we make in churches and in synagogues and marriage ceremonies around this, it's the most important promise you'll ever make. And holding people accountable to those promises and holding people accountable to respecting the promises that other people make...what could possibly be a bigger deal than that in this country?"[7]

Listeners loved *The Mike Pence Show*, but were often confused about Mike's political affiliations. "People [would] call in and say, 'I'm trying to figure you out. Are you a conservative or are you a libertarian?' And I took to saying, 'I'm a Christian, a conservative, and a Republican in that order.'"[8]

CHILDREN FROM GOD'S "PERFECT TIMING"

It wasn't long after he began working full-time in radio that Mike and Karen learned they were expecting their third child, Audrey Ann.

"In retrospect, I look back, and I am so glad that we didn't have our kids when we wanted to have them.... As it ended up, He brought us three kids boom, boom, boom. And it's just been wonderful. It's been such a privilege," Karen says. "Now it's so clear to us that that was the perfect timing, these kids are the perfect kids for us, and we couldn't be more grateful every day that He gave us that privilege."[9]

Having three children under four years old changed Mike, Steger says.

"He was head-over-heels for Karen, of course, but the kids brought a richness to his life, perhaps because he and Karen had faced the real prospect that they would have none," Steger says, citing the difficulties they had in conceiving. "He became a dad—that brought a joy to his life. It was a feeling of completeness. He said, 'I have children. I have a boy and two girls. I am blessed. Everybody's healthy. I've got this fun little family.'"

As Mike's children were born, his own father wasn't far from his heart or mind. He often wondered about his father's military service and how it may have affected his outlook on life. He knew his father had earned a Bronze Star for courage under fire, but it wasn't something he proudly displayed or talked about. After he returned home from Korea, Ed Pence placed the medal in a dresser drawer, never to be taken out or shown to his children.

It wasn't until he had a talk with a cousin who had grown up with his father in Chicago that Mike came to realize the level of pain that had haunted Ed Pence.

"He told me that the war had changed my dad," Mike says. His cousin told Mike, "'Before the war, your dad was the most happy-go-lucky guy I ever met, but...after he came back, he was different.' And then he said words I'll never forget. He said, "I don't think your dad ever got over the guilt of coming home."...In those words, in an instant, I understood every unfinished sentence, every far-away look on my father's face, whenever the war came up. If he talked about it at all, he'd talk about the guys he served with, guys who didn't get to come home, to marry their sweetheart, raise a house full of kids, live their dreams and see their children's children. And that's when I understood the quiet cost of freedom and the burden so many of our veterans bear in their hearts."[10]

With his own busy household and the radio show gaining in popularity, Mike found himself in demand as someone with experience in politics and campaigning.

One day, Mike received a call from David M. McIntosh, who had served in the Reagan administration as special assistant to the attorney general and special assistant to the president for domestic affairs. He'd also served as executive director in George H.W. Bush's administration under Vice President Dan Quayle's Council for Competitiveness.

"I decided I wanted to try to run for Congress myself and we were living in Phil Sharp's district," recalls McIntosh. "So I asked Mike if he'd go to lunch with me to talk about his experience in doing that and get his advice. We met at a Mexican restaurant in downtown Indianapolis; it was a little hole in the wall with Formica tables and plastic chairs.

"We spent a couple of hours talking about it," McIntosh says, "and he drilled me. *What do I believe in? Why am I running for Congress?* I shared with him the work I'd done for President Reagan and Vice President Quayle, basically fighting for conservative issues and that I wanted to run on those issues. He looked at me in the end and said, 'I was going to tell you don't do it. It's too hard to beat an incumbent, but if you're willing to go and talk about those issues and fight for those issues, then you should go do this race regardless of whether you win or lose because you're advancing the cause of freedom and conservative values.' [Mike] also said, 'In the end, you need to go to God and get a sense of what He's calling you to do.'"

Mike had one other piece of advice: don't run a negative campaign.

"He gave me a copy of 'Confessions of a Negative Campaigner,'" says McIntosh. "He said, 'You can run a strong campaign on the issues and raw contrast between your position and a liberal Democrat, but never let it become a negative campaign."

OFFERING SISTER'S HELP

Then Mike mentioned his sister, Annie, could help McIntosh run for office.

"He said, 'By the way, my sister helped me run the race and she's available if you need somebody to help you', at which point I said, 'Absolutely, I don't have any campaign staff.'" Since Annie knew the district, she could be a major asset, McIntosh knew.

McIntosh and his wife, Ruthie, had just moved to Muncie, Indiana, and had been driving around to meet people, but they wanted to make his name more widely known. While they were out networking, to everyone's surprise, incumbent Democratic Congressman Phil Sharp announced that he would not be running again because he had decided to retire.

"Mike could have decided to enter the run then," recalls McIntosh, "and the Republican Party asked him if he wanted to do that because he had better [name recognition] and a contributor list. [But Mike] said, 'No, I want to keep doing and building my radio show and I think David McIntosh would be a great candidate.' He chose not to and therefore gave my campaign the green light to continue."

Knowing a new Democrat who was possibly well-known would step up to the plate, McIntosh knew he needed all of the support he could get.

"So Annie helped me out," says McIntosh. "She became my campaign manager for the primary and we hired a young, college Republican who had just graduated from [Indiana University] and the two of them and my wife Ruthie and I started that journey. Mike was helpful, supportive of me, and gave me his donor list. And really, with his help and Annie's help, we raised the money I needed to win the primary, [which] we won by 450 votes in a close race."

Mike invited McIntosh on his radio show to give him even more name recognition and enable him to share his conservative values with listeners.

"In the course of that, Mike and Karen invited Ruthie and I over to their house a couple of times to really share what it was like for a family to run," says McIntosh. "We didn't have children at the time, but I remember Karen sharing with Ruthie that, 'Now, without children, you can participate and work during the day and go and meet up with David for a campaign event at night and really make it a family event.' And that helped us know how to do it and feel good and comfortable with it."

Mike's advice to McIntosh not to run a negative campaign hit a wall at one point.

"There was a time where the consultants presented an issue to me that was more of a personal attack" on an opponent, McIntosh says. "I was troubled by it and I went and asked Mike what he thought and Mike reminded me, 'Yes, you want to stay away from the negative, personal attacks. Beware of consultants who will flash and burn and then leave you after the election.'"

After a hard-fought race against Democrat Joe Hogsett, a lobbyist, McIntosh was elected to Congress in November 1994.

ENDNOTES

1. Braunstein.
2. Kukolla.
3. Ibid.
4. Brian Blair, "Open Mike: Columbus native's radio show, Saturday TV debut demonstrate he has learned diplomacy," *The Republic*, Columbus, IN, September 17, 1995.
5. Brian Slodysko, "Pence's unflappability could help Trump stay cool," Associated Press/*The Indianapolis Star*, July 12, 2016.
6. McCawley.
7. Samuelsohn.
8. C-SPAN, "Q&A with Mike Pence," January 19, 2006.
9. Braunstein.
10. Remarks by the Vice President at the National Veterans Day Observance, Arlington National Cemetery, Arlington, VA, November 11, 2017.

8

ACCOUNTABILITY

As iron sharpens iron, so one person sharpens another.
—Proverbs 27:17

With three young children and two thriving careers—Mike in radio, Karen painting watercolors and working part-time as a teacher—the couple were able to build their dream home. It was around this time that Mike met Gary Varvel, political cartoonist for the *Indianapolis Star*.

"I had just started as the editorial cartoonist in late 1994 and Mike had a radio and television show," recalls Varvel. "His producer contacted me and asked me to be on the show and Mike and I just hit it off. We both had three kids; we're both around the same age, both starting to gray, and were both Christians. There are just some people you meet, especially believers, where you feel a connection. We started having lunch together and we'd talk about family and the Bible, what we had read that morning. That was an important thing with him."

It wasn't long before the men were confiding in one another and Mike shared his disappointment over his last congressional run.

"He told me he made a big mistake taking advice from political campaign guys," Varvel recalls. "He said, 'We ended up doing things that really wasn't me.' They really attacked his opponent. He said, 'I wasn't comfortable with it, but I went with it and I was embarrassed by it.' He thought his career in politics was over and he'd just end up doing politics from the outside."

As brothers in Christ, Mike and Varvel encouraged one another to walk in their individual spiritual journeys and held each other accountable to walking in the Christian faith.

Karen and Mike began attending a non-denominational fellowship called Grace Tabernacle Church every Sunday. Hubler, meanwhile, was attending the Community Church of Greenwood, where Charles Lake served as pastor. At that time, the church had a thousand members.

"One day, Charles came to me and said, 'Teach a class on the upcoming political cycle,'" recalls Hubler. After agreeing to lead the class, Hubler asked Mike to come and speak to the group.

"Mike came and spoke a week or so later," recalls Hubler. "We had breakfast afterwards and he gave me a prompt. He said, 'You know, if somebody invited me back to that church, my wife and I would go there and see if that's where we want to worship.' He came the next Sunday and then my wife and I hosted them two or three more times. That's when he began coming to the church."

Jim Dodson, who was the assistant pastor and administrator of the Community Church of Greenwood, remembers the Pences' coming to services there.

"As part of assimilation ministries, I always followed up with newcomers," says Dodson. "I'd never heard about Mike, but someone on staff told me he was a guy that had a radio program in town and had visited the church. Our senior pastor, Charles Lake, asked me to make contact with him. I made an appointment and he broke it. He broke it at least five times, but I want to say it was nine times, and he always had a reason. Finally, one time he didn't cancel on me. I got to the restaurant first and waited at a table."

Mike eventually showed up and sat across from Dodson.

"He sat down and looked at me with this wonderful smile he has," Dodson recalls, "and just laid both hands down on the table and said, 'You are the most persistent person I've ever met in my life!' I said, 'I'm just doing my job!'"

The two men laughed, started talking, and hit it off.

"We talked about what he did for a living, his family, and what church he was coming from," says Dodson.

Shortly after that initial lunch, Pastor Lake challenged his staff to look for ways to disciple or teach people who were coming to their church in hopes of seeing spiritual growth. Dodson took this task seriously.

FORMING ACCOUNTABILITY GROUP

"I went to Mike and said, 'Hey, I'm forming an accountability group and I'd love for you to be in it," Dodson remembers. "I told him it would be four people and we'd meet on a weekly basis, [and] that during the week, we'd all study a passage of Scripture, then discuss it. We'd share our lives. We'd share our prayer concerns. We'd share insights into what we study, and we'd eat together and enjoy some fellowship and then go on with our week."

Dodson intended the group to follow the advice of Proverbs 27:17: "*Iron sharpens iron.*" This biblical analogy means that one man can help sharpen another by his life experiences, perception, and views on God and His Word, the Bible.

"Mike was the first guy I asked and I kept waiting for an answer and he didn't give me one, but persistent me, I kept asking," says Dodson. "And finally, he said, 'I'll tell you what, if you can get Howard Hubler to be in the group, I'll join.'"

That was all the encouragement Dodson needed. "I called Howard and told him I needed him in it," says Dodson. "I told him Mike Pence said he'll be in it if you will and so he agreed. I wanted another person in the group so I asked Garry [Smith] to join it because he wasn't really connected in the church."

Smith remembers that day well. "Jim and I had been meeting for accountability and he said, 'Hey, would you mind if I bring a couple of other guys for a foursome?'" recalls Smith. "I asked him who he was thinking and he said, 'Howard Hubler and Mike Pence.'"

The four men met "almost every Friday morning at seven or eight o'clock" at the Four Seasons Family Restaurant in Greenwood, remembers Dodson. "Mike was extremely diligent. Every week that we met, Mike had always read the Scriptures we were doing and he was prepared to comment on them. Not all of us were. He always had insight on the Scriptures. It was so much about everyday life and what we were doing and how we were living."

Initially, Pastor Lake kept a watchful eye on the group. He had heard of Mike and knew he "was accused of some improprieties on the final day prior to the election, which some people said cost him that election," Lake recalls. "So, when I first met him I was a little bit skeptical. That changed very quickly. One of the biggest items that made that change was his desire to be a part of Jim Dodson's small group and be held accountable for discipleship in the Lord.

"Discipleship was our major thrust as a church," Lake explains. "Mike's commitment to the disciplining emphasis of the church was very sincere and demonstrated by his commitment to it. And his growth was accelerated by his willingness to be a part of a small group and be held accountable."

All four of the men matured in Christ as they continued to meet, confiding and leaning on one another for strength and wisdom.

"For me, it was a great time for me to witness Mike's spiritual power walk because I was pretty much the spiritual weakling of the group," says Garry Smith, reflecting back on that time. "I remember sitting there in awe just having these men of God explaining their faith—and they were so grounded. It was important to me at the time because I acted like I was a Christian on Sundays, but the rest of the week, I didn't."

The four men bonded spiritually and emotionally as they challenged and encouraged one another on day-to-day issues.

"You hold each other accountable to certain things," explains Dodson. "If you're in [a] group, you have to be willing to be transparent, you have to be willing to be responsive and honest about things. And you have to be willing to answer hard questions."[1]

"We prayed fervently for each other," says Smith. "We were more than a Bible study. We were an accountability group and prayer warriors for one another. We would reference Scripture and how it applied to various areas we all struggled in. The group totally transformed my spiritual walk."

DEEP, ABIDING LOVE OF PEOPLE

For Mike, it was more than just a weekly get-together to discuss the Bible. It was a bonding of friends and brothers in Christ and Mike treated the other three as such. Lake says part of Mike's allure is his deep, abiding love of people like the men in his accountability group.

"When you're talking with Mike, he's not talking to you and looking in another direction at somebody else to see if something better is going to come along," says Lake. "When you're talking to Mike, you have his undivided attention and you feel like you're the most important person in his world."

In Mike, Smith saw a mentor and spiritual hero.

"Mike was a champion in my eyes; I saw a guy I wanted to be like," says Smith. "He was articulate in his speaking, versed in Scripture, and he liked to say, 'Let your yes be yes and your no be no' (Matthew 5:37). I got to see how Mike ran his radio show and how Howard Hubler ran his automobile businesses on the firm foundation of the Bible and I just thought that was so cool, that the Bible's the rule. Before that, I didn't realize that."

Dodson says Mike challenged his faith walk as well.

"One of the things I appreciated about Mike was the balance and the authenticity and transparency in the way he practiced his faith," says Dodson. "He weighs things and considers them. He's not impulsive in making major decisions without really taking time to discern and listen to the Lord's voice. I've watched him discern what it is God wants him to do. I've watched him be patient as he makes decisions. I've watched him seek the counsel of others rather than just [depending on] himself."

Garry Smith agrees. "He is fervent in his belief and stands on it. He's not two-sided or double-tongued."

Echoing Smith and Dodson, Hubler says Mike was the spiritual rock of the group. "He did a great job of always steering us towards God's Word."

Although the men's wives were not directly involved in the group, Dodson says Karen sought ways to impact the lives of the men and their families and minister to them.

"We had just started our accountability group," recalls Dodson. "I had open-heart surgery and one day Karen called and she said, 'Hey, we want to bring you an evening meal.' As busy as they are, she came and cooked us dinner, stayed and visited, and ministered to my wife, Sharon. She's such a reflection of Mike. She's such a team person with Mike. Our relationship wasn't with Karen. The relationship was with Mike, but Karen came and ministered to my wife and showed care for me. That's just the kind of people they are."

Pastor Lake says the faith of Mike and Karen is an inspiration to all who meet them and get to know them.

"One of the things that impresses me about the Pences is, I think their faith is a very practical one," says Lake. "It's not that they just believe the right things—they apply it and work it out on a daily basis in what I believe to be a very practical manner."

Mike's relationship with Karen was one of the things Lake has admired most about him.

"That's one of his major attributes," says Lake. "From the very beginning to this very day, I don't know of any men that I've seen more committed to a wife, children and family as Mike has been."

Mike took his role in the accountability group seriously and sought ways to encourage, lead, and mentor the men. Smith and his wife had struggled with infertility and were given the opportunity to adopt through the church. While sharing his and Karen's own struggles, Mike encouraged and prayed for the Smiths through the adoption process. Mike also took Hubler under his wing outside the group.

"Part of that time, I was going through a divorce and Mike said, 'You know, I want to mentor you in the Christian faith about your divorce,'" says Hubler. "So there were times Mike came to my dealership. We had one of these big picnic tables and we'd eat lunch and talk about my pending divorce."

Mike used Scripture verses to encourage Hubler to commit to giving his all to the marriage.

"He mentored me," recalls Huber. "Most of the things he said were top-of-mind. All these Scriptures, he had command of just casually as a lay person and they were all Scriptures I'd have to look up. Mike's faith was always three steps ahead of mine. I'm versed enough in the Bible, but Mike has the Scriptures memorized. Mike knows the story and the story behind the story. It was like sitting with a pastor. Mike was very good. He asked questions [such as], 'Before you would ever divorce, is there anything out there, anything that would change the state of affairs?'"

TEASED ABOUT "STANDARD ISSUE"

There was levity among the group as well. Mike's powerful faith had done nothing to quell his quick sense of humor and he often teased the other three men. They dished the ribbing right back at him.

Mike "was always dressed to the nines," recalls Smith. "We called his outfit the Mike Pence Standard Issue, which Howard Hubler came up with."

Hubler laughs as he relates Mike's "standard" outfit: "a navy-blue sports coat, a white shirt, a club tie, khaki pants, and blue military shoes that had the soles worn out and navy-blue socks."

The other men tried to get Mike to push the envelope a little bit with regard to his fashion sense, but he wouldn't budge. He did wear different ties occasionally.

While Mike was meeting with his accountability group, Karen pursued opportunities to serve in the church. Along with taking dinners to the sick, she'd stop and pray for anyone who needed it. She also made her family vulnerable and transparent by asking for help when she or her family needed it.

"That's the kind of person she is, a person who believes in prayer, a godly mother and wife," says Vicki Lake, the wife of Pastor Charles Lake. In fact, "Karen would send out prayer requests to people—to pray for them as a family, that God would give them the strength to do all that they had to do."[2]

Mrs. Lake wrestles with a disease that hinders her red blood cell production and has been a recipient of Karen's continued prayers and kindness.

"I personally get an occasional text asking me, 'How are your numbers?'" she says. Once, while Karen was visiting, "she grabbed my hands and we prayed together in my laundry room."[3]

POPULAR ON CONSERVATIVE CIRCUIT

With every passing year, Mike's radio show grew in popularity and he was continually in demand to appear on other radio and television programs on the conservative circuit.

"He was invited to Heritage [Foundation], gun owners' groups, property-rights groups, pro-life groups, and pro-Israel groups. People started to see an authentic, affable conservative who was not in a bad mood about it," recalls Kellyanne Conway, who was a friend and colleague.[4]

Hubler and Mike continued to meet outside of the accountability group. One morning, Hubler had something for Mike that would begin a chain of events that revealed God's hand working in the Pences' life.

"One day, we were sitting at a restaurant and Mike and I were having breakfast," says Hubler. "When we were done, I handed him a check and it said, 'For the Mike Pence Exploratory Committee.' Mike said, 'Hubler, what are we exploring?' And I answered, 'We're exploring [whether] you should run for office."

But Mike didn't have the confidence in himself that Hubler seemed to have.

"He said, 'Well, I appreciate this, but why do you think I'd be the ideal candidate?'" Hubler relates. And his friend spelled it out for him. "I said, "Mike, you've been on the IPR for as long as I've known you—probably five years there. And you've been doing this WIBC radio program. You know there are state legislators who are not consumed with Indiana politics as much as you are. In fact, unless you're in the government, nobody is entwined in state politics like you are and you transcend a couple of governors, you transcend hundreds of state legislators. There's simply nobody who knows our state like you do. You come and speak about Indiana and you don't need five minutes of research. It's all top of mind. You're going to run against some kid who thought it would be great to run for Congress who knows nothing."

Mike admitted to Hubler, "Well, you make it sound pretty compelling."

Reflecting on that time, Hubler says, "He was that guy. There was no other guy out there. Nobody was as steeped in Hoosier politics as Mike Pence was at that time."

Mike had previously come to terms with the fact that he'd never fulfill his childhood dream of serving in Congress, so Hubler's suggestion took him off-guard. In fact, Mike had told a reporter, "I'm done dreaming. All my dreams today have to do with my faith and wife and kids. I take all the rest a day at a time. I say that from my heart because my lifelong dream was always to serve in Congress."[5]

CONGRESSMAN GIVES UP SEAT

Yet around the time of Hubler's proposal, the Republican Party was recruiting Congressman David McIntosh to run for governor.

"Before I said 'yes' to that, I wanted to know that the seat I had worked so hard to win and build up would stay in a conservative Republican hand," says McIntosh. "I went to Mike and Karen and said, 'I really wish you guys would think about running for [my seat]. I want to say 'yes' to this offer to run for governor, but I want to know that we have a good congressman.' Their first answer was, 'No, I've moved on. I have a new career in media.'"

Mike loved doing radio and the show was a commercial success, both popular and bringing in advertising dollars.

McIntosh, a fellow believer in Christ, knew just how to convince Mike to reconsider. He encouraged Mike to go home and pray with Karen about the matter.

Shortly after his lunch with McIntosh, Mike met with his good friend Bill Smith, a Capitol Hill veteran who had founded the Indiana Family Forum in conjunction with Dr. James Dobson and Focus on the Family.

"You know, Bill, I thought my career in politics was over," Mike told Smith, who committed right then to join Mike and Karen in prayer over the matter.

Mike petitioned other friends to join him and Karen as well, including his accountability group.

"One day in our meeting, he said, 'I want to talk to you guys about a prayer concern.' And it was a different tone, so we all perked up," recalls Dodson. "He said, 'I'm considering running for Congress.'"

Of course, Dodson knew that Mike had run for Congress twice before and had lost both times—"two times a losing proposition." He remembers Mike "had pretty much determined he never wanted to do that again. So when he said it, it shocked me. I was so unprepared for that because he had written it off. I was like, 'A third time? Really?'"

Mike's prayer request also caught Garry Smith by surprise.

"He said he'd been thinking about it for a couple of months," relates Smith. "Then he said, 'I was a different person when I ran the first time and my life has changed.' He said, 'Over the years, I didn't act like a Christian. Since then, I have humbled myself. I'm ready to tackle it now.'"

Dodson remembers Mike admitted to the group that "in his previous two campaigns, he had been extremely negative." And Mike promised, "'If I run this time, I won't do that.' He said that win or lose, he wouldn't do that again. He regretted it."

Mike had to take Karen's views into consideration as well. While she was supportive of Mike, she wanted to make sure it was God's will for them to run again.

Dodson recalls that Mike told the group, "Karen is very hesitant about it…. You know, we need to do this together and I'm really trying to discern God's will."

The men began to pray faithfully and fervently for Mike's prayer concerns and Karen's confirmation that it was what God wanted them to do.

Karen's qualms about running for Congress again also centered around their children and the family as a whole.

"We really had to examine it a lot more carefully," Karen would say. "This would affect five people."[6]

One morning, David and Ruthie McIntosh invited politico Van Smith to their home and they had breakfast together. Smith had been involved with politics since he'd first moved to Indiana in 1956 and had served in several administrations. He also had advised and raised money for countless candidates.

"I had a cup of coffee and some eggs and David said, 'I'm going to run for governor and I'm going to announce it at noon in Indianapolis in a press conference today," recalls Smith. "So afterwards, I went back to the office and I recalled that some years ago when Phil Sharp was the Democratic candidate, in '88 and '90, there was a young couple who had run against him and lost by the name of Pence. So I called Mike Pence."

Van Smith and his wife, Margaret, "had become acquainted with them when he ran against Phil," Smith recalls. "We were impressed. They were very young, relatively, compared to the crowd we were talking about at the time, and inexperienced, but eager, enthusiastic and fresh to the political scene, and intelligent and aggressive in some new ideas. So, we kept track of them."

"I called Mike," Van Smith says, "and I said, 'I'm going to share with you the news that at noon today, David McIntosh is going to have a press conference and he's going to announce that he's going to run for governor. Margaret and I would like to encourage you to think about having a press conference at 1:00 and announce that you're going to run for his congressional seat.' And [Mike] said, 'Oh, my gosh, that's nice of you to think about us, but Karen would just never go for that.' He said, 'I don't think that would happen, but I'll talk with Karen.' I got a call a half-hour later and he said, 'Karen is very excited and we said that we'll consider it if you'll be our chairman.' I said, 'Well, I will do that.'"

It was obvious that God was moving in the hearts of Mike and Karen, but they wanted to be sure it was really *His* will and receive His direction on how to do it His way before making an announcement of such magnitude.

"When Mike and Karen were trying to decide whether he should run for Congress, one of the things they had to consider was, how would it be different from the races they ran in 1988 and 1990?" recalls Bill Smith. "They realized they had put too much of their own effort into it and hadn't relied enough on God and God's providence in those races."

It had been a couple of months since their lunch when McIntosh ran into Mike and Karen at the Brickyard 400 at the Indianapolis Motor Speedway. McIntosh pulled Mike to the side and asked if he and Karen had prayed about it and given the idea of running for his seat more thought. Mike didn't give him a definite answer but said they were "open to it," McIntosh says.

A MOMENTOUS VACATION

To clear their minds in an attempt to hear God's direction, the couple took their kids on vacation to Colorado to mull over the idea and get clarity once and for all about what they should do. For Mike, the best place to do that was in the mountains on horseback.

"Dad often quotes Reagan, who said, 'The outside of a horse is good for the inside of a man,'" says Charlotte, the couple's middle child. "So growing up whenever we had the funds, the time, and Mom let him pick the spot, he always made a point to take us where there were horses, woods, and log cabins."[7]

In the summer of 1999, they vacationed on a ranch in Colorado. Hiking, horseback riding, exploring, and enjoying campfires at night, this time and place "resembled Narnia," Charlotte says, referring to the fantasy world of C.S. Lewis. "Perhaps I caught some feeling in the air on that particular trip, too. My subconscious tapped into the possibilities the future held for my family on those mountainsides and it never really let go."[8]

While horseback riding in the mountains one day, Mike and Karen stopped to look out over the serene plains before them. Mike looked up and noticed two red-tailed hawks soaring above them.

"Look at those two hawks," Mike said. "They look like us."

Karen agreed as they watched the hawks for a few minutes. Then Mike spoke again.

"We need to make a decision," he said. "Should we run?"

"I think we should run," Karen told Mike. "But this time, we should be like those two hawks. No flapping. We should step off the cliff and allow God to lift us up."

Mike later shared this conversation with his friends and accountability partners.

"They weren't flapping their wings; they were soaring," says Bill Smith. "They said, 'We'll win this race if we don't flap, if we don't do it on our own strength. We'll trust Him and we'll run this campaign with integrity and treat people the way we want to be treated.' And that's exactly what they did. I was in the middle of it all. I can tell you, we treated our opponents with respect. There were no negative personal attacks. It was all done with decency, honesty, and treating our fellow man with kindness."

While it seemed like it took them a long time to make a decision to enter the congressional race, Mike and Karen were inspiring those around them.

"I saw how he and Karen both really approached it prayerfully," says McIntosh, "and laid it before the Lord and asked, 'Is this what you want us to do? You want us to give up the comfortable career that had turned out to be successful and take a risk that we might lose again?' No flapping." The impetus for this decision comes from Isaiah 40:31:

Mike's father, Second Lt. Edward Joseph Pence Jr.,
received a Bronze Star for courage under fire during the Korean War.

A childhood photo of Gregory, Edward, and Mike Pence.

Nancy and Ed Pence with their four sons in the 1960s.

Mike Pence celebrates his First Communion.

Mike Pence holds a trophy he won in a speech contest.

Family photo shows Mike Pence, center, as a teen with his parents and siblings.

Mike Pence in his
high school yearbook.

Mike Pence plays the guitar at home in the 1970s.

A college photo of Mike Pence.

Mike Pence graduated from Hanover College in May 1981 with a B.A. in history.

Karen and Mike Pence were married on June 8, 1985,
at St. Christopher's Roman Catholic Church in Speedway, Indiana.

Above and below, Mike Pence with good friend Bill Smith,
who has served as his campaign manager, adviser, and chief of staff.

The accountability group went to Fort Lauderdale, Florida, to celebrate Mike Pence's congressional win and spend time together before the group dissolved. From left are Howard Hubler, Mike Pence, Jim Dodson, and Garry Smith.

Ryan Reger, center, joined Mike Pence's staff after working for former Indiana legislator David McIntosh, left.

*The four Pence brothers—Thomas, Edward, Mike, and Gregory—
at Lucas Oil Stadium on Election Night in 2012.*

Mike Pence embraces his mother, Nancy,
after being sworn in as governor of Indiana.

The Pences visited relatives in Doonbeg, Ireland, in 2013.

Mike Pence takes a turn at the helm of Howard Hubler's yacht.

Vice President Mike Pence with friend and media strategist Rex Elsass, left.

Mike Pence with Jim and Sharon Dodson.

Mike and Karen Pence with family pet Maverick.

While serving in Congress, Mike Pence took to the airwaves to reach constituents.

Twenty-six members of the Pence family gathered on Election Night
in November 2016 to support the Trump/Pence ticket
and celebrate their victory.

Mike and Karen Pence sit for a portrait with their children,
Audrey, Michael, and Charlotte, in January 2013.

Mike Pence prays at the Western Wall in Jerusalem.

But those who hope in the LORD *will renew their strength. They will soar on wings like eagles; they will run and not grow weary, they will walk and not be faint.*

After the Pences' vacation, Mike began to share their decision with those closest to him. Mike told McIntosh at Acapulco Joe's in Indianapolis.

"It made the announcement and run for governor much easier for me," McIntosh says.

To show his appreciation for Mike sharing his donor list with him during his own campaign six years earlier, McIntosh gave him an updated list with a few improvements.

Mike also called Varvel and asked his old friend out to lunch.

"I go and he said, 'I want to let you know, I'm planning on running for Congress,'" Varvel recalls. "Shocked, I said, 'I thought you told me your wife would kill you if you did that again.' He said, 'Well, the Lord [has] changed her mind.'"

The political cartoonist had a word of caution for Mike. "Just don't mess up," Varvel told him. "I don't do 'atta boy' cartoons. If I'm drawing about you, it's usually not a good thing."[9]

ENDNOTES

1. Ryan Trares, "Mike Pence: Group recalls strong roots that helped Pence thrive," *The Daily Journal*, Franklin, IN, January 18, 2017.
2. Parker.
3. Parker.
4. Mayer.
5. Blair.
6. Rudavsky.
7. Charlotte Pence, *Where You Go.*
8. Ibid.
9. Gary Varvel, "Varvel: The day I unfriended Mike Pence," *The Indianapolis Star*, January 17, 2017.

9

DOING IT GOD'S WAY

Commit to the LORD whatever you do,
and your plans will succeed.
—Proverbs 16:3

Mike declared his candidacy for Congress on February 16, 1999, at the Horizon Convention Center in Muncie, Indiana. Karen knew this campaign would be different from the start because both she and Mike had grown spiritually.

"The first couple of times we ran, I think there was a lot of ambition," Karen says. "We thought we could change the world, go to Washington. The [third] time we felt called...We just were different people. We were a lot more mature and it was a lot more of a calling... We felt that 2000 was an opportunity to do it the right way."[1]

Mike and Karen sat down with their three children to discuss their father's potential career change. If he won the congressional race, the family would have to move to the Washington, D.C., area. To help their children understand their spiritual motivation and goals for the job, Mike and Karen showed them the image of a child in his mother's womb. One of their major goals, they told the kids, would be to end abortion.

Mike asked Bill Smith, who had agreed to serve as his campaign manager, to consider serving as his chief of staff if Mike won the seat. Smith agreed.

HIRING A MEDIA STRATEGIST

After announcing his candidacy, Mike began to interview media strategists, searching for someone to produce his political ads. Among them was Rex Elsass, founder of The Strategy Group Company.

"I was immediately impressed with Mike," says Elsass. "He understands theater and television production and knows a little something about media buying, so he was somebody I immediately respected."

The two men connected and Mike was impressed with Elsass's resume, so he hired him and his company to represent him. As soon as they started filming, Elsass says he knew Mike was a Christian.

"We would start a day of filming with our crew and my team and he'd offer a word of prayer, asking for God's wisdom and blessing on our work for that day, [to] transparently be able to show our hearts and use our gifts in the greatest way," recalls Elsass.

He says Mike stood out from every other politician with whom he'd worked in the past.

"I could see this was a guy, frankly, who literally [was] like no one I've ever filmed, turned on with the camera in such an amazing way," says Elsass. "He connected with people from the very beginning. In the first ad we shot, there was a magic in terms to how he handles and reacts to the stage."

Mike had to end *The Mike Pence Show* in September 1999 to enable him to concentrate fully on the campaign.

Elsass credits Mike's years on the radio for his success and ability to reach people's hearts and minds.

"When he's done radio three hours a day, every day, it prepared him amazingly to be able to think on his feet quickly and be able to maintain people's interest," Elsass says. "He knew when humor was appropriate and when an emotional touch was appropriate. I'm sure he would say those years in radio gave him the greatest communication skills and the best honing of communication skills he could possibly have."

After winning the Republican primary with ease, Mike challenged Democrat Robert Rock Jr., the son of a former lieutenant governor, in the general election. Avoiding personal attacks, both men ran issues-oriented campaigns. As he'd done on his radio show, Mike provoked thoughtful discussions and questioned his opponent respectfully, despite their very different political views.

Elsass was continually in awe of Mike as he traveled with him across the state of Indiana on the campaign trail.

"His faith shapes everything he's about," says Elsass. "His faith shapes his relationships with people. His deep faith gives him a rock-solid confidence and empathy for people. How do you know someone's a Christian? You know they're Christians because of their loving nature and he's a person who's very sincere. When we went to a senior citizens' home, it actually inspired an ad just seeing him interacting with people. This isn't just someone using senior citizens solely as a prop. He was there to engage with people and we just happened to capture it. He's always connected with people in that kind of way and I think it's because of his faith. It drives everything he does. It drives every decision he makes. It affects how he relates to people. It gives him the ability to be forgiving and be someone who really lives, very, very truly to the Word"—the Bible.

In one television ad, Mike told viewers that he had matured since his first two campaigns, saying he was committed to talking about himself and his beliefs.

"I've learned a lot in the last ten years," he said. "I've seen my children born, I've built a business, and what I've learned is that negative personal attacks have no place in public life. Whether my opponents agree with me or not, we are committed to run a positive, issue-oriented campaign. Folks want to hear what you're for. They don't want to hear about who you're against."[2]

KAREN'S INVOLVEMENT

According to Elsass, Karen was intricately involved with filming from the beginning.

"She always participated in the campaigns," he says. "She was always involved seeing scripts and storyboards. In all of our ad series she was a central part. Many of our ads were narrated by Karen. One of my favorite stories about the two of them was where we commemorate, and Karen narrates, the day of their first date ice skating in a rink in Indiana. We went back and essentially filmed where their first date was and they both skated that day."

Elsass was impressed with the Pences' solid relationship.

"People approach faith as a coalition. What's nice about Mike and Karen is it's so much who they are and just naturally what they do," says Elsass. "Mike's faith is expressed in what people would consider just normal activities or days because you know he's being lifted up every day by his strength in prayer."

As the Pences are a true team and partnership, Karen was very involved in the campaign.

"It is really 'they' ran for Congress," says Marjorie Dannenfelser, president of the anti-abortion organization Susan B. Anthony List and a longtime friend. "The kind of marriage they have is truly an equal partnership. It is based on their beliefs—their Christian beliefs—that it's a calling, not just a job."[3]

Bill Smith agrees with Dannenfelser's assessment.

"After all they had been through as a family, the difficulties of the losses in 1998 and 1990, they needed to be on the same page in 2000 if they were going to do it again," he says. "They truly did run as a team, even though it was his name, of course, on the ballot."

In their years of marriage, Karen agrees, "we've always been a team. We've always approached it as a team."[4]

Dannenfelser says Karen plays an important role in the Pence household.

"The strength of her stand at the center of the family is true, but it's not this hardened battle-axe thing," Dannenfelser says. "If you are that steady rudder out of love, it's a totally different picture than if you're a steady rudder because you are a military ruler of a family."[5]

In one of his campaign ads, Mike credited Karen for teaching him about education and advocating for teachers.

"Everything I know about education I've learned from my wife Karen," Mike told viewers. "She's been a public school teacher; she's taught in the classroom for more than fifteen years. She really believes in kids and convinced me a long time ago there's nothing that ails our local schools that teachers can't fix if we give them the resources and the freedom to teach. The last thing we need is the federal government to get more involved in our local schools. We need more accountability, competition, and parental involvement. I think she's a great teacher. She's sure taught me a lot."[6]

In a later campaign ad, Karen supported her husband by sharing his love for Hoosiers.

"When Mike leaves in the morning, he's got the people of Indiana on his heart," Karen said. "He's looking for the best way to serve them. It's almost like they're part of his family. I see him get with people and he just lifts their spirits. He's sincere, his faith directs him, and I think what he really wants to bring to people is hope. What I know is that at the end of the day, he's given his all to make it a better community, a better state, a better nation. "[7]

Jane Wainwright, who has known Karen for over twenty years, gives credit to Karen's authenticity.

"There are no pretenses about Karen," says Wainwright. "What you saw and what you see now is what you get. She's a real genuine person."[8]

Elsass says he and Mike looked at their ads as something more than just a way to reach Indiana voters.

"When we were running ads showing very sincerely who the man is and where his optimism comes from, in a small way, we were sharing Christ with hundreds of thousands of people throughout Indiana," Elsass explains. "We were planting a mustard seed of faith. What works best [in ads] is the truth. That ability to show Mike Pence, in that transparent, emotional connection that he has with the Lord, I think motivates many people because there is that sincerity, transparency, and optimism that comes from knowing you have an eternal home that transcends your work on earth."

Throughout the campaign, Mike and Bill Smith reminded each other frequently about their ultimate goals.

"We would constantly remind each other that it's okay to lose the race," says Smith. "And that was the attitude we had all along. He'd always say, 'As long as our integrity and our families are intact at the end of this, we will have succeeded.'"

NEWSPAPER VS. BIBLE

Hubler went out of his way to help Mike raise money for his campaign and shares a story about how Mike specifically touched a group of potential donors during a fund-raising event at Hubler's home.

"We had this large event at our house to raise money for his congressional campaign," Hubler recalls. Mike "got up in front of everyone and he said, 'I am a believer, but I'm also a politician.' Then he said, 'Every morning, I get up and there's two things before me. *The Wall Street Journal* is sitting on the table, which I need to know for my line of work through and through, because everything in it is going to be the topic of the day. [And] sitting next to it is the Bible.'"

Giving an impromptu spiritual lesson to the crowd, Mike held up his Bible in one hand and used a magazine as a prop for the *Journal* in the other hand, Hubler relates. One is "dessert," Mike said, referring to *The Wall Street Journal*.

"Then he held up the Bible and said, 'Meat,'" Hubler says. "What he said was that the devil tugs on us all day, every day, no matter where we are. And he said even for him [the devil's] saying, 'Don't read that Bible.'"

Mike's vulnerability and transparency touched those in attendance. They raised over $43,000 that night.

"A lot of those people were unbelievers, but they came to me after that particular day and just applauded how he made such a human situation relevant to them," Hubler says.

Mike continued to wear "the Mike Pence Standard Issue" outfit that his accountability brothers so mercilessly teased him about, so one day, Hubler offered to buy him some new clothes and suit him head-to-toe. "Any color but navy blue I told him," Hubler says, laughing.

But Mike declined this kind offer. It was against campaign regulations to accept gifts, he explained. Mike said the same thing when Hubler offered the Pences his Fort Lauderdale home for a little retreat from the stresses of the campaign.

"He was adamant about following the rules," Hubler says.

Dodson drove around with Mike to provide moral support while Mike campaigned around the district. But Dodson says Mike really had all the support he needed from God.

"Mike was never far from his Bible," Dodson remembers. "Mike has never been hesitant—ever—to let people know he's a Christian. He would always acknowledge that the Lord was part of his life, that he prayed that the Lord would guide him and help him make decisions."

In the fall, the polls showed that Mike was clearly the frontrunner. He talked to Bill Smith about staying on as his chief of staff.

"As it got closer to October, he asked if I would be his chief of staff if he won the election," Smith recalls. "After several days of discussion, he was gracious enough to give me the flexibility that my family needed. Part of the arrangement was that I could stay in Indiana and commute to Washington as needed."

Mike won the congressional seat by a twelve-point margin after running a successful campaign on conservative values such as opposing abortion and calling for a considerably smaller federal government. He made a pledge to Hoosiers that "a promise made is a promise kept."

Family, friends, and supporters gathered at the Fine Arts Center in Anderson on election night to celebrate Mike's victory with him. Mike told the cheering crowd that there was a big difference between this race and the one that had ended in defeat ten years prior.

"My faith in Jesus Christ, the God of second chances, who granted us not so much victory as the grace to run a campaign of integrity," Mike said. "We'll give him the glory first."[9]

Bill Smith gave Mike a one-year commitment to serve as his chief of staff. He would end up serving with Mike for more than a dozen years. Years later, Mike would jokingly say, "Here's Bill Smith, my chief of staff. He's in his twelfth year of a one-year commitment."

Unfortunately, David McIntosh—the man who made it possible for Mike to serve in the U.S. House of Representatives because he himself stepped aside—lost his race for the governorship. While elated with his own win, Mike felt his friend's sorrow and tried to encourage him spiritually.

"Very specifically, he recommended to me when I lost the race that I read the Bible in a year and start going through it," says McIntosh. "He showed me his Bible and how he'd taken notes. I said, 'Yeah, yeah, that sounds good' and promptly forgot about it."

Later, after a couple other people gave McIntosh the same advice, he saw it as a sign from God and caved in.

"I eventually started reading it and that has completely changed my faith," confesses McIntosh. "That was something that Mike directly gave me as advice that has molded and deepened my faith."

ENDNOTES

1. Rudavsky.
2. Mike Pence, "Straight Talk," 2000 campaign ad with Media Strategy Group.
3. Celeste Katz, "Karen Pence Is Playing the Mother of All Long Games," *Town & Country*, April 19, 2018.
4. Rudavsky.
5. Katz.
6. Mike Pence, "Education," 2000 campaign ad with Media Strategy Group.
7. Karen Pence, "On His Heart," Mike Pence 2002 campaign ad with Media Strategy Group.
8. Rudavsky.
9. Rick Yencer, "Pence wins big; McIntosh loses home precinct, 191-119," *The Star Press*, Muncie, IN, November 9, 2000.

10

BUILDING A LIFE
IN WASHINGTON

*But Ruth replied, "Don't urge me to leave you or to turn back
from you. Where you go I will go, and where you stay I will stay.
Your people will be my people and your God my God."*
—Ruth 1:16

After the congressional race, Karen gave Mike a gift that has
become an important aspect of their home décor ever since.

"My wife presented me with a framed verse" that they hung over
their mantle, Mike relates. "It simply reads some ancient words people
of faith have clung to throughout the millennia. And as we reflect on
the great challenges…that believers [in] Christ face across the globe, I
think we do well to claim this promise again."[1]

The framed verse comes from Jeremiah 29:11: *"For I know the
plans I have for you," declares the* LORD, *"plans to prosper you and not to
harm you, plans to give you hope and a future."*

As the family savored their win, the four men in the accountability group went on vacation together as a last hurrah. They had been
meeting regularly for four years and they knew Mike's life was about to
change drastically as the Pences went off to the East Coast. They also
knew that without Mike's spiritual leadership, it was unlikely that the
remaining three men would continue to meet.

"Sometime in early fall, we decided that if he won, we wanted the four of us to go to Howard Hubler's home in Fort Lauderdale to spend four days alone together," says Dodson. "We knew things were going to change hugely; the group would break up as it was and [Mike would] become extremely busy and largely inaccessible. He wouldn't ever be in town."

In addition to his Florida home by the Atlantic Intracoastal Waterway, Hubler had a seventy-foot yacht off the dock behind it, staffed with a captain and full crew to ensure all of their needs were met. The men spent time trolling in the canals in a twenty-one-foot boat, taking the yacht to a local restaurant on the water, and hanging out at Hubler's home.

"We did three or four things every day," recalls Dodson. "One of them was we spent time together just enjoying each other's company." They also ate meals together, "spent time talking about the Lord," and "did some Bible reading. And then we'd pray for each other."

They talked about the challenges facing Mike in his new job as a congressman.

"We talked about Mike's new role, his responsibility and his new platform, and his decision to take his family to Washington," says Dodson. "We wanted to make sure he knew that even though we wouldn't be with him, we'd be praying for him."

GOOD ADVICE FROM DAN QUAYLE

There were several things to take into consideration, so Mike and Karen decided to confer with Vice President Dan Quayle and his wife, Marilyn. The Pences had become friends with the Quayles over the years; Dan had served as a congressman from 1977 to 1981 and a U.S. senator for Indiana from 1981 to 1989. Dan and Marilyn warned Mike and Karen that if they stayed in Indiana and Mike tried to commute home on the weekends, he would never have any peace. At every soccer game he attended, constituents would come over to speak with him. He wouldn't be able to enjoy watching his children play. And the

Quayles also pointed out that one spouse living in the D.C. area while the other stayed in Indiana could be hard on a marriage.

At the time, the Pences' children were only six, seven, and nine years old, and Mike wanted to be as much a part of their lives as possible. "I just know my kids need quality time to be with their dad," Mike would say.

Mike reported back to his accountability group that they'd decided to keep a modest home in Indiana for when Congress was out of session and get a rental in Washington.

"There are so many guys who go and leave their families at home and they face temptation, they get accused of stuff, they find themselves in compromising situations, or they have marital or family problems," says Dodson. "Michael just said, 'That's not me. It's God, then my family, and then the job.'"

Varvel and Mike met for lunch one last time before the family moved to Washington, D.C., full-time and he had a prayer request. "He told me, 'Gary, pray that when I go to Washington that my 'yes,' will be 'yes' and my 'no' will be 'no,'" Varvel relates. This encouragement comes from Jesus in Matthew 5:37. Varvel says Mike had "seen too many congressmen go there and then fudge the truth. He didn't want to be that guy."

In fact, Charlotte says the family adopted a Bible verse at this time that they would hold on to over the coming years as Mike's job in politics progressed and took them back and forth across the country:

> But Ruth replied, "Don't urge me to leave you or to turn back from you. Where you go I will go, and where you stay I will stay. Your people will be my people and your God my God." (Ruth 1:16)

"This verse, commonly quoted in the Pence family, holds the truth of how we navigate life and all it brings. It is our beacon. It has defined our vision, led us forward, and kept us from turning too frequently sideways or backward in the midst of struggle," says Charlotte.[2]

The Pences trusted God in the same way Ruth did. Neither they nor Ruth knew what the future would bring, but they believed God would make everything right.

"When Dad was elected as an Indiana congressman in 2000, we followed him to live in Washington, D.C.," Charlotte relates. "Many congressional families decide to stay in their home states instead, but we didn't want Dad to travel back and forth so much. The best thing about growing up was not that Dad was in Congress. It was that he was home for dinner almost every night. We got to see him; we knew him."[3]

All of the Pences moved to the D.C. area "just to keep our kids and our family close," Mike says. "I always told people, 'You can have some pretty heady days in Washington, D.C., but it was always such a blessing to be maybe in a meeting at the White House, maybe a hearing on Capitol Hill, maybe a national television interview, but I could walk into that little house that we had outside Washington, D.C., and I knew that there were four people who were absolutely unimpressed with me."[4]

Patricia Bailey had separate conversations with Mike and Karen about how moving back and forth between Washington and Indiana affected the children.

"We talked to them about the whole concept of, when your children come back to Indiana, is that easier or harder?" she recalls. "And they both said, independently of each other, how much harder it is when they came to Indiana because when they come here, they are Mike Pence's child and there's some notoriety that comes with that. And when they're in Washington, everybody's the kid of a congressman or Cabinet member, so there's not that sense of, 'I'm special, people are staring at me, or people are watching me,' because everybody's that kid."

The family rented a modest home in Arlington, Virginia, where they found a private Christian school for the kids where Karen could also work part-time. It was the first time Karen had ever lived outside of her home state.

Mike began his new job on January 3, 2001, as the 107th Congress convened. With his family and closest friends watching, he took the oath of office stating, in part, that he would "defend the Constitution of the United States against all enemies, foreign and domestic; that I will bear true faith and allegiance to the same."

BUTTING HEADS WITH BUSH

Three weeks after taking the oath of office, Mike attended the inauguration of George W. Bush. He didn't know it at the time, but he and Bush would frequently be at odds on policy. In doing so, Mike became instrumental in changing the heart and views of the new president.

The same week Bush took office, Mike's leadership skills were immediately noted and he was named assistant to House Majority Whip Tom Delay, R-Texas. Then Mike's colleagues elected him to serve as chairman of the House Republican Study Committee. Hoosiers were watching with pride as Mike rose in the ranks and was honored, sharing in his achievements as if they were their own.

"There seems to be no stopping U.S. Rep. Mike Pence as he rises to the top of the freshman class of the U.S. House of Representatives," noted a newspaper in Muncie. "Last week, Pence picked up the chairmanship of the regulatory reform and oversight subcommittee of the House Small Business Committee. He was the only freshman member of the 107th Congress to receive a subcommittee chair, usually reserved for more senior members." Mike noted the position "will permit me to be a more effective voice for small businesses and family farms, not only in Indiana but all across the nation."[5]

From the onset, Mike had a special relationship with his staff and sought to mentor them to be more like Christ, specifically by being servants.

Andrew Phipps, a long-time friend and Mike's director of district communications, recalls the office atmosphere as being one of servanthood.

"Mike wanted his staff to take a servant's attitude in their job description," says Phipps. "They were there to do a service for the people. He was an example of that. There was a time when some demonstrators had come to the Anderson, Indiana, office. They were from the union and he went out and took coffee and doughnuts to them. And someone said, 'Why are you doing this? We're here protesting!' And he said, 'Well, you have the right, I guess, to protest, but we don't have to be ugly about it on our part. We can still take a friendly attitude. We can allow you to do your job. We just thought while you were here demonstrating your particular concerns, we'd offer you coffee and doughnuts.' I've been around him a lot and he'd refer to a Bible verse about serving. In one instance, he was talking about Christ washing the disciples' feet [in John 13:1–17]. It was the Lord humbling himself as a servant. Mike wanted to set that example of humility. He was always the one in a reception line who would offer the people their plates. He always had a servant's heart."

Phipps says Mike knew that to be a leader, you had to first be willing to follow someone else. Mike sought to follow and imitate Christ.

As Mike continued to build his staff, he insisted that they follow one rule to work for him.

"I know an [individual] who at one point was discussing with Mike the possibility of joining his staff," recalls evangelical power broker, Ralph Reed. "This person was married with children and they lived in another state. When the person called to say he was going to take the job, Mike said to this young man, 'I hope this won't be a deal killer for you, but I just want you to know that it's mandatory for me. If you come to Washington to work for me, you're bringing your wife and kids. And if you're not bringing your wife and kids, you're not coming to work for me. I want your family here. I want you going home at the end of the day and hugging your kids and eating dinner with your family. I don't want you to be commuting and living alone during the week in Washington, D.C., which is a place of numerous temptations, and exposing yourself unnecessarily to those risks.' And this young man, who happens to be a believer, by the way, told me how much he appreciated that. Not just to preserve Pence's character and priorities, but also he kind of felt it was on a very personal level that he was looking out for him."

Among the people Mike brought on staff was Stephen Piepgrass.

"Mike came in as a freshman congressman and was looking for someone to serve as a press secretary," says Piepgrass. "Someone to be in charge of all communication with media, speech writing, local radio and TV stations, and give statements to the press. I came into the job knowing I'd already gotten into law school at UVA [University of Virginia School of Law] at that time and I decided to defer a year so I could work for him."

UNASHAMED OF FAITH

Like everyone who first comes into contact with Mike, Piepgrass immediately noticed just how much Mike's faith is a part of his life.

"He's very personable and someone who was a very strong believer and wore his faith on his sleeve and was completely unashamed," says Piepgrass. "As his speech writer, he would always encourage me, among other staff, to weave into whatever we were putting together for him, bits and pieces from Scripture wherever possible. Every day at the kick-off of Congress, the congressmen are able to make a one-minute speech on just about anything they want to. The vast majority of [Mike's] speeches, if you know Scripture well, have snippets of [Bible verses] weaved throughout them. And if I couldn't come up with something, he could, because he had a pretty exhaustive knowledge of Scripture."

Taking every opportunity he had to proclaim Christ, Mike once told his colleagues, "I believe that God created the known universe, the Earth and everything in it, including man. And I also believe that someday scientists will come to see that only the theory of intelligent design provides even a remotely rational explanation for the known universe."[6]

A few years later, in a television interview, Chris Matthews asked Mike if he believed in evolution. Twice, Mike answered by stating his views with conviction. "I believe with all my heart that God created the heavens and the earth, the seas and all that is in them," Mike said. "How He did that, I'll ask Him about some day."[7]

In Mike, Piepgrass quickly found someone he could look up to spiritually.

"Everything he did, all of his policy-making, was informed from his faith perspective," recalls Piepgrass. "It's at the core of who he is as a person. Whatever decision he made, he wanted to make sure it was consistent with what he believed. It was very clear. He would not take positions that he felt were inconsistent with his core beliefs with who he was and what his faith was."

Like several of Mike's staffers, he felt as though Mike was investing in him in a deliberate, purposeful, and personal way.

"I definitely saw Pence as a mentor," says Piepgrass. "He encouraged me to go to law school. He was really pleased I was going to UVA and he said, 'That's a great school' and, 'Do well there and you can do anything.' He was an inspiring figure in my life and someone who I looked up to a lot and still try to emulate in different ways. I think God puts people like that into your life at different points and times and I was just blessed to be able to work for him at that formable time in my career. He was very, very encouraging to all of his staff members. We all felt like he built into us as people, not just staff."

In stressing the importance of integrity to him, Piepgrass says Mike talked freely about his second run for Congress and what a disaster it had been for him morally.

"The article, 'Confessions of a Negative Campaigner,' was influenced very much by his faith and it was a turning point in his life," says Piepgrass. "He had a copy of it hanging in his office. He pointed to that often as a turning point for himself personally and he talked to me a number of times about that experience and how going forward, he had really made a commitment to bring his faith and convictions into everything, no matter how encouraging others were to go negative."

Shortly after they moved to Edinburg, Virginia, Mike and Karen sold the home they'd had built in Indianapolis and bought a modest home in Indiana so they could afford to have homes in both their home state and the D.C. area. Dodson helped the family move to Edinburg.

"I've always appreciated one thing a lot about Mike: he's a very humble man," says Dodson. "When he says he's humbled, he really is. He was always so grateful and appreciative to people, in some ways taken aback that people would do things for him. I'm sure Mike could fight the battle of being conceited, but I've never seen him struggle with that battle."

Dodson believes that humility stems from his faith in Christ.

"He's always genuinely been, 'I'm just God's person here. It's just me. I'm Mike. I just want to be a person who's a servant to the Lord. I want to do what He wants. I want Him to use me,'" says Dodson. "That's one of the things that has always attracted me to him."

The Pence family began to attend Immanuel Bible Church in Springfield, Virginia. They went to church every Sunday, regardless of any demands Mike's congressional work might have placed on him. He was determined to keep his family intact and continue to stoke the flames of fire in his marriage with Karen. He did not shift his priorities.

Mike's modus operandi was "vote right and then go home for dinner."[8]

Another former staffer, Ryan Reger, had worked for McIntosh and contacted Mike's office when McIntosh lost the gubernatorial race.

"I reached out to Mike's campaign and told them I'd like to remain in Indiana and work for Mike," says Reger. "I just believed in what he believes in. Personally, he was great, but when I knew what he was going to be advancing in Congress and what he stood for, it made me want to work for [Mike even more as] someone I believed in and do something personally fulfilling."

Reger became Mike's field representative in Indiana. When he went to Washington, he served as Mike's district scheduler, planning all of his events back in their home state.

"We had this van that had his name written on the side of it that [would take] us to the areas of the district where he didn't have an office," says Reger. "We had nineteen counties that we'd drive to the library or town hall...meeting people to talk with them. Seeing him meet people for the first time, it's evident he cares for people. He's so kind and caring. He takes his eyes and kind of squints and looks at someone deep in them like he's really caring about what they're saying. He'd focus on that one person. He cared about each person who had an issue and it was just evident.

"For me," Reger adds, "as I got to know him, he really honestly cared about me as a person. I wasn't just his driver, wasn't just the guy who was supposed to grab his coffee or take notes in a meeting or keep him on time. We had many deep conversations because I was with him long hours. I'd pick him up at six or seven in the morning, sometimes earlier when in Indiana, and we'd be gone all day long until late at night. Many times, he was on the phone, but sometimes, there's no one to call after eight o'clock at night, so we'd just be chatting. Sometimes, we'd have worship music on. To me, he was a mentor and very helpful."

Stevens says Mike "is one of the most personable people I've ever met. If he's talking to you, he zones everything else out. I've only met a handful of people in my life who have that ability and he's one of them."

When Mike talks to you, it's like you're "the only person in the room," Stevens adds.

SOUGHT OUT AS A MENTOR

Like several of his staff members, Reger looked up to Mike.

"One of my favorite things and memories of working with him was the early mornings I'd pick him up at his house and he'd just got done with his devotional time in the morning," Reger says. "We'd talk about the passage and devotion he read on the way to our first meeting. That was precious time to me because I got to pick his brain about what he thought about stuff and it helped me in my faith. He doesn't just talk faith—he lives it. He made the Word of God a priority in his life. Mike made me realize that if someone like that can make it such a priority, I have no excuse. Just seeing his devotion challenged me. Sometimes, if he didn't have a chance to have his devotions before I picked him up, he'd do it right then as we were driving to our first event. But he had his Bible a lot. He liked to write his own speeches and many times used Scripture."

Reger recalls Mike talking frequently about Karen and their unusually solid marriage.

"He did a great job of prioritizing that relationship," says Reger. "Karen was involved with the scheduling process and she was super protective of making sure he wasn't gone too many nights from home. He gave her that authority. [Mike said], 'Look at my schedule and if there's something you don't like...' He gave her the veto power and she exercised that. She was protective of his time and of him personally to make sure he didn't get too tired. She would look and make sure he wasn't in a hotel for too many nights in a row. She tried to set the schedule so he could be home almost every single night when he was back in the district. He had short district trips.

"When he was on the way home after an event late at night, he'd call Karen and after talking to her, she'd pass the phone to all the kids," Reger relates. "He'd tell his son, Michael, 'You're the man of the house, so make sure you lock the doors.' I heard him say at numerous events that his job of being a congressman was important, but the most important job to him was Dad."

If his staff knew anything about him, it was that Mike was a strong believer in God and the Bible and that he cared for his staff like family.

"We were brothers in Christ and close friends," says Bill Smith. "He would started staff meetings with prayer. Did he quote Scripture? Not in a sense that he'd pull out his Bible and quote to us, but it would come off his tongue in normal conversation. It never felt like a forced thing or uncomfortable in any way because it's just within his manner.

He always kept his Bible on the desk, the one he actually read. Anyone who would look at his desk would always see the well-worn Bible that he referenced often."

A FILM ABOUT SOUL'S DILEMMA

While Mike was away at Congress, *Indianapolis Star* cartoonist Gary Varvel and his son, Brett, delved into the film business and started House of Grace Films. For their first venture, the two wrote and directed a film called, *The Board*, a dramatic film that explores the human soul, represented by a six-member board of directors. One by one, the soul's power brokers—Mind, Memory, Emotion, Heart, Will, and Conscience—discuss and vote on seemingly mundane events, until a co-worker poses a dilemma with eternal consequences. One ChristianCinema.com reviewer says the film offers an "excellent explanation of the turmoil within us when we are presented with accepting Christ as our Savior." Varvel sent Mike a copy of the film, hoping he would watch it.

"He got it and saw it," says Varvel. "He told me later that he was afraid to watch it because he was afraid it would be terrible, then he knew he'd see me at some point and I would ask him what he'd thought. He said, 'This movie literally brought tears to my eyes. I want you to come to Washington and show it to our congressional interns.'"

Varvel flew to D.C. and held a film showing for several interns, all of whom gave it glowing reviews. *The Board* ended up having a successful run on the independent film circuit and was translated into five languages. Varvel went on to co-write and produce a second film, *The War Within* (2014), which won seven film festival awards.

While in Congress, Mike adamantly searched for ways to influence his senior colleagues. He continually found himself challenging House members from both parties when they strayed from the conservative path.

The accountability group—Mike, Dodson, Hubler, and Garry Smith—continued to keep in contact with one another, despite that they could no longer meet weekly. Mike attended Community Church of Columbus, a daughter church of the church in Greenwood they had attended, whenever he was in town.

A CULTURAL WARRIOR

Mike quickly garnered the respect of colleagues on Capitol Hill. "His reputation as a culture warrior was unsullied," one reporter wrote.[9]

Mike championed efforts for a limited government, fiscal responsibility, economic development, educational opportunities for those less fortunate, and the enforcement of the U.S. Constitution.

And just as he stressed to his aides, Mike demonstrated servanthood in his relationships with constituents and fellow Republican lawmakers, taking every opportunity given to him to reach out to them and minister to them if they were going through a difficult personal issue or dealing with tragedy.

Phipps says Mike's compassion and empathy for people inspired everyone around him.

"If someone got hurt or there was a tragedy involving one of the contingents, maybe overseas, he wanted to get to the family and say something, maybe visit them," says Phipps. "And maybe at least let them know he was praying for them. His faith was very important to him. He wanted his life to reflect that."

Phipps says Mike's ability to relate to others stems from his heart of selflessness.

"Mike Pence is very unique in manner and in respect to the political process," Phipps says. "He has a good way of making those around him feel better about themselves. He is the kind of person who will do what he can to lift you up without all of the attention being on himself. In fact, he's rather deliberate to take the attention off himself and put it on the individual to whom he's speaking."

Mike frequently took friends' children under his wing as interns or pages. Among them was the son of Mark and Patricia Bailey.

"Our son did a summer internship for Mike," says Patricia Bailey, "but one of the things when the interns came in that Mike communicated and everyone on his staff communicated is that, 'We are not in charge here. We are here to serve the public.' So whenever anyone came in, it didn't matter if it was from their district or not, they answered all questions for them and coordinated all Capitol visits and everything else because it was a place of public service. To me, it was such a remarkable reflection of that servant-leadership: This is a little piece of Indiana in this office and when people come here, we extend Hoosier hospitality to them. Unlike other congressmen's offices, when you go in, if you're not a part of their district, if you haven't called ahead or done X, Y, or Z, you're just out of luck. If you went in [Mike's office], he had a little popcorn machine and you could have popcorn and if they had someone who could help, you could get a Capitol tour, even if you were from Boise, Idaho. It just really impressed a lot of people who went through there that there was a very different sense of who he was, that servant-leadership was a real thing."

Mike often spoke words of encouragement to staff members, investing in their lives and serving as a mentor to several men under his command.

"As a man of faith, Mike would talk spiritually and affectionately about his staff," Hubler says. "Mike always knew these people on a personal level. Mike told me he was called to serve them and he did a great job at it."

Mike credited both his biblical views and his upbringing for shaping his attitude of servanthood. He sought ways to give others the opportunities he'd been given as a child.

"We really did focus on those success factors of growing up in a family with a loving mother and father, getting a decent education, having a grounding in faith, and having things that improved the odds of success in America," says Blackwell. "We talked about making sure [those] contexts existed for more and more children."

Mike tells people, "If you work hard, you study hard, and you never give up on your dreams and listen to people that care about you, you can live those dreams."[10]

Even in his first year in Congress, Mike's staff knew how important Karen was to him.

"She's the backbone of that family," says Reger. "He talked about how when he lost the first couple of races in '88 and '90 and he was depressed, how Karen basically kicked him in the rear and said, 'Get up off that couch and do something.' Not in a harsh way, but in a loving way, telling him it was just an election. He talked about her lifting him up in that time."

Friends back in Greenwood watched to see if becoming a congressman would change Mike, but he remained the same man they'd come to know: affable, humble, and godly.

One of Mike's pages was Hubler's son, Greg.

"My son would call me every couple of days from Washington, D.C.," Hubler recalls. "He said, 'You know, Dad, I go to these meetings in the Longworth Building and I go to occasional meetings in the Senate. And I'm called to be there at a certain time. I go there and here's all these black cars all lined up and you know what the fourth car is? Mike's Chevy S-10 pickup truck.' He carried that humility to Congress."

CONVICTIONS OF STEEL

Anyone who took Mike's humility for weakness would be mistaken. Friends say he had a "steel" about him that was impenetrable. "Michael is firm in times when he has to be firm," says Steger, and "he'll state his position" as such.

Colleagues saw that steel on a regular basis. In Mike's first year in Congress, he gained a reputation as being someone with strong convictions who was also a maverick. He earned respect and attention by challenging his own party's leaders, both in Congress and in President George W. Bush's administration.

"Bush was pushing for this prescription drug benefit and he was trying to get Pence's vote," says Varvel. "Mike told me that Bush had him down to the White House and he said, 'They bring me into this room and then the president comes in. He sits right across from me and is real friendly and asks about [my] kids and names them.' He'd done his homework. Then he said, 'Look, Mike, I really need your help on this bill.' And I remember Mike saying he said, 'Mr. President, I respect you, but that's not why I came to Washington. I didn't come to Washington to grow government.' At the end, Mike said they agreed to disagree."

FIGHTING HUMAN EMBRYO RESEARCH

It wasn't the first time Mike went toe-to-toe with the president. From his first days as a freshman congressman, he petitioned Bush to reinstate a ban on federal funding of human embryo research. The debate between the two men rested on a conflict between "scientific progress" and religious conviction. Mike firmly believes that life begins at conception.

In a July 2001 address on the House floor, Mike said, "Adult stem cell research is pro-life, but destroying nascent human beings for research is not pro-life.... Not one medical treatment has been developed from research done on stem cells from human embryos. Virtually every advancement cited today on this floor was accomplished with adult stem cell research." He concluded by urging Bush to "do justice, enforce the law, and choose life so that we and our children may live."[11]

With few supporters backing him in his efforts, Mike stood tall and wouldn't back down. Ultimately, he swayed the heart of the evangelical president. Bush decided to allow federal funding for research only on existing stem cell lines "where the life-and-death decision has already been made."[12]

In explaining his decision, Bush said, "My position on these issues is shaped by deeply held beliefs. I'm a strong supporter of science and technology, and believe they have the potential for incredible good—to improve lives, to save life, to conquer disease.... I also believe human life is a sacred gift from our creator. I worry about a culture that devalues life, and believe as your president I have an important obligation to foster and encourage respect for life in America and throughout the world."[13]

During his years in Congress, Mike continually advocated on behalf of human embryos. Speaking on the House floor in 2006 on the Castle-DeGette bill, which would have expanded the use of federal funds for research on new embryotic stem cells, Mike forcefully said it was "morally wrong to create human life to destroy it for research, and... morally wrong to take the tax dollars of millions of prolife Americans who believe that life is sacred and use it to fund the destruction of human embryos for research."[14]

Despite his plea, the House and Senate passed the measure. Bush promptly vetoed it, however, and the House failed to override that veto.

Mike would frequently and passionately seek President Bush's support on all pro-life issues, frequently securing it. It was clear to his colleagues that God had given him favor with Bush.

FORMING CONSERVATIVE CAUCUS

Mike didn't just stand up for his convictions; he gathered others together who shared his beliefs to reinforce the conservative cause.

"My son told me that one day, Mike had a meeting with George W. Bush and a handful of people and Mike called George Bush to question," says Hubler. "As a result, Mike gets together with a handful of people they ended up calling the Conservative Caucus—ninety-two men and women who are in the House of Representatives who chose to stand and tie down fast conservative causes in Congress as Bush was taking it moderate. They said, 'We need a spokesman' and it ended up being Mike Pence."

Not everyone in Congress appreciated Mike's boldness on the House floor or when dealing with the president.

Mike "said he kind of got spanked because he stood up to the president," recalls Varvel.

One day, while meeting constituents at an Indiana fairgrounds, Mike had a negative encounter with a fellow congressman who didn't share his political views, Varvel says. "He told me there was a person who was in Congress who walked by and said, 'This guy was a thug to me.' Mike's not that way. I've never seen him say really angry things about anybody else. He'll say he doesn't agree with them."

Blackwell, the senior fellow at the Family Research Council, served as a mentor to many up-and-coming politicians, including Mike, and his wisdom and guidance were always welcome.

Blackwell would remind Mike of how baseball legend Satchel Paige "used to say it's very difficult to steal second base if you want to keep one foot on first base." Blackwell says he told Mike, "You actually have to take risks in life to do the right thing. It's through failure that you become better. Not too many people come up with their ground-breaking invention on their first try. But they had this insatiable belief of doing something new, doing something different, taking a risk. And that's what political leadership is about."

When things didn't go as Mike hoped on the House floor and he felt discouraged or defeated, Blackwell often gave him an encouraging word.

"We've had conversations about getting up off the ground once you've been knocked down," says Blackwell. "Having to experience standing up and speaking out has cost him, whether it's been legislative setbacks, whether it's been leadership in the House, and when that sort of speaking out cost him the scorn of Republican leaders who were more establishment-oriented, more embracing of the status quo that needed to be changed. I know how ostracized inside circles treat tree-shakers and disrupters of the status quo. I know during those points of setbacks or defeats, he turned to God."

The lessons Mike learned as a radio show host were also in the back of his mind.

In October 2001, the U.S. House paid tribute to Rush Limbaugh a few days after the radio talk show host and conservative political commentator announced he was going deaf. Mike stood on the House floor to thank Limbaugh for emboldening him to launch his own radio program.

"I was, in every sense, Rush Limbaugh's warm-up act in Indiana, airing every time from 9 a.m. to noon as his lead-in on many Hoosier stations," Mike said then. "Rush Limbaugh has made a difference in my life, and I say without apology that I believe he has made a difference in the life of the nation. He has given us an example of a life that is about ideas larger than personal advancement, a life that tries to bring the reality of God's grace in each of our lives and in the history of this nation before the citizenry every day. My word to Rush is stay the course, encourage, tear down the strongholds, only be strong and courageous, do not be discouraged, for the Lord your God will go with you wherever you go."[15]

Mike knew his faith and conservative views in Congress and the disdain of those who didn't share the same beliefs impacted his children, so he talked frequently about his convictions and the policies he supported and opposed while with his family, usually at the dinner table.

"It warms my heart sometimes when my kids will talk about understanding that sometimes, Dad is a little less popular with his colleagues than he might like to be because he has taken stands consistent with his beliefs and his core principles," Mike says.[16]

Richard Land, President of the Southern Evangelical Seminary, met first met Mike during his freshman year in the House.

"I found him to be a completely genuine, 24-karat gold evangelical who was a man of his word, a man of impeccable integrity, and who was there for the right reasons and wanted to do things right," says Land. "It was easier to find people who weren't like Mike Pence [in politics] than those who were like Mike Pence."

Land credits Mike's faith for shaping his political views.

"He's a man who strives to have a biblical worldview as an evangelical, Bible-believing Christian would see it," says Land. "In terms of his character and demeanor, he's a lot like what I imagine the apostle John was like. Mike has a very calming influence. There was a reason John was called the beloved disciple. Mike is a conscience builder, a guy who tries to think the best of people until proven otherwise."

As Mike settled into his first year in Congress, all seemed to be well…until the media got involved.

ENDNOTES

1. Carly Hoilman, "VP Mike Pence: 'No People of Faith Today Face Greater Hostility or Hatred Than the Followers of Christ,'" *FaithWire*, May 12, 2017.
2. Charlotte Pence, *Where You Go: Life Lessons from My Father*.
3. Ibid.
4. "A Visit with Governor Mike and Karen Pence," *Dr. James Dobson's Family Talk*, October 5, 2016 (www.drjamesdobson.org/Broadcasts/Broadcast?i=3a5c4909-4083-4633-9436-cd2ff97b3132).
5. *The Star Press* Staff, "Side Remarks: Pence Moves to Top of House Class," *The Star Press*, Muncie, IN, February 11, 2001.
6. Mike Pence, "Theory of the Origin of Man," *Congressional Record, Proceedings and Debates of the 107th Congress, Second Session*, House of Representatives, Vol. 148, No. 93, Washington, July 11, 2002.
7 . *Hardball with Chris Matthews*, MSNBC, May 5, 2009.
8. Lawrence Kudlow, "2005 Man of the Year: Rep. Mike Pence," *Human Events*, December 22, 2005.
9. David Hawkings, "Who's Mike Pence and Why Has Trump Picked Him?", *Roll Call*, July 14, 2016.
10. Kirk Johannesen, "Pence, Trump share 'belief in the American dream,'" *The Republic*, January 13, 2017.
11. Mike Pence, "The Law and Ethical Standards Demand Discontinuation of Federal Funding of Destructive Human Embryo Research," *Congressional Record, 107th Congress, First Session*, Vol. 147, No. 96, Washington, July 11, 2001.
12. "President George W. Bush's address on stem cell research," *Inside Politics*, CNN, August 9, 2001.
13. Ibid.
14. Mike Pence, "Veto Human Embryo Research," *Congressional Record, 109th Congress, Second Session*, Vol. 152, No. 95, Washington, July 19, 2006.
15. Mike Pence, "Tribute to Rush Hudson Limbaugh, III," *Congressional Record, 107th Congress, First Session*, Vol. 147, No. 139, Washington, October 16, 2001.
16. C-SPAN, "Q&A with Mike Pence," January 19, 2006.

11

CONGRESSMAN PENCE

Whoever wants to become great among you must be your
servant, and whoever wants to be first must be your slave—
just as the Son of Man did not come to be served, but to serve,
and to give his life as a ransom for many.
—Matthew 20:26–28

During his first few months in Congress, Mike began adhering to what the media called the "Mike Pence Rule" of conduct and received a lot of flak for it. In reality, Mike was following Billy Graham's code of conduct, which the renowned evangelist preacher first began to follow himself in November 1948. Approaching thirty years old, Graham started a discussion with his close friends about problems among other evangelists that undermined the integrity of the gospel message, revealing hypocrisy and ruined lives. He encouraged them to go to their hotel rooms for an hour and list all of the problems they could think of that they might encounter. Graham recounts the conversation in his autobiography:

"When they returned, the lists were remarkably similar, and in a short amount of time, we made a series of resolutions or commitments among ourselves that would guide us in our future evangelistic work. In reality, it was more of an informal understanding among ourselves—a shared commitment to do all we could do to uphold the Bible's standard of absolute integrity and purity for evangelists."[1]

The first problem Graham's friends cited was a lack of account-ability for finances and donations. The second was sexual immorality. Graham wrote:

"We all knew of evangelists who had fallen into immorality while separated from their families by travel. We pledged among ourselves to avoid any situation that would have even the appearance of compro-mise or suspicion. From that day on, I did not travel, meet or eat alone with a woman other than my wife. We determined that the Apostle Paul's mandate to the young pastor Timothy would be ours as well: '*Flee...youthful lusts*' (2 Timothy 1:22, KJV)."[2]

Although he has been mocked for not dining with other women unless Karen is there, Mike has often refused dinner or cocktail invi-tations from male colleagues as well.

"It's about building a zone around your marriage," he says. Referring to D.C., he adds, "I don't think it's a predatory town, but I think you can inadvertently send the wrong message by being in [cer-tain] situations." Back home in Indiana, "Little old ladies come and say, 'Honey, whatever you need to do, keep your family together.'"[3]

OTHERS HAD AFFAIRS

The reality is, Karen and Mike saw "some examples right in front of their face where congressmen or senators had gotten into affairs," says Steger. "Michael would say, 'It really is a cesspool, it really is a swamp.' So they just made a decision as a very mature, Christian couple, that we are now in a very unhealthy environment from a Christian point-of-view and the idea that a man would be in Congress from Monday through Friday and maybe fly home, but very often times not, and going a week or two weeks without seeing your family, they just thought, 'This is not a natural way to live.' It was done as a way to respect Karen and I would use it as a discipline in the way you would say, I'm a disciple. I am disciplined and intentional" as the apostle Paul who wrote, "*I discipline my body like an athlete, training it to do what it should*" (1 Corinthians 9:27 NLT).

Doug Deason, a long-time friend of Mike's and president of Deason Capital Services in Texas, says applying the Billy Graham Rule is a standard every married man should follow.

"Number one, it's the most Christian thing you can do for your wife and in honor of your wife," says Deason. "But number two, the left side of the aisle, they're going to be standing there as the elevator opens and he gets off with another woman and then the rumors start. It's a smart, logical thing to do. It's just so refreshing to see it in Washington in leadership like that."

Despite his reasons for implementing the spiritual boundaries in his life and his friends' support, "critics argue that this reduces women to sexual temptresses, and precludes him from working with women on an equal basis," Varvel says. "But the Mike Pence I know is living by a biblical principle. First Thessalonians 5:22 says, '*Abstain from all appearance of evil*' [KJV]. In our overly sexualized society, a photo of Pence dining alone with a woman would be enough to suggest infidelity. Paparazzi make a living doing this."[4]

McIntosh looks at the chaos and pain that ignoring the Billy Graham Rule could cause.

"You look at what happened with the Brett Kavanaugh hearings and separate from faith, [the rule] makes no sense," says McIntosh, referring to the 2018 U.S. Senate hearings to confirm Kavanaugh's appointment to the U.S. Supreme Court. "You expose yourself to future allegations. But it also meant, 'I want to set the right relationship here and make it very clear that this is a professional relationship with the women I'm working with.' To the secular world, it seems odd that someone would think this way and act this way, but in God's economy, it's a completely different way of making decisions."

MORE NEED TO FOLLOW RULE

Dr. James Dobson, founder of Focus on the Family and the Christian-focused organization and radio channel *Family Talk*, says he has great love and respect for Mike and Karen. Talking about the Billy Graham Rule on his radio program after Mike was criticized for adhering to it, Dobson admonished more men to follow Mike's example.

"I have known Mike Pence for twenty-five years. He is a godly man, a good man, a good family man, a good husband and father....

He lives by the highest standards of ethics," Dobson said. "I have seen some crazy things, but this [attack on Mike] has got to be one of the stupidest that I have heard."[5]

The media complained that the Billy Graham Rule was sexist and hindered women who were trying to advance in the workplace. Most married women would not level such criticism, Dobson maintained.

"Ask a woman how she feels about it," Dobson suggested. "Ask a woman who loves her husband and is trying to live a godly life as a wife and mother. Ask a woman who has children if she wants her husband to honor her in this way.... This is not coming from women; it's coming from these reporters that are looking for something negative to say. Are [job] promotions more valuable than a lifetime together in a committed, loving marriage? I mean how silly is that? It just takes my breath away."[6]

All of Mike's staff members knew he followed the Billy Graham Rule.

"He was adamant about not being alone with another woman," recalls Reger. "It was hard to do, but it showed you how much he valued his marriage that he would put those kinds of safeguards up."

Those who make fun of Mike "for the protections he puts on his behavior must not know the people I know or suffer the temptations I face," says Mollie Hemingway, senior editor of *The Federalist*. "They must not read the headlines about marriages ending due to infidelity. I have far too many friends who found their inhibitions lowered by alcohol and distance from a spouse. The end result of their lapse in judgment has in some cases been the destruction of their marriage.... Pence's smart tactics for avoiding the kind of marital failure that could destroy him, his wife, their family, and the lives of those around them is to be commended and celebrated."[7]

NOT JUST WOMEN

Steger says there's another reason Mike doesn't eat alone with a woman other than Karen.

"It's so bent out of shape and the motives that are imputed on Mike for that decision are so unfounded," says Steger. "It's not so much that he doesn't go out to dinner alone with a woman; it's that he doesn't go out to dinner alone with hardly anybody. All the time he was in Washington [in Congress], he'd say, 'All I want to do is work hard. Vote. Go home for dinner.' He never desired to be a part of the D.C. cocktail scene. He didn't want to be wined and dined by lobbyists. What was in his heart's desire was to get home to Karen and the kids."

Mike isn't the only Christian man who adopted the Billy Graham Rule in his life. Others include Pastor Rick Warren, author of the best-seller, *The Purpose Driven Life*, and Ralph Reed, founder of the Faith & Freedom Coalition.

"For those of us who came up in the evangelical world, that [rule] was well known," says Reed. "Millions of men for over fifty years have followed that rule. As an example, an orthodox rabbi will not shake the hand of a woman and I have met orthodox women who would not shake my hand. There's some version of this in the Jewish community and you never hear about it being commented on as treating women as second-class citizens or it being disrespectful."

Kellyanne Conway, who has worked as one of Mike's top advisers for years, defends his position, saying she "never felt excluded or dismissed.... Most wives would appreciate a loyal husband who puts them first. People are trying to bloody and muddy him, but talk about narrow-minded—to judge his marriage!"[8]

Pastor Charles Lake laughs as he talks about those who persecute Mike on this issue.

"I think it's hilarious," Lake says, "that it wasn't long after they made a mockery of him having that rule that some of them were saying that if some of our politicians today would follow that rule, we'd have less scandal in politics than we have."

Late one night, after watching the news together and hearing the media criticize her father for following the Billy Graham Rule, Charlotte shared her heart with Mike, telling him, "Thank you...for only having dinner with my mom my entire life."[9]

That put it all into perspective for Mike.

Joining a bipartisan group of sixty faith-filled members of Congress, men and women, Mike began attending the Congressional Prayer Caucus in which members gathered for prayer before important votes. Mike also began attending a Bible study with thirty to sixty other representatives. It was held at the Capitol every Wednesday morning from 8:00 to 9:00 a.m. Republican Congressman John Carter of Texas began to attend as a freshman representative.

"The men each took turns teaching the study and went around the room if there was time and we prayed for each other," says Carter.

Mike's faith in God became evident as he counseled and led other men in the study by invoking Scripture, Carter says. "Pence used to say, 'Iron sharpens iron' [Proverbs 27:17] when we'd hit a wall in Congress and used to preach on the verse that when our nation repents, God will heal our land" from 2 Chronicles 7:14.

STILL HAD SENSE OF HUMOR, FUN

Congressional work and his faith did not make Mike a somber person. He never lost his playful sense of humor. On one occasion, Mike, Carter, and Representative John Culberson snuck through a top window in the Capitol and climbed on top of the roof.

"There was a couch with a tent over it and beer bottles scattered everywhere where workers who had been repairing the roof took breaks and relaxed after work," Carter recalls with a laugh. "Mike joked that's where Senate leaders went after work."

McIntosh says Mike was playful and full of joy.

"We liked to do backyard barbecues, roasting wienies over the pit," McIntosh recalls. "One night, my son, who was probably four or five at the time, disappeared into the garage and came back with two sticks with a bunch of old rags tied to [them] and he and Mike turned them into torches and they were running around the backyard. I was thinking to myself, 'Not too many four-year-olds get to play *that* game with a congressman!' Mike turned to me afterwards and said, 'We don't usually get to go to events where I have a bunch of old underwear rags tied up in a torch!'"

Mike's friends attest to the fact that he's the same man day-to-day that he is on Sunday mornings.

Faith is "the most important thing in my life," Mike would say during his days in Congress. "My relationship with the Lord, the way that expresses itself in real ways, day in and day out, the way I conduct myself at home and at work, is really what I would like to make my end-all."[10]

Mike stands out from other politicians who say they have strong religious convictions.

"What makes Mike different from other politicians who claim to be Christians is he walks the walk," says Deason. "He truly, truly walks the walk. He does less talking the talk and does more walking the walk than any politician I've ever known. There's just not a kinder or gentler politician with strength than Mike Pence."

While serving in Congress, Mike referred to himself as a "happy warrior" for conservative principles. His views and the votes he cast always traced back to the Bible and the United States Constitution.

FIGHT AGAINST ABORTION

Wielding both like swords, Mike stood against abortion and co-sponsored the Right to Life Act, which offered constitutional protection, under the 14th Amendment, to "each born and pre-born human person."[11] Addressing the 2001 March for Life rally—held every year since the U.S. Supreme Court ruled abortion legal in *Roe v. Wade* in 1973—Mike said, "A fundamental axiom of Western civilization is to believe in the sanctity of human life. The 107th Congress must be about the business of reasserting this crucial principle in our law. Roe must go."[12] At later marches, Mike said he was committed to reducing *Roe v. Wade* to "the ash heap of history."

Mike made national news when he threatened to shut down the federal government unless it defunded Planned Parenthood. As his biblical values and conservative views about abortion were highlighted in the media across the nation, conservative Christians began to take notice, heightening Mike's national profile.

Mike gamely attempted to defund Planned Parenthood even in January 2009, when the Democrats held majorities in both houses of Congress.

With his original sixty-three cosponsors, Mike reintroduced the Title X Abortion Provider Prohibition Act in the House, saying, "It comes as a surprise to many to learn that the largest recipient of non-abortion federal taxpayer dollars through Title 10 is the largest abortion provider in America. Most Americans don't realize that.... Now, Planned Parenthood, that recipient, will be very quick to say that, well, Title 10 can't go to providing or promoting abortion services, and that is certainly true, but it doesn't change the fact that the largest abortion provider in America is also the recipient of literally tens of millions of dollars in federal taxpayer money that go into their non-abortion related activities. Our legislation, reintroduced today with broad support and in the last Congress, cosponsored by nearly 200 of our colleagues, would restrict any federal family planning funds from going to organizations like Planned Parenthood, who perform abortions on demand or for any reason. And I urge my colleagues to support this measure."[13]

Unquestionably, Mike is "pro-life," Phipps notes. "He feels his view is consistent with Bible teaching—life is sacred, life was created by God. When we start the slippery slope of devaluing life and its sanctity, then we are headed for great peril. I think his moral outlook, based on his interpretation of Scripture and how he feels the God of the Bible would have him feel about life, I think that's been the guiding star that directed his path."

STRONG SUPPORTER OF ISRAEL

Mike has also taken a strong, continuous stand in support of Israel. For instance, in May 2001, he joined other House representatives in committing to relocate the U.S. Embassy in Israel to Jerusalem. Later that year, citing newspaper reports that "the State Department is preparing to pressure our friends in Israel to make territorial concessions including yielding part of Jerusalem to the establishment of a Palestinian state," Mike urged the president and the State Department "to clarify the unqualified support of the United States of America for Jerusalem as the inviolate and eternal capital of Israel; and that the United States of America, Christians and Jews and all of Americans stand for the territorial integrity of Israel and so should this Congress."[14]

In February 2004, Mike sponsored a resolution supporting Israel's construction of a security fence to prevent Palestinian terrorist attacks. In 2007, he co-led the bipartisan Congressional Anti-Semitism Task Force.

"My support for Israel stems largely from my personal faith," Mike told the *Congressional Quarterly* in 2002. "In the Bible, God promises Abraham, *'Those who bless you I will bless, and those who curse you I will curse.'*"[15]

Matthew Brooks, executive director of the Republican Jewish Coalition, says Mike's pro-Israel stance has saved and changed the lives of innumerable Israelis.

"He became one of the most important pro-Israel voices in the Republican caucus," says Brooks. "He was a leader in supporting Israel's decision to construct the security barrier under Prime Minister [Ariel] Sharon and that was particularly controversial at the time, but has since proven to have saved countless lives from terror attacks from the Palestinian terrorists. He was one of the leaders at the forefront of supporting Israel and Israel's right to secure its citizens and to build the security fence."

Brooks believes Mike's passion for Israel is found in his passion for his Christian heritage.

"Israel is the home of Judaism and it's also the home of Christianity and the birth place of Christ, and so much of Christianity weaves through the streets of the old city of Jerusalem," says Brooks. "I think people go there and feel like they're coming home."

He believes Mike will "always be a stalwart friend and defender of Israel....not only based on shared values and shared goals in terms of our two nations being aligned, but I also think it's because of his commitment in his heart that it's a Jewish homeland but also his homeland as a devout Christian."

Mike's association with the American Israel Public Affairs Committee (AIPAC) dates back to 1988, when he first ran for Congress, and continued after he became a congressman in 2001. Addressing AIPAC in 2009, Mike said, "Like the overwhelming majority of my constituents, my Christian faith compels me to cherish the state of Israel. In the year 2000, when I was first selected to Congress, Israel was already a priority to me. I really looked forward to being in a position where I knew I could help fulfill what I believed was not only right for America but the right thing to do."[16]

In a speech at the Washington summit of Christians United for Israel (CUFI), a non-profit founded by Pastor John Hagee, Mike stated, "Though Israel was built by human hands, it is impossible not to sense that just beneath its history lies the hand of heaven."[17]

ADVOCATE FOR SENIORS, VETERANS

Mike made it his mission in Congress to speak for those who could not speak or advocate for themselves. Regarding the elderly and their medical needs, he said the Medicare Modernization and Prescription Drug Act of 2002, which he supported, "protects Hoosier seniors from having to choose between putting food on their tables and buying the prescription drugs they need. Forcing seniors in our prosperous nation to make such a choice is morally wrong. America is better than that, and Americans have the right to expect better than that from their government."[18]

Mike also fought for better health care services for veterans throughout his years in Congress. When news came out about some of the poor conditions at Walter Reed Army Medical Center and bureaucratic delays for veterans trying to receive medical treatment, he told his colleagues, "Let us work in a bipartisan way in this Congress to fundamentally bring changes to our health care system that serves our military, that serves our veterans, that ultimately will rise to the level that each one of them deserves. The Old Book says if you owe debts, pay debts; if honor, then honor; if respect, then respect. One of the ways that our nation discharges a debt that we cannot ever fully repay to those who have worn the uniform is to ensure that they receive the medical treatment that they so richly deserve."[19]

Steger says, "Mike just sees free enterprise as in line with biblical principles: help out the widows, help out the orphans, help out the poor."

As Mike fought for Hoosiers' rights in our nation's capital, he came face-to-face with tragedies that changed countless lives forever.

ENDNOTES

1. Billy Graham, *Just As I Am: The Autobiography of Billy Graham* (New York: HarperCollins Publishers, 1997).
2. Ibid.
3. Mike Pence, 2002 interview with *The Hill*, Washington, D.C., quoted by Emma Green, "How Mike Pence's Marriage Became Fodder for the Culture Wars," *The Atlantic*, March 30, 2017.
4. Gary Varvel, "Varvel: Rebutting *The New Yorker* caricature of Mike Pence," *The Indianapolis Star*, October 24, 2017.
5. Dr. James Dobson with guest Eben Fowler, "Boundaries: Protecting Your Marriage," *Family Talk*, April 10, 2017.
6. Ibid.
7. Mollie Hemingway, "Don't Mock Mike Pence For Protecting His Marriage, Commend Him," *The Federalist*, March 30, 2017.
8. Mayer.
9. Charlotte Pence, *Where You Go*.
10. C-SPAN, "Q&A with Mike Pence," January 19, 2006.
11. H.R.618, Right to Life Act, 110th Congress (2007-2008).
12. User-created clip of Mike Pence at March for Life, C-SPAN, January 22, 2001 (www.c-span.org/video/?c4617276/mike-pence-2001).
13. Mike Pence, "Abortion," *Congressional Record, 111th Congress, First Session*, Vol. 155, No. 12, Washington, January 21, 2009.
14. Mike Pence, "Pledging Support for Israel," *Congressional Record, 107th Congress, First Session*, Vol. 147, No. 137, Washington, October 12, 2001.
15. Coppins.
16. www.aipac.org.
17. "Remarks by the Vice President at Christians United for Israel Washington Summit," July 17, 2017 (www.whitehouse.gov/briefings-statements/remarks-vice-president-christians-united-israel-washington-summit).
18. "Indiana Congressional Races, Congressional District 6," *The Howey Political Report*, Vol. 8, No. 39, July 1, 2002.
19. Mike Pence, "Our Military Health Care System," *Congressional Record, 110th Congress, First Session*, House of Representatives, Vol. 153, No. 38, Washington, March 6, 2007.

12

"THE UNFORGETTABLE 107TH CONGRESS"

We are hard pressed on every side, but not crushed; perplexed,
but not in despair; persecuted, but not abandoned; struck down,
but not destroyed.
—2 Corinthians 4:8–9

On the morning of Tuesday, September 11, 2001, having served in Congress for just nine months, Mike headed to a House Agriculture Committee meeting at the Capitol after having breakfast with a member of his staff.

Without warning, at 8:46 a.m., American Airlines Flight 11 crashed into the north tower of the World Trade Center in New York City. Government officials thought it was a fluke accident until minutes later, when United Airlines Flight 175 rammed into the south tower. Chaos ensued. And just as shell-shocked Americans were still gasping for breath, American Airlines Flight 77 hit the Pentagon, less than an hour after the first crash.

"I got into the office right after the first plane had hit the World Trade Center," recalls Piepgrass. "When I walked in, everyone was glued to the television."

Mike was in the office, just across the street from the Capitol.

"The memories of that day seem like they were fifteen minutes ago to me," Mike says. "I'd heard about the first aircraft hitting one of the World Trade Center's [towers] and I was in my office when my assistant, Jennifer...dropped the phone and reeled back and said, 'The Pentagon's been hit.' Our office was on about the fourth floor across the street from the Capitol. Immediately, I thought it would be appropriate for us to move out of the building against the possibility [of] an even widening attack on the Capitol. There was no order for evacuation, but I told the team, 'We need to move out.' But we stopped for a quick prayer."[1]

The Pences attended a church in Washington "with a lot of people that worked at the Pentagon and we just knew there was heartbreaking loss of life and bravery under way and we just prayed one of those quick prayers," Mike says.[2]

He told his staff "to move away from the Capitol, but for my part, I felt like I needed to report for duty," Mike recalls, "and so I walked onto the Capitol grounds and the sights and sounds of that day, I'll never forget—half of the sky was filled with mud-brown columns of smoke billowing out of the Pentagon and aircraft, jet aircraft, flying at low levels, sirens everywhere, pandemonium."[3]

Mike was concerned about what else to expect. Officials knew there was a fourth plane and suspected that its target was the U.S. Capitol, so they prepared to evacuate.

EVERYONE RAN

"I will always remember the scenes of that day, watching the Capitol complex being evacuated," Mike vividly recalls. "It was as though the building was literally hemorrhaging with people running in every direction."[4]

"At some point, we got word that we had to evacuate and they pulled the alarms in the building," remembers Piepgrass. "We prayed together first and then we all evacuated, leaving everything in the office. Everyone ran from the building and we kept running for blocks and blocks because we thought one of the next planes would hit the Capitol building or one of the House office buildings that we were in."

Mike's chief of staff, Bill Smith, was in a meeting two blocks from the White House.

"The secretary rolled a television screen into the room and said, 'Mr. Smith, I think you and your group will want to see this,'" recalls Smith. "Just then, the second plane hit the tower. Then a message came over my government-issued BlackBerry from Mike, saying, 'Where are you?' I told him and he said, 'You need to get out of there because they think another plane may be coming towards the White House.' We communicated back and forth with each other over our BlackBerries throughout the morning. We were praying for each other, our families and country. Obviously, we were all concerned about what was actually happening."

That morning and Mike's words are etched in Steger's memory.

JOINS CONGRESSIONAL LEADERS

"He looks out from the Capitol across the National Mall, past the Washington Monument towards the Pentagon. Pitch black smoke was billowing. Michael has this catharsis that the country is completely vulnerable," says Steger. "The first thing all the congressmen were told is to 'spread out, go home, go somewhere, but don't stay at the Capitol.' Mike immediately pushed back and said, 'Where is leadership gathering?' And he had to ask the question several times because they were saying, 'Congressman, don't worry about that, just go.' But he was insistent and he finally got someone to tell him where leadership was meeting [and] he immediately went to that place."

There was a reason Mike was fearless.

"Standing there on the plaza in the midst of that pandemonium and in the days that followed that," Mike says, "I thought of that verse [from Isaiah 26:3] that says the Lord will surround in perfect peace the man who trusts in Him. And I can honestly tell you, my wife will attest to it, that as I stood there on the Capitol grounds, I knew we were all going to be okay. I had peace in the midst of that pandemonium and I'll carry that the rest of my life, but it was a peace that even in the midst of that, that God's grace was extending, not only to my little family, but to this nation."[5]

Mike joined the House and Senate leaders who were meeting at the United States Capitol Police (USCP) headquarters across the street from the Capitol. Charged with protecting the United States Congress, USCP is the only full-service federal law enforcement agency responsible to the legislative branch of the United States government. It was overwhelmed with what was occurring and its inability to reach all of its police officers on the ground.

USCP had hand-held and car radios on an analog system that didn't work in several "dead spots" around congressional buildings.[6]

Mike "gets there and he was a young congressman, a first termer," says Steger. "So here he is, just a rookie, and he's insisting on getting with leadership at this moment of devastation. He's shocked, but thinking clearly, saying, 'I have a responsibility. I'm an elected congressman. I'm not running for the hills and I'm going to fulfill my duties here.' He gets to the office and leadership can't make calls because the cell lines are all jammed. Michael had a BlackBerry at the time. One of the leaders is saying, 'Why can't we get a line out? We've got to make a call!' And [this] little rookie congressman is over there [getting messages out] because he had a BlackBerry that runs on a different [wavelength]. So Michael could get out, but leadership couldn't."

Mike was making calls to Karen and his staff, assuring them of his safety, making sure they were safe, and praying with all of them. As he was communicating with them, Mike and the other members of Congress with him were told their lives were in danger.

"Shortly after I arrived, the chief of police set the phone back down and informed the leaders gathered there that there was a plane inbound for the Capitol, and he said it was 12 minutes out," Mike says, recalling the threat on their lives. "In that moment, the room became silent, and as people began to make plans, I found myself looking out the window, where just across the street was the Capitol dome, with that majestic statue of freedom standing a top it. A dome that's a symbol for the ideas of this nation—of the freedom and democracy for all the world."[7]

THE LONGEST 12 MINUTES

Mike prayed silently as they all held their breath with their lives in the balance.

"So we waited," Mike says. "It was the longest 12 minutes of my life. But it turned into 13 minutes. Then 14. Then we were informed that the plane had gone down in a field in Pennsylvania."[8]

Selflessly, the thirty-three passengers and seven crew members of United Airlines Flight 93 fought back against their four terrorists. All on board lost their lives as the plane crashed in rural Somerset County, Pennsylvania.

Mike says the forty "heroes of Flight 93" were "men and women who looked evil squarely in the eye and without regard to their personal safety, they rushed forward to save lives."[9]

Years later, moved to tears by the heroism of the passengers and crew of Flight 93, Mike would say, "I will always believe that I, and many others in our nation's capital, were able to get home that day to hug our families because of the courage and selflessness of the heroes of Flight 93. The American people will forever be inspired by their courage and resolve. We honor them by remembering them...and by doing everything in our power as a nation to prevent such evil from ever reaching our shores again."[10]

On the afternoon of September 11, 2001—the day that simply came to be known as 9/11—Mike talked to a reporter back home in Indiana from his D.C. area home in Arlington.

"We need to fashion a response that is swift and violent," Mike said. "We know where these people live. We know who the likely suspects are. I am hoping that the sun doesn't come up again in that part of the world without smoke billowing from one of their targets."[11]

House leaders knew Osama bin Laden's organization was likely behind the attacks because of a phone call and a fax that read, "Atten: Bin Laden will destroy your capital."[12]

Mike urged Americans to pray, adding, "They should be confident in the strength of our national leadership, in our president. We will get through this. We will prevail and we will respond."[13]

Mike made sure every one of his staff members were safely evacuated and in secure locations. He prayed for those who had lost their lives, their family members, and the safety of American citizens.

"Through the whole thing, he kept his cool and his demeanor," says Bill Smith. "He knew God was in control."

"It's in our strength in the service to others that you work through crisis and you work through communal setbacks," says Blackwell. "America's enemies see our diversity as a threat and, therefore, any time they can foster division among us, they do. Mike was one of these leaders who understood the nature of the threat and what made us threatening as a nation and that we couldn't actually give our detractors and the terrorists what they wanted by turning on each other. I remember Mike using the line, 'Instead of turning on one another, we should turn towards one another.' And that's the sort of leadership that he's always offered."

Steger says the 9/11 attacks on American soil showed Mike the susceptibility of our nation.

"It just steeled Mike with a real understanding of how vulnerable we are and how important it is that we stay strong as a military, as a nation now," says Steger. "He believes America is a shining city on a hill and a beacon of light for the world. I don't mean that in just Reaganesque terms. I mean that more in spiritual terms of being light to the world. He also understands that light has to be protected."

Mike made his feelings about the terrorists' assault on America quite clear. Recalling how the ground shook after the plane hit the Pentagon, he was filled "with a deep and resolute anger that this would not stand; that America would respond.... The butchers who carried out these attacks see themselves as warriors, and it would be wrong of us to deal with them otherwise. What they are about to learn is that America's fighting men are the most powerful warriors in the history of the world. Tonight I will solemnly and with deep humility vote to give our president the power to use all necessary and appropriate force to vanquish the enemies of our peace. May God have mercy on their souls, because the United States of America will not."[14]

The terrorist attacks caused the deaths of nearly three thousand people and injured more than six thousand others.

In a united front, Congress immediately focused on fortifying America's borders, strengthening security measures at airports, and initiating a war on terrorism.

TOURING WORLD TRADE CENTER

Days later, on October 1, Mike and dozens of other members of Congress toured the remains of the World Trade Center, meeting with firefighters and rescue workers as they sorted through debris.

"It is almost too difficult to describe," Mike said. "There is literally 15 stories of twisted steel, still burning with fires that we were told were 1,500 to 1,600 degrees underground. This is a war zone.... I can't imagine if a weapon of mass destruction had been used here in New York that the damage would have been any different."[15]

Mike knew President Bush had to be feeling a lot of pressure after the attacks. Feeling empathy for the heavy burden of America and her safety that weighed on the president, Mike approached him at the White House Christmas party with assurance of his spiritual support.

"The first time I saw President Bush after 9/11, I told him I was praying for him, by name, just about every day on my knees," Mike says. "He looked at me and he said, 'Mike, keep it up. It matters.'"[16]

"Many times, in the political arena, you have people say things because they feel it's the right phraseology, like 'God bless America' or 'Our prayers are with you,'" says Phipps. "But Mike was the kind of fellow who if there was a little boy who was crying at a memorial service, he was the kind of person who would go and hug the child himself personally. If a kid got hurt or something, he'd take that situation and show great compassion, an almost fatherly attitude. He really identified with suffering people who lost loved ones or who had tragedy. He always offered kind remarks and he always wanted to say something to uplift the spirit and he was never ashamed of his faith in Christ."

As America was reeling from the overwhelming pain and devastation of 9/11, and Congress was focusing on the war at hand, Mike endured another test of his faith and leadership skills.

LETTERS WITH ANTHRAX

Soon after the attacks, anonymous letters laced with anthrax were delivered to media outlets and government offices in the District of Columbia, New York, and Florida. The one sent to Senator Patrick J. Leahy of Vermont was typical. Dated "09-11-01" and printed in block lettering, it read, "You can not stop us. We have this anthrax. You die now. Are you afraid? Death to America. Death to Israel. Allah is great."[17]

The anthrax-laced letters killed five Americans and sickened seventeen others. The ensuing investigation was one of the largest and most complex in the history of law enforcement.

In the search for anthrax, investigators found that Mike's office and two others in the Longworth House Office Building had been exposed to the dangerous, infectious bacteria. Mike's and Bill Smith's desks had trace elements of anthrax on them. Following FBI instructions, Mike's staff left everything behind and created a make-shift office in the Capitol basement, where they drew up a list of people who could have been exposed.

"It was on a Friday night that we received the telephone call that they had found the chemical anthrax bacillus in our office and that of other members of the House and Senate," Mike recalls. "It began a mad dash, a scramble that went all night long as we tried to reconstruct who had been in the office during the affected two-week period of time. I was on the phone with people literally around the world who had come through our office in that time, urging them to seek medical attention. It was a frightening time with our three small children close by [and] with young men and women who served us in those offices. It was an anxious twenty-four hours."[18]

Mike and his staff were told to immediately report to the Capitol physician to be checked for symptoms, which could begin to manifest themselves as early as one day after exposure and up to two months later. Despite not seeing any signs of an infection, the doctor put everyone on a sixty-day prescription of ciprofloxacin or Cipro—a powerful antibiotic that stops the growth of bacteria—as a precautionary measure.

"Michael was concerned," says Steger. "What he conveyed to me was, 'The right people have it, they're analyzing what it was and were putting in processes, but this is now a reality we have to live with and we have to deal with it.' He said, 'Well, you know, first of all, I don't want to leave behind a wife and three children. How far does this thing go now? The kids are at school. What do we do at home? How exposed are we and how focused is our enemy?'"

The Capitol physician suggested that the Pence children be examined in case they'd been exposed to anthrax while visiting their father at work. "Poison powder" was found in Daddy's office, Karen told the kids. They prayed, read from the Bible, and talked about what to expect in case they had to take antibiotics.

"We wanted to assure them that Mommy and Daddy were OK and that all the staff people they know are well," Mike recalls.[19]

The next day was a Sunday and the Pences went to church.

"I'll never forget that weekend," Mike says. "Ensconced as we were in our nation's capital, we slipped away to a suburban church. We were there on a Sunday morning as Karen and I stood in the pews, away from our home church in Greenwood, Indiana. Somewhere in one of the songs lifting up praise...I felt that warm waterfall of [God's] presence.... I turned and looked at my wife and she had tears in her eyes before I ever looked at her and I knew she felt it, too.

"We didn't think any more of it other than a moment of passing grace, but when we came back to our little townhouse, we sent the kids off to play in their rooms, we saw the light flashing on the answering machine and we hit play. And there over the voice of the answering machine came those dulcet tones of Pastor Charles Lake."[20]

Without knowing the trial the Pences were enduring, the Holy Spirit had revealed to Lake that they were struggling with something serious.

Recalling the message, Mike says, "And Pastor Lake said, 'I just called to tell you, since you're on our hearts, that this morning about 10:15, we prayed for you and Karen and Michael and Charlotte and Audrey in the middle of our service. And I just wanted you to know that.' And I picked up the phone with tears in my eyes and I called Pastor Charles and I said, 'You didn't have to tell us. We knew.'"[21]

Because of the peace he and Karen had in their hearts, they had surety that God was in control, so Mike was able to be strong for his family and staff and forge forward in faith.

CALM IN A CRISIS

"Again, in a crisis situation, he handled it with a cool head and calm demeanor that you would expect of someone who puts his trust in Someone bigger than himself," Bill Smith says. "He showed himself to be able to hold up in a time of stress. Sometimes you show your faith not just by quoting Scripture or by getting on your knees in the moment. Sometimes you show your faith by caring for others more than yourself. And that's what I saw in both the 9/11 attacks and Anthrax scare. His first instincts were to ask, 'How are the people around me? Does anyone have a need I can fill?' He showed his faith in real-life situations. In any crisis situation, if you want to know if a person's faith is genuine, look to see if they show care and compassion to their fellow man. Mike certainly shows that in droves."

Mike had always drawn strength from his spiritual heroes during difficult times and found strength in their words.

"My favorite quote about prayer comes from one of my favorite authors, C.S. Lewis," Mike says. "He said, 'I pray because I can't help myself. I pray because I'm helpless. I pray because the need flows out of me all the time, waking or sleeping.' And then he said, 'But prayer doesn't change God. It changes me.' And so it is in my life."[22]

Steger says Mike knew people were praying for them, telling his friend, "Karen and I feel kind of a shield of prayer around us."

The overwhelming stress of the prior two months, along with day-to-day activities in Congress, were daunting. But Mike found refuge in his private time with God and at home with Karen and their children.

Michael's staff found strength in his example of fortitude and spiritual leadership.

"The way he modeled handling difficult and stressful situations inspired me," Piepgrass explains. "He was gracious and calm and very thoughtful about it—and fairly unflappable. And I think a lot of that came from his faith and that was a good model for me in that position and has been throughout my career. When I get in stressful positions, as you get with any kind of job where there's a lot on the line, I've thought back, 'This is how Mike would handle things.' And all of that, too, was informed with his knowledge that he's really not in control. I've tried to take that lesson and apply it to my career."

Mike wasn't any less vocal to those responsible for the anthrax scare than he'd been to the terrorists after 9/11.

"To the people who did this, wherever they are, our message to you is simply this: You have failed again," Mike said. "You have failed to reach your target and you have failed in a much more profound way. For by this act, you have further steeled the resolve of every member of this national government whose duty it is to either bring you to justice or seal your fate."[23]

After a lengthy investigation, authorities believed that Dr. Bruce E. Ivins, a microbiologist at the United States Army Medical Research Institute of Infectious Diseases, was behind the attacks. However, Ivins died of an overdose in July 2008 before criminal charges were filed against him.

As his faith continued to be tried over time, Mike would say, "My faith has been tested, relied on, more times than I could possibly count. All I know for sure today is I need Him more than ever and He's really the center of my life and the center of my family's life."[24]

The tragedies only brought Mike and Karen closer as a couple. Friends say they became even more inseparable.

"Their relationship is very close and very real," says Bill Smith. "It is about as close as you can get in a husband and wife. They literally have combined their lives in a way that is very rare in the political world. In many ways, they are a normal couple in terms of highs and lows, but they always work through it together and come out better on the other end. Mike and Karen always made their relationship the top priority and no decisions of any significance were made without the other person being on board."

Piepgrass agrees with that assessment.

"They are a very good match; they balance each other very well," he says. "Mike can be serious, but he also has a good sense of humor and she does, too. Family is incredibly important to both of them and they're very well suited to each other."

Mike and Karen knew their staff had been through a rough first year in Congress and sought ways to encourage them.

"After 9/11 and the whole anthrax incident, Mike wanted to show his appreciation and show us that he really saw us as more than staff and employees, but as an extension of his family, which is how he really saw us," Piepgrass explains. "Many of his staff knew them for years because they came from Indiana. I had gotten really close to them because I traveled with Mike. So he had us all over for a barbecue in his backyard at their little place in Arlington."

AVOIDING SNIPER ATTACKS

Just as things were beginning to settle down for Mike and Karen, they had a scare that would make them appreciate one another even more.

In October 2002, during Mike's second year in Congress, two snipers, John Allen Muhammad, and his teenage cohort, Lee Boyd Malvo, were terrorizing the Washington, D.C., area for weeks from their makeshift sniper nest in the trunk of Muhammad's car. Together, the pair would kill ten adults and wound a 13-year-old boy. They targeted their victims at random as they went about their daily lives at gas stations, outside shopping malls, and on the streets.

Late one morning, Karen went shopping at the Home Depot in Seven Corners, Virginia. Hours later, Muhammad and Malvo picked that location for one of their sniper attacks.

"That really shook up Mike because Karen had just been in that same parking garage on that same floor within just a few hours," recalls Feigenbaum. "It just had a huge impact on him and Karen." They thought about what might have happened if she had gone shopping later that day. "Mike said, 'We prayed over the fact that we weren't involved in that and weren't there at that time.'"

Although work on Capitol Hill was demanding, Mike made a point to be at the kids' games and activities as often as possible and remain active in their lives, even if it meant he had to leave the House floor and then return later that night to vote.

When Congress wasn't in session, Mike and Karen would take the kids back home to Indiana. During the six-hundred-mile drive to and from Washington, they'd listen to inspirational stories from Focus on the Family, such as *Adventures in Odyssey*. When at home, they enjoyed family activities suggested by the organization.

"One of the most cherished memories of our children's youth is the Family Nights booklet that we got from Focus on the Family," Mike says. "It inspired us to spend every Friday night with our little ones, usually on the living room floor, a little bit of pizza in the waiting, and we would huddle around a fun story, we'd learn a biblical message. And that Focus on Family family night booklet is on the shelf with lots of notes from those moments with the little ones."[25]

BOLDLY PROCLAIMING FAITH

While Mike continued to show his resolute faith on the House floor, aides and politicians often saw him reading his Bible as well. Using Scripture to validate his policy arguments, he told one staff member, "These have stood the test of time. They have eternal value."[26]

"He's just very bold," says Piepgrass. "He speaks his mind and doesn't pull punches, especially when it comes to who he is as a believer. That's one way he challenged me in my faith. He was just unashamed of the gospel and lives his life that way and will talk about it boldly, openly, with anyone. It was very striking to me. I try my best to do the same in my job and in daily life, having seen that as an example."

Because BlackBerries did not have phone functionality until 2002 and the phones at the office were shut down at 5:00 p.m. every day, Karen gave Mike an antique red phone one Christmas, connected to a number only she knew, so she could reach him at any time in the event of an emergency.

Karen was such an effective leader that she was asked by the Congressional Spouse Club to co-lead the spouse orientation with a Democratic spouse for the husbands and wives of new members of Congress. Although she never thought others should necessarily make the same decision she and Mike had made to move their entire family to Washington, Karen wanted the new spouses of House representatives to know all of their options so they could make informed decisions for their families.

Steger says Karen was committed to her new role. The new members of Congress would go off to one room, he says, "and Karen would take the spouses in orientation in a different room and just talk with them about the enormous pressures of Washington. She'd say how unnatural the situation is [to be separated] and just be a realist about the situation—no blinders on, just here's the real situation and how to be a good a couple if your husband or wife is an elected congressman and how to work through that. They believed that the congressman needed to go home at night to a home-cooked meal and, frankly, bat things around with their spouse. It's unhealthy for a congressman to be in Washington and spending his nights grinding too hard on policy issues or being with lobbyists."

SUPPORT FOR "IN GOD WE TRUST"

Mike continued to attend the weekly Bible study in Congress. During that time, the architect of the U.S. Capitol Visitor Center was engraving various words and sayings on the stone walls. Mike and the men in the Bible study asked him to include the nation's motto, "In God We Trust," but he refused. After several pleas were rejected, the men took it before leadership. Fellow believer and Congressman Dan Lungren of California introduced legislation directing the architect to carve the important motto on the wall. The legislation garnered the support of 410 members of the House.

"This motto is now permanently etched in the center, which now serves as the gateway into the United States Capitol building," Mike says, "and it is my hope that this will always be a visible reminder of the faith from which we come and the God who has so greatly blessed our nation."[27]

Three years into his tenure, on Saturday, September 11, 2004, Mike was on his way to the Indianapolis Airport when he saw a tragic accident on the freeway. He had no idea that his friend Ed Feigenbaum was in the carnage.

Ironically, Feigenbaum was coming from a meeting with Jim Atterholt, then an AT&T lobbyist—and Mike's future gubernatorial chief of staff. Feigenbaum slowed down to avoid a mattress that had just flown off a vehicle in front of him. The driver behind Feigenbaum slammed into the back of his car, which was hit so hard, it came to an abrupt stop on top of the mattress.

"I saw the collapsed car with the mattress underneath and I distinctly remember breathing a prayer for the driver, completely unaware that it was my friend of many years," Mike later wrote to Feigenbaum in an email.

In the ambulance, on the way to Indiana University Methodist Hospital, Feigenbaum was clinically dead and revived twice. Diagnosed with a traumatic brain injury, he spent ten days in the neuro-intensive care unit and another month in rehabilitation after his release from the hospital.

When Mike heard through the grapevine that Feigenbaum had been in a tragic accident and then realized it was the same one he drove past only days earlier, he was shocked and devastated. He immediately reached out to his friend, not certain when Feigenbaum would be able to read his email.

"When I heard you were the driver," Mike wrote, "I can't help but believe—from what I saw—that it was truly a miracle of God that you were spared."

Mike assured Feigenbaum that he and his family would be praying faithfully for his recovery and offered to help in any way they could. After a year of physical therapy, Feigenbaum fully recovered from the accident.

Mike continued to get reelected by comfortable margins. *Esquire Magazine* rated him as one of the ten best members of Congress, saying, "From immigration to earmarks, Pence is one of the most principled members, from either party, and his unalloyed traditional conservatism has repeatedly pitted him against his party elders."[28]

Everyone knew Mike would go toe-to-toe with anyone in order to stand by his convictions, one of which was marriage.

During a House debate on the Marriage Protection Amendment, Mike said, "Like millions of Americans, I believe that marriage matters, that it was ordained by God, instituted among men, that it is the glue of the American family and the safest harbor to raise children.... Several millennia ago the words were written that a man should leave his father and mother and cleave to his wife and the two shall become one flesh. It was not our idea; it was God's idea," referring to Genesis 2:24 and Mark 10:7–12.[29]

VISITING THE TROOPS

Throughout his tenure in Congress, Mike would take an annual trip to visit American troops overseas and rally support for them.

"I've had the privilege to visit our troops in Afghanistan and Iraq nearly every year since the wars began," Mike said. "They're the bravest men and women I've ever met.... Their service and sacrifice is a blessing to America."[30]

These ventures also honed Mike's approach to issues in the areas of national security and diplomacy, giving him a passion and commitment to ensure democracy for Americans.

Every trip overseas made a lasting impression on him. It meant even more as Mike recalled his father's own service under combat and how it had changed his life.

"He was affected," says Steger. "What he came back with was a deep and awesome respect for the sacrifices that our soldiers go through. Mike had a real clear understanding that there's really no battle lines anymore with post-traumatic stress disorder popping up in so many young guys.... The gratitude that comes from that on Mike's part, to see what these guys sacrificed to keep us free over here, he developed a deep respect and really a passion to do what he can for the guys."

Mike garnered respect in Congress and among those closest to him as a man who made sound decisions after a lot of thought and counsel. Friends say Mike reaches out to others for their opinions because of the biblical advice from Proverbs 11:14: *"In an abundance of counselors there is safety"* (ESV).

"I do know him as the type of person who does not move on rumor or feelings.... He is not the type of person who can evaluate things without seeing them firsthand," says Donald Manzullo, a former congressman from Illinois who served on the House Foreign Affairs subcommittee on the Middle East and South Asia with Mike.[31]

In 2006, Mike decided to run for House Minority Leader, but lost to Ohio's John A. Boehner, who had served as House Majority Leader. Boehner has praised Mike as "an exceptional leader, and an even better man.... With his heart, honesty, and integrity, he won the trust and respect of everyone with whom he served."[32]

"I think Mike impressed John Boehner [with] how he conducted that race," says McIntosh. "He never made it personal. He supported Boehner after he won and that led John, who needed a conservative on his leadership team, to ask Mike, 'Would you step forward and join me?'"

Boehner's respect for Mike became evident when he asked Mike to serve as the Republican Conference Chair, the party's third-highest-ranking post in the House. Mike would preside over weekly meetings where fellow Republican House members would discuss policy and legislative goals.

In fact, most of the men and women serving in Congress who worked with Mike had a deep respect for him regardless of their political views. Steger attributes this to Mike's affability and how he treats everyone.

STEPS IN TO HELP IMMIGRANT

While home in Indiana one day, Mike heard about a Muncie mother of two who was pulled over during a traffic stop and arrested on a long-standing deportation order initiated by an ex-husband.

Federal authorities kept Fatu Flake at an Illinois detention center and were threatening to send her back to her native Sierra Leone, leaving her new husband and children behind. Mike knew he had to intervene—she was a Hoosier after all and he had made a commitment to the people of Indiana that he would help them in any way he could. He took that responsibility seriously.

Mike and Reger went to the family's home to talk with them about the situation. Later, back in Washington, Mike contacted Senator Evan Bayh.

"He said, 'Evan, I need your help,'" recalls Reger. "We had people on our staff doing tons of work, making phone calls. It was really neat to see [Mike] using his authority and power to bless this one family. They were able to stop the whole process."

An immigration hearing was granted and resulted in Flake winning a new immigration status that allowed her to stay long enough to be designated a resident alien.

"He cared about people in Indiana," says Reger. "He didn't care what their politics were. We would help, no matter who you voted for. If you needed help with Social Security or Medicare or immigration stuff, if you were a member of his district, Mike was there to help."

ENDNOTES

1. First Baptist Church of Jacksonville, September 18, 2016.
2. Ibid.
3. First Baptist Church of Jacksonville, September 18, 2016.
4. Allan Smith, "Pence recalls the 'longest 12 minutes of his life' on September 11," *Business Insider*, September 11, 2017.
5. First Baptist Church of Jacksonville, September 18, 2016.
6. Mary Beth Sheridan, "Outdated Radios Fail Capitol Police," *The Washington Post*, June 2, 2008.
7. Allan Smith.
8. Ibid.
9. Ibid.
10. Gabby Morrongiello, "Mike Pence tears up recalling heroes of Flight 93," *Washington Examiner*, September 11, 2017.
11. John Clark, "Pence: Response Must Be Swift and Violent," *The Republic*, September 12, 2001.
12. Ibid.
13. Ibid.
14. Mike Pence, "Authorizing Use of United States Armed Forces Against Those Responsible for Recent Attacks Against the United States," *Congressional Record, 107th Congress, First Session*, Vol. 147, No. 120, Washington, September 14, 2001.
15. John Clark, "Hill, Pence tour devastation at New York's Ground Zero," *The Republic*, October 2, 2001.
16. Mike Pence, "National Day of Prayer," *Congressional Record, 109th Congress, Second Session*, Vol. 152, No. 52, Washington, May 4, 2006.
17. From Federal Bureau of Investigation report, "Amerithrax or Anthrax Investigation," in History, Famous Cases & Criminals (www.fbi.gov/history/famous-cases/amerithrax-or-anthrax-investigation).
18. Mike Pence, 2013 Indiana Leadership Prayer Breakfast.
19. John Clark, "Pence family takes steps vs. 'poison powder,'" *The Republic*, October

28, 2001.

20. Mike Pence, 2013 Indiana Leadership Prayer Breakfast.

21. Ibid.

22. Mike Pence, 2015 Indiana Leadership Prayer Breakfast (www.youtube.com/watch?v=CCiVBg53AkY).

23. "Congressman Mike Pence Responds After Anthrax Scare," October 27, 2001, courtesy of *WISH/Indianapolis*, posted by *TheClassicSports* (www.youtube.com/watch?v=u-bpLtrYmM0).

24. "Trump and Pence Send Video Messages to the Nation's Churches," *CBN News*, November 5, 2016 (www1.cbn.com/cbnnews/us/2016/november/trump-and-pence-send-video-messages-to-the-nations-churches).

25. "Remarks by the Vice President at the Focus on the Family 40th Anniversary Celebration in Colorado Springs, Colorado," June 23, 2017, The American Presidency Project (presidency.proxied.lsit.ucsb.edu/ws/index. php?pid=126529).

26. Meghan O'Gieblyn, "Exiled: Mike Pence and the evangelical fantasy of persecution," *Harper's Magazine*, May 2018.

27. "Pence Statement on 'In God We Trust' in Capitol Visitor's Center," *Standard Newswire*, October 1, 2009.

28. "The 10 Best Members of Congress," *Esquire Magazine*, October 15, 2008.

29. Mike Pence, "Marriage Protection Amendment," *Congressional Record*, 109th Congress, Second Session, Vol. 152, No. 94, Washington, July 18, 2006.

30. Mike Pence, "Service and Sacrifice," Pence4Indiana/Media Strategy Group, July 12, 2012.

31. Steve Eder and Thomas Kaplan, "Trump and Pence: One ticket that tries to merge two worldviews," *The Atlanta Journal-Constitution*, July 21, 2016.

32. David Sherfinski, "Paul Ryan on Mike Pence: 'I can think of no better choice' for our V.P. candidate," *The Washington Times*, July 15, 2016.

13

GOVERNOR OF INDIANA

Whoever can be trusted with very little can
also be trusted with much.
—Luke 16:10

After spending twelve years serving Indiana in Congress, Mike was approached by a group of conservative donors who saw his leadership skills as presidential material for the 2012 election.

"Mike was working with a group of conservative donors who really didn't think that [former Massachusetts Governor Mitt] Romney was going to be a very good candidate and they were looking for someone else," says McIntosh, who was part of the committee. "We did an exhaustive search." The committee "thought through" people like former House Speaker Newt Gingrich of Georgia and "new people" like Mike and U.S. Senators Marco Rubio of Florida and Ted Cruz of Texas. "The group settled on Mike Pence being the best candidate to go up against Barack Obama."

The group called Mike and asked for a meeting. Mike went and listened to what the committee had to say, but he wasn't convinced that running for president was the right thing to do.

"My argument to him was that the upside to running for president was that he might win because Obama could be beat if the right race was run," says McIntosh. "And if he didn't win, he would have a national platform to be the leader of the party of the conservative movement."

Doing what he always did in times of serious decision-making, Mike followed the Bible's advice and sought out wisdom from others: *"Plans fail for lack of counsel, but with many advisers they succeed"* (Proverbs 15:22).

"He was open to running for president," says Bill Smith. "It wasn't something we talked much about. The reason I say that is because even though he would consider it, usually it was because others had approached him and asked him to run. His heart is such that if someone asks him to serve or consider serving in a certain role, he's going to think and pray about it, and that's what he did."

Mike called Ralph Reed to discuss the idea with him.

"He was in Atlanta and he was meeting with people and his staff reached out to me and said Mike would like to meet with me," recalls Reed.

The two friends met at a local restaurant in mid-afternoon between lunch and dinner when it would be quiet and they could talk freely.

PRESIDENCY A LONG SHOT?

"We sat at a table and that's when he shared with me that he was considering the possibility of running for president in 2012," Reed says. "He asked my advice about it. We talked and I gave him generic advice that I would know based on working on a lot of presidential campaigns. I said, 'You know, I'm not telling you not to run as a member of Congress. I think you ought to do whatever you feel the Lord is calling you to do. But we haven't elected a sitting member of Congress [elected] to the White House since the 1840s and there's a reason. Number one, you don't have a statewide fund-raising base like a senator or governor. Prominent [Ohio] Congressman John Kasich made a bid for the presidency in 2000 and failed. Number two, you don't have any executive achievements. You've never held an executive position. You've been a legislator, but you've never run anything. Thirdly, you don't really have a built-in fund-raising base.

"I remember telling him a story of how [former President] Bill Clinton was going through a dry cycle during the Gennifer Flowers allegations and he was running out of money and [the Clintons] would get on a plane to Little Rock and hold a fund-raiser and put another half-a-million dollars in the bank and then get back on the plane and get back on the campaign trail. You can do that if you're a governor. You can't do that if you're a congressman. I said, 'You might want to think about going back home and running for governor.'"

Mike told Reed "in a specific and almost matter-of-fact type reference," that he and Karen were praying about it and "seeking God's will for his life."

And as he'd done with every other career move, Mike called Steger.

"The morning of January 3, 2010, Mike called me out of the blue," remembers Steger. "He said, 'Do you have a couple of minutes? I'm on my way to meet with a pastor, but I have something I want to talk with you about.' I said, 'Sure, fire away.' He said, 'Well, I'm giving it some serious thought to running for president or governor. So I'm trying to make up my mind and I just wanted to talk about it a little bit.' We had a lovely conversation and then he said he had to get to his appointment. He said he'd call back in an hour."

Steger watched one hour turn into several. "I said, 'He's not going to call back. He's on to the next thing,'" says Steger. But Mike did call, later that afternoon.

"We talked for two and a half hours," recalls Steger. "During that time, he's seeking a different perspective, seeking a different point of view, and wanting to drill down and look at pros and cons, his strengths and weaknesses. We talked about how he was younger than the other candidates and how he had time. Basically, my message to him was, 'If the time picks the man, my answer would be [to] run for president, but if man picks the time, you're not ready to be president, so run for governor.' Mike was very open-minded about it and commented to me that several of his close advisors also thought the governorship was the better fit for him at his age and at that time in his career. It really was a conversation about where can you best serve, where are you supposed to be right now and, in essence, back to that whole helper's view. The driver for Mike is, 'Where can I help people?' and that's a real key point."

In Indiana, governors are limited to serving eight years in any twelve-year period. Mike's friend, popular incumbent Governor Mitch Daniels, was term-limited and his lieutenant governor decided not to run. That left the opportunity open for Mike to be nominated.

"His ultimate decision was not to run for president," says Bill Smith. "He said, 'It's not the right time and if there is at some point in the future, God will make it clear to me or give me a peace about it.'"

GAINING EXECUTIVE EXPERIENCE

McIntosh says Mike's decision to run for governor instead of president ended up being the best option. "He chose the more humble experience, but honestly wanted to get that executive experience before going on the national stage and it ended up serving him well."

Blackwell, who had continued to advise Mike on his political career, says the House of Representatives had been looking at moving Mike up through their ranks.

"When he was making the move from Congress to run for governor, there were a lot of us who saw him as a Speaker-of-the-House-in-waiting," says Blackwell.

However, Mike shared his interest in running for governor and Blackwell encouraged him to seek God's will as the two men prayed together. "We prayed that God would give him and his family the clarity of decision."

Mike and Karen decided to follow the advice of several of his confidants and seek the Republican nomination for governor of Indiana in 2012. The Republican Governors Association showed their support by giving him $1 million in PAC money to help finance his campaign.

SELECTING A RUNNING MATE

In the spring of 2012, Mike met with several people he was considering for running mate. Dr. Sue Ellspermann, a highly successful businesswoman, was on that short list. After graduating from Purdue University in 1982 with a Bachelor of Science in industrial engineering, she received her Ph.D. from the University of Louisville in 1996. Ellspermann founded a business consulting firm and was the founding director of the University of Southern Indiana's Center for Applied Research. Succeeding in every arena, she was elected to the Indiana House of Representatives in the 74th District in 2010. It was clear to Mike that with Ellspermann's experience and education, she would be a good choice for lieutenant governor.

Jennifer L. Ping, principal at the Bose Public Affairs Group, believes Mike was impressed by more than Ellspermann's education and accomplishments.

"I think it was her credentials and personality and willingness to roll up her sleeves and do sometimes not always the most popular [thing], but what was needed to move the state forward, that put her on the list," says Ping. "And that's exactly the position that Mike wanted to put his candidacy for governor in."

During the interview process, Ellspermann thought for sure she'd shut the door on the opportunity to run with Mike by sharing her convictions about political campaigns.

"The thing that I thought would get me off of the short list was that the non-negotiable for me was political civility in the race," says Ellspermann. "To be the lieutenant governor candidate, that was my non-negotiable. After that day, I thought I was probably done with the interview at that point and then a few days later, I got the call asking if I would in fact be his lieutenant governor candidate."

Ellspermann noticed the level of Mike's commitment to God from the beginning.

"In everything from the time that the vetting began to when he offered me to be his lieutenant governor candidate, it was important to him that this be family decisions we made, so he and Karen and my husband, Jim, and I met for dinner and it was very much one of those of making sure that everything we did was aligned with our family values and on faith values," Ellspermann says. "We were very aligned."

KIDS HELP ON CAMPAIGN TRAIL

From the beginning of Mike's career in politics, he and Karen always had their kids helping in their father's campaign in some capacity. This one was no different, but now, the kids had busy schedules of their own. Michael was then a twenty-one-year-old student at Purdue and studying to be a pilot, while Charlotte, then nineteen, was a freshman film student at DePaul University in Chicago. Meanwhile, Audrey was finishing up her last year of high school. In spite of their schedules, the kids did whatever they could to support their dad.

"This has always been a family affair for us," says Mike, "from the very first campaign headed out to county fairs, while Karen and I would be shaking hands at the Republican tent, the kids would be standing out in front of the tent, handing out flyers and shaking hands."[1]

In the past, the kids took turns introducing their father at fairs, speaking events, or campaign fund-raisers. When Mike announced that he was going to run for governor, Steger says, Audrey volunteered to introduce her dad's candidacy on May 5, 2012.

AUDREY'S SPEECH A HIT

"Michael's announcement was in his hometown of Columbus, Indiana," recalls Steger. "I'm not sure if he asked all the kids, but one way or another, Audrey says she's going to be the child who introduces her dad. Three weeks before the announcement, Karen comes to her and asks, 'How are you doing on your introductory speech? Want to run it by me?' Audrey said, 'Nope. I'm good. I'm thinking about it.' Mike goes to her a couple of days later and says, 'How's it going?' Audrey said, 'Don't worry about it, Dad.' Now the day comes and she doesn't have it ready and everybody knows it. So she's writing it on the way to the announcement. The place is jam-packed. A guy introduces this eighteen-year-old young lady, who gets up in front of a gigantic convention-style room and proceeds to knock it out of the park. She was funny. She was witty. It was just the way any dad would love for his daughter to be talking about him and she delivers it with poise and grace. If you had asked me listening to her, I'd [have] said she must have been working on this for months and recording herself on video."

Just over two weeks later, Mike announced Ellspermann as his running mate.

On the campaign trail, before Mike walked out on to a stage to speak, friends say he would pull his family and inner circle together to pray for the event, each other, and America.

"So many politicians live one life in public and one life in private," says Dan Murphy. "But one thing I can tell you about Mike is that he's the same in both worlds. There's no contradiction."

NO NEGATIVE ADS, PERIOD

As he'd insisted repeatedly when running for his congressional seat over the years, Mike was adamant that his campaign would be free of negative ads and comments.

"He felt there is a good way to do things and he wanted to do it the right way," says Phipps. "For example, I think he wanted to keep politics out of the gutter. I've never heard him call the opposing candidate a bad name. Matter of fact, I've never heard him use a smutty word or a word you might think is the slightest caliber of being obscene.

"To some people, their faith is something they refer to like they're proud to be an American," Phipps adds, "but when Mike says he's a Christian, that symbolizes his real beliefs. He takes prayer seriously. He tries to live life according to biblical precepts. I think he really believes in his heart that his Christian faith is one of utmost importance and everything else is secondary."

Steger says 2012 was the perfect time for Mike to run for governor.

"At that point, Michael had been in Congress for twelve years and from an electoral point of view, he's untouchable," Steger says. "By the time he runs for governor, he was fortunate in that his district was spread out such that he had to buy television [ads] in Indianapolis, Cincinnati, Ohio, and Ft. Wayne, Indiana, to reach the whole district. This also meant that three quarters of the entire state of Indiana had been seeing his ads for twelve years, which set him up beautifully. If you didn't know Mike Pence as your congressman, you knew him because he was on your TV all the time even if you weren't in his district. Even so, he didn't take it for granted. He worked incredibly hard."

Mike ran his campaign like clockwork. He told Elsass that he wanted his ads to have a "morning in America" feel about them. He meticulously watched and edited the commercials to fine-tune them and ran them all by Karen and the kids for their input. Mike wanted to win the gubernatorial election, but he wasn't willing to abandon his principles to do so.

The race against former state Representative John Gregg was tight as Election Day loomed. Mike was under enormous pressure from his consultants to take things negative. Mike refused. He used Scripture to show them that it wasn't biblical to talk negatively about another person.

Reger, who had worked for Mike for the first seven years he was in Congress, remembers meeting him on the campaign trail while he was running for governor.

"Mike has made time to encourage me many times as we were driving around when he was a congressman, but [when] he was running for governor, my wife and I had a conversation with him and told him we were having some issues with having a child and we'd had three miscarriages," says Reger. "He encouraged us that he and Karen had issues like that and he said he'd personally put that on his prayer list. And I believe he did. He meant it. I've heard him say that to many folks, many times, that he'd pray for them and he did."

Reger and his wife conceived and were able to carry the baby to term, giving birth to a son.

MIKE'S "THE REAL DEAL"

While campaigning, Mike's friends were frequently approached by others and asked about his character.

"I've had a fair number of people ask me, 'Well, what is he really like?'" says Mark Bailey. "I'd tell them, 'He's the real deal. He is absolutely genuine. He's genuine in his faith.' I think sometimes people are skeptical because there are certain public figures who tend to use their faith to further their popularity, or because they think they need to be seen a certain way, but when you hear Mike talk about his faith, that's who he is. That's been who he's been since I've known him. His faith is very, very important to him and he's not ashamed, but very forthright in telling people."

Reger agrees with Bailey's assessment of some politicians and their professions of faith.

"A lot of people say they love the Lord, or they're Christians, or you hear athletes say thanks to God or Jesus," says Reger, "but you never really know. But you can't spend as much time as I did with Mike without knowing they're sincere."

Assembling a gubernatorial staff in the event that he won, Mike asked Bill Smith to continue to serve as his chief of staff. Smith agreed; he enjoyed working with Mike because of their friendship and Mike's faith and values.

"Mike is solid, compassionate, and thoughtful," says Smith. "He's someone who not only knows what he believes, but he knows why he believes it. His worldview is consistent. His faith informs his decisions. He doesn't hide his faith under a bushel and he also doesn't wear it on his sleeves. He reminds me a lot about what Chuck Colson used to say about faith in the public square, 'You don't have to carry your Bible into the legislature because if the principles you support are based in biblical truths, people will want to know where you got it.' It's just a part of who he is."

Working side-by-side with Mike for over twelve years in Congress, Smith knew him as well as anyone else in his life and says Mike's faith was evident in every aspect of his life.

"His faith was evident, first of all, in the way he lived his life," says Smith. "He modeled, I think, what you'd hope for from a man who proclaims faith. So the man I saw in meetings behind closed doors was the same man who would be working soup kitchen lines or reaching down to tie a child's shoe. He's servant-hearted."

DEALING WITH LIES FROM OPPOSITION

Along with The Strategy Group Company, Elsass continued to produce ads for Mike's gubernatorial campaign, just as he'd done when Mike ran for Congress. As the opposing party and news outlets said negative things about Mike and his conservative policies, Elsass wrestled with what he says were the lies being perpetrated against his friend.

"Frankly, it was something I struggled with because it was very frustrating to me to hear people say things that just aren't accurate," says Elsass. "Mike realized after this race that the reality is that you have to defend your honor."

Simcox says not everyone can make the transition from congressman to governor successfully, but he knew Mike wouldn't have a problem.

"He was an intellectual conservative who from college on up thought deeply about issues," says Simcox. "I think you can be a member of Congress and not go real deep on issues because you touch on different issues about every other minute. You don't have to implement them, you just vote on them. Being the governor is different. You have to run something. When I see congressmen leave Congress and think that all that knowledge and all that experience transfers to being in the executive branch of government, I hold my breath because some can do it and do it well and some simply can't. It's as different as night and day."

Simcox says he has witnessed Mike's ability to make that transition firsthand.

"When I was on his executive campaign committee, I would go to these briefings where he had these various teams, one on health care and one on pre-school issues and various other issues," says Simcox. "I remember this one particular day that we had a meeting. It was really long and people would get up and give fifteen- or twenty-minute summaries of where the team was on these issues and make recommendations for the campaign. He was sitting there and there were fifteen or twenty of us sitting around a U-shaped table and what I noticed the whole day long is that his attention was locked on these people speaking. There was no fumbling with his cell phone, no turning to whisper to someone else, no getting up and saying, 'I'll be right back, just keep going.' None of this that you'd typically see. He listened to every word. He asked all the right questions. He took notes. He suggested follow-up."

As Election Day arrived, the Pence and Ellspermann families, friends, and campaign staff all gathered in a room at Lucas Oil Stadium in Indianapolis to watch the election results come in. When Mike's victory was announced, they gathered in a large circle to pray. Afterward, wanting some privacy, Mike, Karen, and the kids went into a bathroom to huddle together, thank God, and exchange gifts, a custom Karen had started when Mike first began campaigning for Congress.

A SURPRISE GIFT FOR KAREN

"Mom did this after each election when we were growing up," recalls Charlotte. "There would always be some present, a memento, to thank us for what we had done—win or lose."[2]

This time, the kids had a surprise for their mother that caught Karen off guard.

"We each wrote our favorite 'Mom quote' from the campaign trail on a note card and framed them. They were all things she had said to us along the way, and they sum her up almost perfectly."[3]

Michael wrote: "I'm not going to let what's going on out there affect what's going on in here."

Charlotte's note read, "You teach your kids how to fight for their dreams by fighting for your own."

And Audrey shared the soothing words, "I'm listening. And I hear you."

Karen later said, "It is probably the greatest gift I have ever been given or will ever get in my entire life."[4]

The Pences left the bathroom and joined the victory rally on the field of Lucus Oil Stadium. As Mike would later say, "Everything has changed, and nothing has changed."[5]

Mike took the oath to office as governor of Indiana on January 14, 2013.

"When I raised my right hand to become governor of the state of Indiana," says Mike, "I had my hand on Benjamin Harrison's Bible and right underneath it was my Bible. I opened it to the verse that he took his oath of office as president on and I marked a verse in mine." After offering to give Solomon whatever he wishes, Mike reflects, "the Lord said, '*What do you want?*' And young Solomon said as he was accepting authority, '*Give me a discerning heart to distinguish between right and wrong, for who is able to govern this great people of Yours?*'"[6]

When President Harrison took the oath of office in 1889, his Bible was opened to the first verse of Psalm 121: "*I will lift up mine eyes unto the hills, from whence cometh my help.*"

Mike asked other leaders in Indiana to intercede for the state.

"I ask you to pray that we would have hearts of compassion, ever softened with deep concern for the aged, the sick, the infirm, the disabled, for those in prison," Mike said, noting in Matthew 25, "Jesus speaks a story of when He's commending those on the other side about how they served Him when He was hungry, when He was naked, when He was in hardship, and they said, 'When? When did we do that?' And He said, 'Whatever you did for the least of these brothers and sisters of mine, you did for Me.' So, I pray for your prayers that we might have hearts of compassion for the least of these."[7]

Pastor Charles Lake of Greenwood Community Church gave the invocation at Mike's inauguration as governor, praying in part:

"Give Governor Pence wisdom beyond his own, as You have promised to give divine wisdom to anyone who acknowledges their need and asks. Give him patience and perseverance as he faces the challenges of state government and the stressed economy we experience as a nation. Give him Your vision for what life in Indiana should be. Give him the strength and the courage to stay true to the moral convictions and spiritual commitments that have guided his life to this day. Help him to be true to his faith and give him the joy of serving unselfishly as he seeks to better the lives of thousands of Hoosiers. Help him to choose conviction over compromise, purpose over pride, and principles over political correctness."

MOVING INTO GOVERNOR'S RESIDENCE

Ironically, Karen had been commissioned years earlier to do a painting of the governor's residence on North Meridian Street in Indianapolis. A group of individuals were having dinner there and gave the painting to First Lady Cheri Daniels, wife of Governor Mitch Daniels, while others in attendance received prints of it. Oddly enough, Karen had previously tried to paint the Governor's Residence for an art contest, but when she started photographing it from multiple angles, security asked her to leave.

So for Karen, moving into the governor's residence was a homecoming of sorts. She knew becoming first lady of Indiana would mean a loss of privacy, so she turned to a former first lady for advice.

"You know, Judy O'Bannon [Governor Frank O'Bannon's wife] told me, 'Just get over it. Just get over it,' so I am taking her advice," Karen said. "I am just going to get over it and realize…we are going to be in the public eye and we want to make the most of it."[8]

Many voters who knew Mike liked to ride motorcycles had encouraged him to ride into the state on a Harley for Inauguration Day, but he joked that they were more likely to see him on horseback.

"I know word's already out that the Pence family likes to ride and so I can tell you my ambition as governor, any free time [on] a Saturday morning is to slip down to Brown County or find another place to where we can saddle up and ride," Mike said.[9]

Throughout the family's twelve years in Congress, Karen missed Indiana, so she was glad to be back home.

"Indiana is just a very special place," Karen says. "There are no other people like Hoosiers."[10]

A BUSY FIRST LADY

After moving over a dozen times, Karen was eager to settle in as first lady. Reaching out to all of her living predecessors, she sought their advice in how to best serve in her new role and support her husband. She was encouraged to just be herself and assured Hoosiers would love her.

Within days of their move into their new home, Karen had emergency gall bladder surgery. As soon as she was able, she started a weekly Bible study.

Karen started painting again and won several awards for her work. She also took a chance on starting another small business. After swimming in a cold Indiana lake, she was surprised to find that someone had taken her towel from the spot where she'd left it. So she designed "That's My Towel" charms and sold the hook-on identification towel tags online.

The new first lady never forgot her early childhood living on an Air Force base and always made time to support and speak to family members of service personnel.

In her first year as Indiana's first lady, Karen established the Indiana First Lady's Charitable Foundation, a 501(c)3 to promote individuals and organizations that encourage children, families, and the arts through grants and scholarships. During the first three years Mike served as governor, the foundation gave out more than $600,000, including $100,000 to Riley Children's Foundation for the art therapy program at Riley Hospital for Children, $65,000 to Feeding Indiana's

Hungry, $100,000 for the Indiana Bicentennial Commission, and many other grants to a variety of organizations.

Karen was passionate about the benefits of art therapy, particularly for children who are too ill to express the often-unspoken frustrations and pain they experience emotionally, mentally, physically, and spiritually. She became a board member for Riley Children's Foundation and honorary chair of the art therapy program at Riley Hospital for Children, and donated her prints for various fundraisers.

Karen also served on the board for Tracy's Kids, an art therapy program at children's hospitals in Washington, D.C., that uses the arts to help young cancer patients and their families cope with the emotional stress and trauma of cancer and its treatment. The organization's mission is to ensure that the children and families are emotionally equipped to fight cancer as actively as possible—and prepare them for the time when they are cancer-free.

Marilyn Logsdon first met Karen and became her friend when they were elementary school teachers at the same school in the late 1980s and later served on Karen's charitable board. She recalls Karen as a woman of prayer as she helped Mike lead Indiana.

"She would say, 'Before we look at these grants, let's just ask God for wisdom and discernment,'" Logsdon says.

CHURCH AND BIBLE STUDY

Mike and Karen began to attend College Park Church, which began in 1984 with only four families. By the time Mike became governor, however, it was considered a megachurch, defined as any Protestant Christian church that has or exceeds two thousand or more people in average weekend attendance. Mike's friend and former fraternity brother, Drew Murray, and his wife, Jane, also attended College Park Church. With a security team in tow, the Pences were there most Sundays.

Immediately upon becoming governor, Mike initiated a weekly Bible study at the governor's mansion. Simcox was one of a handful of people invited to join it.

"For four years of his governorship, with rather few exceptions, I was one of six people who met with him every Thursday morning in the governor's residence for an hour of Bible study and prayer," says Simcox. "So I had the opportunity to not just to listen to the platitudes, the speeches, and public prayers and all of this, but see the real man.

"We became a covenant group and by that I mean we shared intimate details and concerns for family and health issues," Simcox adds. "We prayed for each other and laid hands on each other at times. We got to know each other very well beyond the surface. There are two things that I saw in that setting that stood out. One is, his Bible—every page of this Bible was dog-eared and obviously been gone through I don't know how many times. Every page had underlines and margin notes. The kinds of things that leads one to see that a person had opened that Bible on numerous times and had studied it.

"The other thing I noticed was perspective of Bible study or discussion of Bible passages or events of the Bible characters whose lives are laid bare in the Bible," he says. "There was never a concept that we discussed or a Bible character or figure in the Bible that we discussed that Michael hadn't thought of before and didn't have something to say about it. Wherever we went in the Bible, it was clear he'd studied it beforehand.

"I saw a term once that defined certain kinds of people as seasoned saints," Simcox says. "And a seasoned saint is someone who has worn calluses on his elbows going through Scripture and reading literature that defines and interprets the Scripture. I concluded that Mike had been very serious about studying Scripture and he's well acquainted with prayer and the power of prayer."

Just a few months into his governorship, Mike was ranked as the second most conservative governor in the country by an analysis of Republican governors conducted by Nate Silver of *The New York Times*.[11]

Hoosiers were proud of their decision to make Mike the leader of Indiana's executive branch.

LED BY FAITH AS GOVERNOR

Ellspermann believes Mike's faith led him in his role as governor.

"He was always a Christian first in everything he did," she says. "As a governor, his Bible was always on his desk and virtually every meeting we had, he would reference Scripture that he had been reading and discerning from his morning prayers. He wove his faith into many of the conversations we had and it was apparent it was how he led and that his level of discernment was very deep on things and his Bible study really helped inform how he took on the day. Every staff meeting we had began with prayer."

Serving as his lieutenant governor, Ellspermann saw that Mike's faith was prominent, but not intrusive or offensive.

"It was very clear to everyone that Mike was guided by a Higher Being and that he was accountable to his faith and his Lord," she says. "He captured a level that if you were not a devout Christian, you were not offended by it, but if you were a Christian, you really appreciated it. He hit a nice balance."

Mike brought the same limited government and low tax philosophy to his role as governor of Indiana that he had fought for as a congressman. He honored veterans, sought to abolish abortion, advocated for educational opportunities for the poor and financial provision for the elderly and less fortunate, and relentlessly focused on jobs for the unemployed. The state's unemployment rate fell steadily, from 8.5 percent in January 2013 to 4.1 percent in November 2016.

Everyone benefited under Mike's leadership, Ellspermann says.

"Mike was very thoughtful and very respectful of every person he met," she says. He "was very much aware of [how] he believed the state needed to go and helping prepare the way and bring people along. I don't ever remember being in a meeting in those more than four years [together] where he didn't show great respect and humility of himself. Though he could have controlled many meetings, he didn't. Even in the contentious part of the House leadership, Senate leadership, minority, majority parties, sitting in small groups, he was a very humble presence. He would listen. He would always take a personal interest in people."

Ellspermann says Mike's ability to be even-tempered through different circumstances made meetings and their offices serene.

"Never in those years did I hear him ever raise a voice, never did I make someone look bad," she says. "Never did I see him put his own ego or spin on things. He would never let his ego get in front of making someone else more important. He just naturally had and has a way of making everyone feel their value and their importance and that they're making a difference in what they are doing. It's one of the great gifts he has."

Mike's strong, impeccable leadership and speaking skills didn't go unnoticed. There continued to be whispers on among people of both parties and among conservatives that Mike should run for president of the United States in 2016.

Deason recalls first meeting Mike at a leadership retreat in New York City when Mike was governor.

"My first impression was that he should be our next president of the United States," Deason says. "He was that impressive of a speaker and he had such a passion for this country and for moral, conservative values."

ENDNOTES

1. Julia Moffitt, "Pence family comes home to Indiana," WTHR Channel 13/NBC, Indianapolis January 14, 2013.
2. Charlotte Pence, *Where You Go*.
3. Ibid.
4. Ibid.
5. Ibid.
6. Mike Pence, 2015 Indiana Leadership Prayer Breakfast.
7. Ibid.
8. Moffitt.
9. Ibid.
10. Rudavsky.
11. Nate Silver, "In State Governments, Signs of a Healthier G.O.P.," *The New York Times*, FiveThirtyEight Blogs, April 16, 2013.

14

STICKING TO PRIORITIES

But seek ye first the kingdom of God, and his righteousness; and
all these things shall be added unto you.
—Matthew 6:33 KJV

Karen's influence on Mike continued to exceed the confines of their home and her initiatives as Indiana's first lady. She was credited by many in the political arena as Mike's key advisor. Karen was "the highest ranking official in the state of Indiana," Mike often said.

"I would characterize her as the silent, omnipresent partner," says Brian Howey, publisher of Howey Politics Indiana, a nonpartisan political news website. "You knew she was there, you knew there was some considerable influence she wielded, but, boy, she was not public about it."[1]

Peter Rusthoven, a lawyer active in Indiana Republican politics says Mike and Karen "are in a strong, supportive marriage bound by common faith. I don't think they make decisions separately."[2]

The couple are known among friends and colleagues as go-getters who would go to great lengths to serve others individually and as a team.

"Some people have that air that they're just going to get it done," says Van Smith. "We felt that way about Mike and Karen."[3]

As Mike led the state of Indiana with passion and stoic leadership, the couple would surprise Republicans and Democrats alike as they went against political norms in numerous ways. For example, the Pences frequently hosted dinners to which both Democrats and Republicans were invited.

"It wouldn't occur to us to just have Republicans," Karen emphasized. "You know, most of my family is Democrat. So we don't even think that way."[4]

As governor, Mike had more responsibility and had to appear at public events more often than he did as a congressman. Inevitably, that meant he'd run into more Hoosiers expressing their opinions and needs. He always enjoyed meeting people of faith.

"The sweetest words I ever hear as governor and I hear them all the time.... People walk up to me and they tend to lower their voice just a little bit to make it personal and they say, 'I'm praying for you,'" Mike said. "It hits me in the heart every time because I know they mean it. They don't say it in a casual way, they say it with intent, and they say it to inform. And then invariably, the sweetest request I ever hear [is]... 'How can I pray for you?'... I invariably say, 'Pray for my family' because I know people are praying for me."[5]

Although their children were grown, like all parents, Mike and Karen still worried about them, so Mike would frequently ask constituents to pray for his family.

Mike's mother, Nancy, continued to be an important part of their lives. Years after Ed died and she had finished raising her girls, she married retired pharmacist Basil Fritsch, who hailed from Chicago. With her new husband's encouragement, Nancy received her bachelor's degree in psychology from Saint Mary-of-the-Woods College in her sixties.

Still spunky, Nancy refused to let age slow her down, Steger says.

"The governor of the state of Indiana has a little cabin cottage in Brown County State Park, which is in the southern part of Indiana with beautiful rolling hills," says Steger. "We were there and Nancy was over there dancing with her granddaughter and she was somewhere around seventy-eight, just having a great time. If you want a public persona, there's a familiarity of Barbara Bush in Nancy Pence. It's that strong kind of no-nonsense kind of wit."

DATING AND EXERCISE

Despite his growing responsibilities, Mike continued to make his marriage front and center in his life and made a deliberate effort to take Karen out on dates. The couple usually had a supreme, thin-crust pizza and non-alcoholic beer for dinner on Friday nights and went to the movies.

"Both Mike and Karen love film," says Steger. "When they need a break and just need to veg a little bit and take it easy, they go to a movie theater. They watch the film and then they like to knock it around afterwards, [assessing] how good of a film it was. They're amateur film critics."

To enable them to work out together in the mornings during inclement weather, the Pences bought twin treadmills and had them installed in the governor's residence. They frequently rode their bikes around on the grounds and throughout the historic district of Indianapolis.

"They would go riding as often as weather would allow and their security detail would just ride along with them," says Steger. "These kinds of things are very much Karen bringing her husband back from the craziness of being governor and saying, 'Let's develop some good habits and stay grounded.' Karen tries to bring a sense of normalcy and consistency into their lives."

Mike also made a point to include Karen in his travels whenever he had the opportunity, taking her with him when he went on trips abroad to Germany and Japan.

"I've always appreciated so much the way Mike treats Karen," says Deason. "He's always so respectful of her and so concerned about her and her feelings and that she's front and center with him. He never stands in front of her. He never walks in front of her. He's always the perfect gentleman. He always thanks and honors her. Always. He honors her in such a way that it's his faith that drives that."

Mike's staff could see how intertwined he and Karen were and realized how important her presence was to him.

"The people in the governor's office who worked for him, including one of my sons, came to realize that in furthering the goals of the administration or in serving the governor, they were also serving Karen because she was right there with him," says Simcox. "It's a genuine relationship. I'm convinced she's his number one advisor. I don't think he's ever made a decision that was not a product of the two of them making it together. It's impressive."

Ellspermann says while she served as lieutenant governor, Mike honored both her and Karen in the way he conducted business when they were together.

"Our general rule of thumb was that our doors would be open," she says. Mike "had a big office and we had plenty of privacy to talk about what we needed to talk about. If there was something very sensitive, we would close the door. It didn't happen very often; I can count them on one hand. But it never bothered me. He never said why the door was [left] open, but I think I knew him well enough and respected him enough that it didn't matter to me. It was a non-event. I am a feminist. If it had gotten in the way, I'd have been the first one to let him know it was a problem, but it really just was not."

DEDICATED TO INTERCESSION

Those closest to Mike and Karen saw how her dedication to intercession—the act of praying for others—impacted him and his faith.

"Karen obviously was a big part of his faith journey," says Mark Bailey. "He's often talked over the years in various settings about her [faith]. I've been a member of the steering committee for the Indiana Leadership Prayer Breakfast since 1984, so I've had an opportunity to witness various governors in the capacity of their faith and a little about what prayer means in their life. The night before the prayer breakfast, we would [normally] have a meal at some kind of private restaurant-type facility, but when Mike became governor, they invited us to have that event at the governor's mansion, which we did for all four years Mike was governor. As part of the evening, whenever we were getting ready for the meal, typically you'd have one of the members of the committee pray, but Mike would always ask Karen to pray for the meal and he'd always introduce her as the real prayer warrior of the family."

Mike's prayer life also matured over the years as he pressed into the Lord by reading and memorizing the Bible and implementing it in his daily life.

"Mike was obviously involved with the Indiana Leadership Prayer Breakfast as governor and the way we set those up is, typically, the governor would have about ten minutes where they gave remarks before he introduced the main speaker for the morning," says Bailey. "Usually those remarks were related to prayer in that person's life. Mike would have done that four times as governor and some of the talks he gave about prayer and the importance of prayer in his life were absolutely moving. I've been on that committee for over thirty years and I can't think of any other governor who would have surpassed Mike's comments in terms of genuine and heartfelt and well-thought-out and clearly demonstrating the works of prayer in his life than Mike Pence."

A few months into his governorship, Mike and Karen left the church they'd been attending and began attending a church with the Baileys on the north side of Indianapolis. Affiliated with the Church of God, "it's a fairly conservative denomination that split off from the Methodist Church in the late 1800s," Bailey says.

CHIEF OF STAFF CHANGE

After serving twelve years as Mike's chief of staff while he was in Congress and two while he was governor, Bill Smith stepped down from the position to start a government relations and media production company. Smith had been driving almost an hour and a half round-trip each day from Elwood and the commute was taxing. He agreed to stay on as a political adviser to Mike as needed.

In line to replace Smith was Jim Atterholt, a former state representative and chair of the Indiana Utility Regulatory Commission. He was also a fellow believer. But although Mike was familiar with Atterholt's faith in God, he wanted to be sure that he was God's choice for the position. Over a course of a month, the men talked about everything under the sun, including family, faith, sports, and politics. Eventually, Mike invited Atterholt and his wife, Brenda, to join him and Karen for lunch at the governor's mansion. Later, Mike offered the position to Atterholt, but encouraged him to go home to his wife and pray over the decision together. Atterholt did exactly that before joining Mike's team shortly afterward.

"It has been a blessing to observe the positive tone Governor Pence and his team have set for Indiana and their commitment to servant leadership," Atterholt said at the time. "The governor has a heart for all Hoosiers and a well-deserved reputation for showing kindness to even those who may disagree. I am honored to serve in this new role."[6]

SHARING THE POWER OF PRAYER

Mike took every speaking opportunity he could as governor to talk about faith, the power of prayer, and conservative policies.

"We are to approach the throne of grace with God and we are informed that in everything, by prayer and petition, with thanksgiving, we are to present our request to God. We are commanded to pray for those who have been entrusted with responsibility and leadership," Mike says. "One of my favorite verses is: 'Far be it from me that I should sin against the LORD by failing to pray for you' [1 Samuel 12:23].... The Author of the Universe, the Author of Life, hears...the ultimate Authority is always available.... C. S. Lewis said memorably, 'I'm not always sure that prayer changes things, but I'm always sure prayer changes me.'... One of the most compelling things I've ever read out of the writings and words of President Lincoln are when he said, 'I've often been driven to my knees in this position, when I have come to the conclusion that I have nowhere else to go.' Lincoln was a man of prayer. Prayer changed him and he saved the nation."[7]

Mike credits Karen and her prayer life as an essential aspect of the stability of their home.

"I actually try to start every morning with a little bit of prayer and a little bit of time in [the Bible]. They call it a quiet time in my tradition," Mike shares. "Other than the cat wandering around my feet at the kitchen table, usually meowing loudly for something, it's quiet. The Old Book actually tells us to devote ourselves to prayer.... Lord Tennison said it well two centuries back. He said, 'More things are wrought by prayer than this world dreams of.' And I believe that. But for me and my house, nobody believes that more than Mrs. Pence. And I want to share a little bit of my experience with my devoted wife.... Now, when I tell you that Mrs. Pence believes in prayer and practices it regularly, I don't overstate that. Although some...might say quickly, 'Mike, anybody married to you would have to believe in prayer.'"[8]

Karen always attended the prayer breakfasts for Indiana's leaders, recalls Ping, who worked as a consultant to Karen. "During that time, the young woman that Karen and I had hired to run the First Lady's Luncheon as our event planner was going through cancer. Karen was very prayerful during that and before every one of our First Lady's Luncheon committee meetings, we would pray for that young lady."

PRAYER JOURNALS FOR KIDS

In fact, Karen kept journals in which she wrote down her prayers for each of her three children, starting in November 1994, just before Michael Jr.'s third birthday.

After several years of praying for children, Mike says, "when those kids finally came, we were used to prayer at our house.... When they came along, my wife...bought a little journal that she would write prayers in after she put the little ones to bed.... When each of them left for college, Karen would give them a copy of the pages of this journal."[9]

In that first entry for their son, Karen wrote, "I'm starting this journal one week before you turn three. I'm not sure how it'll unfold, but I have a few ideas as I start. I want to first of all keep this as a prayer journal to document as prayers are answered so you will see someday how inexplicably and intimately the Lord is involved in your fabulous life."

Mike says, "To this very day, she prays and it is the strength of our family and the strength of our life."[10]

While serving as governor in 2013, Mike and Karen decided to take their three kids with them on vacation to Ireland to visit their great-grandfather's homeland. They wanted the kids to have the experience that Mike had in 1980 as a college graduate, to visit distant relatives and see where they came from. While the two-room house where Mike's grandfather had been raised was long gone, they were able to see the farm land where it once stood and visit the tavern their relatives still owned thirty-three years later.

PROTECTING THE UNBORN

When the family returned home to Indiana from overseas in March 2016, Mike continued his spiritual battle on the front-lines to protect life, signing a bill prohibiting abortions based solely on the unborn child's sex, race, color, national origin, ancestry, or disability, including Down syndrome.

The bill, House Enrolled Act (HEA) 1337, "is a comprehensive pro-life measure that affirms the value of all human life," Mike said after the signing. "Some of my most precious moments as governor have been with families of children with disabilities, especially those raising children with Down syndrome. These Hoosiers never fail to inspire me with their compassion and these special children never fail to move me with their love and joy. By enacting this legislation, we take an important step in protecting the unborn, while still providing an exception for the life of the mother. I sign this legislation with a prayer that God would continue to bless these precious children, mothers and families."[11]

While a majority of Hoosiers celebrated the move, Mike's efforts weren't appreciated by everyone. A federal judge ended up blocking the law.

Steger says Mike's view on abortion doesn't exclude a woman's rights to her own body, but it also doesn't exclude the rights of the unborn.

"Mike would have great empathy for any woman in that situation," says Steger. "He would say, 'There are two people here, both of whom have rights, and we need to be sensitive and empathetic and merciful with both people, [but] one person can't talk. Mike just has a big heart for these young children of God, sons and daughters of the Creator, so he's a very strong defender of the least of our brothers and admits that it's tough, but both should have rights."

PROTECTING RELIGIOUS FREEDOM

In the spring of 2015, Mike was reviewing Indiana Senate Bill 101, entitled the Religious Freedom Restoration Act (RFRA), which had been on state lawmakers' table for years. The legislation would amend Indiana's constitution so that individuals and businesses could assert, as a defense in legal proceedings, that their exercise of religion has been, or is likely to be, substantially burdened. The state House of Representatives approved it by a vote of 40-10.

When RFRA came across his desk on March 26, Mike decided to sign it into law. More than eighty people crammed into the governor's office for the signing ceremony, including evangelical leaders, nuns, monks, orthodox Jews, and representatives of pro-family groups who had lobbied for the bill.

When a photo of the signing ceremony was posted on social media, it quickly went viral and caused an uproar among gay rights groups and others who said the law hurt the lesbian, gay, bisexual, and transgender community. Proponents of the law claimed it protected free exercise of religion and freedom of conscience.

Gay rights groups from across the nation condemned the law, calling it discriminatory, and urged tourists and businesses to boycott Indiana.

Mike argued that the purpose of the law was to give individuals a chance to go to court if they felt the government encroached on religious liberty. Critics balked at this explanation, saying Mike wanted to deny basic rights to homosexuals.

As a result of the conflict, companies and organizations that advocated and supported gay rights began to cancel conventions in Indiana and threatened to reverse plans to expand in the state. Even fellow Republicans turned on Mike.

Mike continued to stand his ground.

"If you read the bill instead of reading the papers, you would see that the Religious Freedom Restoration Act, which is now law in Indiana, is simply about giving the courts guidance and establishing the same standards that have existed at the federal level for more than 20 years," Mike said. "I understand the concerns that have been raised by some, because frankly, some in the media have tried to make this about one issue or another."[12]

Mike's explanation only fueled the fire of the gay rights movement. Other cities and states across the nation began lining up to express their disapproval.

"There were two billion tweets in over about a month period," says Ellspermann regarding the backlash about RFRA.

BACK AGAINST THE WALL

Friends and colleagues say Mike's back was up against the wall. The bill wasn't his idea and similar laws had previously been adopted in several states. In fact, Congress had passed comparable federal legislation into law in 1993 that President Bill Clinton signed without anyone batting an eye. But for some reason, Mike was now under fire.

"It was not our agenda," says Ellspermann. "Because it protected religious freedom, of course, Mike would support it. The spin after that was by far the most challenging time for him during our time in office together. He listened to everyone. I know how prayerful he was during that time. It was painful. It was a very difficult time, but he led with great integrity."

The pressure on Mike was overbearing as he felt trapped between what he knew he should do and what he felt he was being forced to do.

"There have been times when Mike's been misunderstood," says Blackwell. "You can believe that marriage is a union between one man and one woman, but it's not Christian to hate people who are homosexual or who believe in same-sex marriage. You fight, but how do you do that and at the same time show a respect for the dignity of others? If you're living in a God-driven way, you search for that dignity in others.

"Rabbi Abraham Heschel, who was one of Dr. King's trusted advisors, would always say, 'Respect discovers the dignity of others,'" adds Blackwell. "Even someone you argue with, someone who you have a fundamental difference with, if you're living in a God-driven way, you search for that dignity in others because that's the context in which you can respect them. But that's not always easy to do when people are throwing hand grenades at you and misdefining you. And that's the real test of your Christian strength. Mike is good at standing on his moral ground and loving and respecting others."

The outrage over RFRA "was a real critical time for Michael," says Steger. Blackwell "really took him under his arm and leveled Mike."

"I was always frustrated that the legislative leaders, the [Indiana House] speaker and [state Senate] president pro tempore, who brought the bill forward and passed it, took none of the heat," says Ellspermann. "It was the general assembly that passed it and yet it was not until Mike signed it that the heat and targeting began. He was not the author or co-author of the bill. Knowing his faith and belief in religious freedom, of course he's going to sign a bill for religious freedom. Vice versa, he would not have signed an openly divisive, prejudicial, discriminatory bill."

Mike would later point out, "We live in a diverse country with people with different viewpoints and different lifestyles and I don't believe in discrimination or mistreatment of anyone. I believe we should love our neighbor as ourself, but neither do I think that anyone should ever fear persecution because of their deeply held religious beliefs. When those two things come into conflict, that's what we have the courts for. The courts sort out those issues and have done so throughout the history of this nation."[13]

But the more Mike tried to explain himself and his perspective, the worse the problem became. Members of every level of government weighed in with their opinions, as did sports leaders, gay rights advocates, and businesses.

PUSH FOR AMENDMENT

Within a week, the Indiana legislature pushed an amendment to the bill intended to protect LGBT people and clarify that RFRA did not authorize any discrimination by "a provider" or "establish a defense to a civil action or criminal prosecution." Provider was defined as "one or more individuals, partnerships, associations, organizations, limited liability companies, corporations, and other organized groups of persons." Excluded were "a church or other nonprofit religious organization or society, including an affiliated school, that is exempt from federal income taxation" and "a rabbi, priest, preacher, minister, pastor, or designee of a church or other nonprofit religious organization or society when the individual is engaged in a religious or affiliated educational function of the church or other nonprofit religious organization or society."[14]

Under intense pressure, Mike signed the revised bill on April 2, 2015. Fellow conservative Republicans and many church leaders saw this as a betrayal.

"Coming to that was a very difficult thing. He was confident that it didn't denigrate significantly the intention of the bill," says Ellspermann. "There had to be symbolic words that changed. Something had to be done. He certainly tried to do what was best for all and recognizing and respecting all Hoosiers and I know how much he prayed about it."

FRIENDS RALLY AROUND MIKE

Several friends came to Mike's defense. Some left prominent jobs in government to join his staff; others offered Mike their support and prayers.

"I visited Mike when he was having some low moments as governor," says Phipps. "He was taking a lot of heat over the LGBT legislation in Indiana. There were a lot of pastors who felt let down and were saying they weren't sure they could support him anymore. So, I went to his office and I told him, 'Mike, I know you've got a lot of concerns on your mind. I don't know all your concerns, but I know what's in your heart' and I pointed to his heart. I said, 'I'm praying for you so that God will help you during this time and I just want you to know I'm not going to throw you under the bus.' And he turned around and walked about two or three feet, then turned back around and he said, 'I love you.'

"Anybody in leadership is on display," Phipps continues. "That comes with the territory. You live life in a fishbowl and maybe rightfully so because you're asking for the public's confidence. You're asking them to trust you to do a certain job, but if I were rating somebody as far as their moral turpitude, I'd put him right at the top in terms of just good character, decency, someone you wouldn't mind having your children around because of how he conducts himself. Mike lives his life aboveboard. There's not going to be any scandals with Mike Pence. I think he's going to make sure every avenue is protected because he's going to live his life in an ethical and moral way."

Like many of Mike's friends, Lake says he becomes frustrated when Mike is portrayed as anything other than the godly man he is.

Lake becomes upset "when I hear Mike criticized for his hatred of homosexuals, lesbians, and bisexuals" because "there isn't a bone of hatred in that man's body towards anyone. Just because he disagrees with same-sex marriage doesn't mean that he hates the people involved in them."

Responding to a Democratic presidential candidate's accusations that Mike is anti-gay, the U.S. ambassador to Germany, Richard Grenell, who is openly gay, defended Mike on *Fox & Friends* in April 2019.[15]

Grenell called Mike "my friend" and said he is "a great man, an honorable man, a man of Christian faith, and somebody that I admire."

Gays face death or imprisonment in the seventy-one countries where homosexuality is considered a crime, Grenell noted. "Mike Pence is on board with decriminalizing homosexuality around the world. I think that speaks volumes."

Friends repeatedly say they've never seen Mike rattled by his circumstances, but the backlash he received from RFRA came close.

"Ultimately, when you talk about a man and his faith, you measure his countenance," says Hubler. "I have known Mike in bad times, I've known him through great times, but Mike Pence's countenance has never changed. I've never seen him mad. I've never seen him provoked. The man never loses his Christian countenance. I've never seen Mike crack for a minute."

Blackwell says Mike's ability to push through the onslaught of verbal attacks made him a better leader.

"In the long haul, a [leader] who has taken one on the chin and bounced back, I think becomes an even more effective leader," says Blackwell. "It's how you handle those setbacks and those disappointments that define you as a person."

When it comes to personal attacks on his faith and character, Mike says he trusts in God, regardless of the outcome. After leaving the White House in 1893, President Benjamin Harrison said, "It's a great comfort to trust God, even if His providence is unfavorable," Mike notes. "A prayer steadies one when he's walking in slippery places, even if things asked for are not given. But you know my greatest evidence [for prayer] comes not from the noteworthy history, or the noteworthy leaders in our history that…I like to read about. It really comes from my experience as governor."[16]

Gay rights activists maintained that RFRA would remain a stain on Mike's legacy as governor, but those who know him best say the harsh criticisms of Mike's character after he signed the law are unwarranted.

"The Mike Pence I know," says Varvel, "lives his life by the two commandments written in Mark 12:30–31. 'Love the Lord your God with all your heart, mind, soul and strength' [and] 'love your neighbor as yourself.' Pence treats people who disagree with him with grace."[17]

SUPPORT FOR ISRAEL

As time passed, the criticism over RFRA died down and enabled Mike to focus on other issues, such as supporting Indiana's Jewish community. Mike encouraged economic ties between Hoosiers and Israelis.

"Israel and Indiana share many concerns that Hoosiers cherish," Mike said at the second annual Indiana-Israel Business Exchange in June 2016. "As our nation's strongest and most important ally in the Middle East, Israel is also a key partner in our state's economic growth, which is why we're proud to welcome Israeli business leaders to Indiana. Hoosiers and Israelis are linked by our self-reliance, determination and entrepreneurial spirit, aiding us all in collaboration to grow our economies and create more great-paying jobs."[18]

Mike visited Israel several times and signed into law a bill that would ban Indiana from having commercial dealings with any company that boycotted Israel.

"We have known and worked with Mike Pence for years," says David Brog of Christians United for Israel, which helped to sponsor Mike's 2014 visit to Israel. "His faith and worldview have made him one of Israel's most steadfast supporters, both in Congress and as governor."[19]

OPPORTUNITIES FOR INMATES

Mike also focused on giving inmates in prisons across Indiana the opportunity to transform their lives for the better.

"He opened the prison system when he was governor to a lot of ministries and to a lot of other activities that were very, very helpful," says Simcox. "He was not insensitive to the plight of the poor. All of that came from a biblical context."

For accountability purposes, Mike often spoke to his inner circle of friends about his marriage to Karen and their unified relationship as one in Christ.

"Mike and I have talked about marriage often," says Blackwell. "We've talked about the three-stranded braid in Ecclesiastes [4:12] where it is man and woman that is united in that three-stranded braid around God that you get strength, that those two people are just much stronger as individuals and as a union because God is at the center of their marriage."

Blackwell says Mike's belief in moral absolutes fuel his passion for human rights.

"I've heard him a number of times basically define himself by saying he was a Christian first," says Blackwell. "At the end of the day for me, it's the way Mike has a fundamental belief in biblical truth and in belief that there are moral absolutes. And by embracing God's truth and moral absolutes, that gives fuel to a fight for the universal recognition of fundamental human rights.... The only way you overtake forces of racial division and ethnic subtractions is that you believe."

Blackwell recalls visiting the National Museum of African American History and Culture in Washington with Mike and some other people.

"Walking through, we were looking at the exhibits and talking to one another and it was Dr. King's fundamental belief in the universality of God's truth that gave the civil rights movement and its leaders the stamina to fight," Blackwell says. "Mike understands it now and he understood it as we were going through that museum. In spirit of conversation, it was evident again that his faith frames everything that he does and he's not apologetic."

THE EXECUTIVE NUDGE

Ellspermann notes Mike's sense of humor was always present while they were working together and he was quick to take part in a joke or prank.

"We had a daughter who was twenty-six and my husband, Jim, believed she should get married," recalls Ellspermann. "She'd been dating this guy for a couple of years and it was time for him to make a commitment to her. Just before Thanksgiving, we were together and Jim said, 'Mike, I need your help. I need an executive order to have this guy propose to my daughter.' Mike just laughed at first, then he looked at Jim and said, 'Okay. You write it up and I'll sign it!' So my husband wrote it and Mike signed it, deciding to call it 'The Executive Nudge.' We had it framed and gave it to them at Christmas that year. It's a real executive order. It has a number. It's the real deal. When they got married in the fall of 2016, we sent Mike and Karen a picture of them holding the Executive Nudge."

After the RFRA conflict, left-wing media sources provoked Mike by saying if he hoped to run in the upcoming presidential election, his chances of winning were dismal. Despite the RFRA fallout, many politicians, conservatives, and Republicans still encouraged Mike to seek the nation's highest office.

Mike was humbled by the idea. As a youth, he had dreamt of serving in Congress, but he had never even thought about serving as governor of the state he loved so well, let alone serving as president of the United States.

ANOTHER TERM AS GOVERNOR

After seeking counsel from several friends, Mike decided to seek a second term as governor. Ellspermann agreed to run for lieutenant governor again, but later, she had an offer that she thought would serve the state better.

A trustee at Ivy Tech Community College "approached me to ask me if I would be interested in being considered for president," she recalls. "I first brushed it away, but was approached again. Going into that fall [of 2015], I began to discern where I was supposed to be. Late November, I said, 'Mike, I think I'd better serve Indiana in this capacity. Ivy Tech is the nation's largest single-credited community college.' When I first took it to him, he wasn't so sure he wanted to hear about it, but I came back a second time and we talked through it again. He then supported me on doing it."

Mike and Ellspermann privately spoke to a couple Ivy Tech trustees and Mike assured them "that he was supporting me if I wanted to do this," she says. "Then, as happens in statehouses, that conversation leaked and went public and the big drama was 'Did he throw me out' or 'Did I leave him?'"

Ellspermann interviewed for the Ivy Tech position. In faith, she stepped down as lieutenant governor on March 2, 2016, knowing Ivy Tech would not make a selection for several months. Mike asked Eric Holcomb to step in as his running mate as rumors swirled around that he'd kicked Ellspermann out of office.

"I actually ran into somebody [in November 2018] in northeastern Indiana who said, 'I'm still mad because the governor pushed you out!'" Ellspermann relates. "And I said, 'The governor didn't push me out! This was my decision.' We came in good together and we left it in a good spot and I still think the world of him and I know the country needs him where he is now."

Mike and Holcomb ran unopposed in the May 2016 Republican primary. In a rematch of the 2012 election, Mike faced John Gregg, a Midwestern Democratic lawyer and former speaker of the Indiana House of Representatives.

Polls showed Mike and Gregg in a dead heat.

ENDNOTES

1. Parker.
2. Ibid.

3. Craig Fehrman, "INcoming: Mike Pence," *Indianapolis Monthly*, January 2, 2013.

4. Maureen Hayden, "Karen Pence forging her role as Indiana's first lady," *The Herald Bulletin*, Anderson, IN, March 18, 2013.

5. Mike Pence, 2015 Indiana Leadership Prayer Breakfast.

6. Laura Arnold, "Indiana Governor Pence Names IURC Chairman Jim Atterholt as New Chief of Staff," *IndianaDG*, Indiana Distributed Energy Alliance, May 13, 2014.

7. Mike Pence, 2013 Indiana Leadership Prayer Breakfast.

8. Mike Pence, 2016 Indiana Leadership Prayer Breakfast.

9. Mike Pence, 2016 Indiana Leadership Prayer Breakfast.

10. Mike Pence, 2016 Indiana Leadership Prayer Breakfast.

11. "Governor Pence Statement on HEA 1337," IN.gov, March 24, 2016.

12. Tony Cook, "Gov. Mike Pence signs 'religious freedom' bill in private, *The Indianapolis Star*, March 25, 2015.

13. "A Visit with Governor Mike and Karen Pence," *Dr. James Dobson's Family Talk*, October 5, 2016.

14. Indiana General Assembly, Conference Committee Report Digest for ESB 50 (iga.in.gov/documents/92b34f58).

15. Caleb Parke, "Ambassador Grenell 'quite pleased' Buttigieg stopped pushing 'hate hoax' about Pence," *Fox News*, April 23, 2019.

16. Mike Pence, 2016 Indiana Leadership Prayer Breakfast.

17. Gary Varvel, "Varvel: Rebutting *The New Yorker* caricature of Mike Pence."

18. Alex Brown, "Pence Welcomes Israeli Leaders at Business Exchange," *Inside Indiana Business*, June 28, 2016.

19. Sean Savage, "Indiana Gov. Mike Pence, Trump's VP choice, roots support for Israel in Christian faith," *Jewish News Service*, July 15, 2016.

15

CHOSEN

The saying is trustworthy: If anyone aspires to the office of over-
seer, he desires a noble task. Therefore an overseer must be above
reproach, the husband of one wife, sober-minded, self-controlled,
respectable, hospitable, able to teach, not a drunkard, not violent
but gentle, not quarrelsome, not a lover of money.
—1 Timothy 3:1–3 ESV

While Mike ran for reelection as governor of Indiana, Donald Trump began to campaign for the primaries as one of three Republicans—a number that grew over time. He didn't have a lot of support from evangelicals or conservatives, including Mike.

McIntosh talked to Mike during the 2016 primary election season. "We were not supporting Trump and I urged him to support Ted Cruz, which he did," McIntosh recalls.

Once Trump started to rack up primary wins, he began to search for a vice presidential candidate. Former House of Representatives Speaker Newt Gingrich and Chris Christie, then governor of New Jersey, were on the short list. So was Mike, which surprised him.

On Friday, June 10, 2016, just a day before the Indiana Republican convention, Mike got word that Trump was considering him for his running mate. Mike's campaign was hosting a reception in downtown Indianapolis; he and Karen were talking with different supporters when Mike got a phone call from Stephen Hilbert, former CEO of Conseco and a good friend of Trump's. He asked Mike, "If you were to be considered for vice president, would you be open to it?"

Mike went straight to Karen with the news. Later, he contacted Jim Atterholt, his gubernatorial chief of staff, who told him he should at least consider Trump's offer.

"Donald Trump wants to talk to me," Mike told his brother, Gregory, over lunch one day. "I told him, 'You have to go, you have no choice.'" As Gregory saw it, "when your party's nominee asks you to be the running mate, you have to do it."[1]

In the meantime, Trump released a list of twenty-one potential Supreme Court nominees with strong pro-life records and began to amass an evangelical, spiritual advisory committee of high-profile faith leaders across different Christian denominations.

TRUMP'S SPIRITUAL ADVISERS

"The spiritual advisory committee was initially a couple of people [Trump] has been close to for a long time," says Dr. Jay Strack, president and founder of the Youth Pastor Summit and Student Leadership University. "It's made up of different denominations with different beliefs."

Trump added additional people to the committee on the advice of its initial members.

"When it was clear Mr. Trump had the nomination, they formed this evangelical spiritual advisory committee and they asked me to join it," recalls Richard Land, president of the Southern Evangelical Seminary in Charlotte, North Carolina. "I said, 'Well, you do understand that Trump was my last choice in the Republican primaries.' And they said, 'Yes, we understand, but Trump is now the nominee.' I said, 'Yes, if you're asking me if I will give Trump advice on what I think he should be doing from a spiritual perspective.' Then they said, 'What would be your first piece of advice that you would give Mr. Trump?' I said, 'Pick Mike Pence. There's not one more thing you can do that would signal evangelicals more clearly that they are going to have a place at the table in your administration and that they're not going to be kicked to the back of the bus. There's not one single person who has been in Washington who has more respect and more trust than Mike Pence.'"

Mike and Karen prayed and mulled over the idea of him running for vice president before sharing it with their kids. Finally, while at the governor's cabin in Brown County one weekend in June 2016, Charlotte overheard her parents talking about something.

"We were sitting on the front porch of Aynes House," recalls Charlotte. "Dad turned to me and said he was being considered, along with a long list full of other well-qualified people, to be Donald Trump's running mate. I don't know why, but I wasn't surprised.… I told Dad I wasn't shocked and that he would be a good pick. He laughed, a little speechless, and commented how he was starting to think he was the only person in our family genuinely surprised by the news."[2]

While Trump weighed his options for running mate, Mike and Karen had two very important topics they needed Trump to address before they'd even consider an offer. First, they wanted to know what Mike's duties would entail as Trump's vice president. The second topic was of a more personal nature. Mike and Karen "felt we would need to know the Trumps as a family in order to make a decision," Charlotte says.[3]

A FAMILY WEEKEND TOGETHER

Trump's campaign chairman at the time, Paul Manafort, arranged for Mike, Karen, and Charlotte, who had just graduated from DePaul, to fly to the Trump National Golf Club in Bedminster, New Jersey, to spend a weekend in July with Trump, his wife, Melania, and their son, Barron.

"I didn't know him [Trump] at all" before that weekend, Mike later admitted. "I had met him twice [and] shaken his hand."[4]

One of those times was in 2011, when he was running for governor of Indiana. Mike went to Trump Tower in Manhattan and asked Trump for a campaign contribution, which he received.[5]

Mike's longtime friend and adviser Kellyanne Conway also served as an advisor to the Trump campaign. Knowing this, Mike sought her advice on what to expect when meeting Trump and how to best converse with him. Conway urged him to be himself and talk about things other than politics.

"I knew they would enjoy each other's company," Conway said later. "Mike Pence is someone whose faith allows him to subvert his ego to the greater good."[6]

Trump and Mike spent the weekend sizing each other up as potential running mates and played golf together. Mike later said Trump "beat me like a drum."[7]

The two men connected politically over conservative issues and personally over their shared passion for their families. While Trump was considering his options, Mike called McIntosh for his advice.

"He said, 'Do you think it's a good idea? People are telling me it might ruin my career and I should just stay here [in Indiana] and run for governor,'" McIntosh recalls. "I said, 'Look, you should absolutely do this if he offers it. One, you might become vice president, but two, if you don't, you'll be the leading candidate for president four years from now.'"

Mike sought out others for their advice as well, but no one's opinion mattered as much as Karen's. Together, they continued to pray for discernment of God's will.

"After that weekend, we headed back to Indiana and would go on to discuss the events in the weeks to come," recalls Charlotte. "Mom and Dad decided that if an offer was made, they would accept. We were trusting God with whatever happened, and we felt blessed to have had the experiences we did up to that point."[8]

Trump narrowed his choice down to Christie and Mike and seemed torn about who to pick as his running mate. To test his compatibility with both men, he decided to campaign with them separately, first with Christie. The day after he campaigned with Christie, Trump flew to Indiana to campaign with Mike. At the end of the evening, when Trump prepared to return to Manhattan, he learned that his plane had a flat tire and a new one would have to be specially flown in overnight. Trump and his son, Eric, who had accompanied him, decided to spend the night in Indiana.

The Trumps joined Mike and Karen for dinner at the Capital Grille in Indianapolis. They arranged to have breakfast together the next morning at the governor's mansion.

LATE-NIGHT FLOWER GATHERING

Mike and Karen went back to the governor's mansion in somewhat of a panic.

"Mike told me he and Karen got back to the mansion that night and they were literally out in the backyard with scissors and a flashlight [from his cell phone], cutting flowers off" the bushes for floral arrangements to decorate the mansion, says Reed. "It was ten or eleven o'clock at night and they said to one another, 'If we get picked, no one's going to believe this.'"

The governor's residence didn't employ a chef, so Karen contacted their residence manager, who called a local eatery that they used for catering and asked if they could do some individual egg dishes early the next morning.

The morning of July 13, Mike and Karen got up early in anticipation of the Trumps' arrival.

"They walked in and said, 'Wow! You're making breakfast!'" Mike later told Reed.

Reed recalls, "Mike said, 'And you know, the funny thing is, everybody thinks they have all this domestic staff and they're all wealthy New Yorkers, but they're all down to earth.' He said, 'I'm not saying it closed the deal, but I was told they got a big kick out of it.'"

That evening, Mike met with his advisers to discuss their plans going forward. Soon after they started talking, one of Mike's top aides got a call from the Trump campaign and was told that Trump would be calling within a few minutes to give him his answer. So, Mike and his aides began to pray together, asking for God's guidance, His peace that surpasses all understanding, wisdom, and a hedge of protection around the Pence family. Afterward, Mike went home so he could be with Karen, Charlotte, and Michael Jr.'s fiancée, Sarah, when the call came in.

Charlotte says the family had sat down and discussed what it would mean for them if their dad was chosen.

"We talked about it a lot," Charlotte says. "I was kind of lucky because I was the only kid living at home at the time. So I got to really see my parents actually go through this thought process and I honestly had a lot of peace about it because I saw them just pray about it a lot, to really trusting God to go down this path that they felt called to. So honestly I felt really good about it and I was kind of along for the ride the whole time."[9]

THE CALL FROM TRUMP

The phone finally rang at 11:00 p.m. As soon as they heard it, Mike and Karen took the phone downstairs so they could have some privacy.

"I heard that familiar voice over the phone," Mike says. "We had been told that the call might come. But we prayed through it as a family, we talked to our children. I said 'yes' in a heartbeat."[10]

Trump knew Mike and Karen were a team; he knew Mike relied on her, so he wanted her to know of his belief in her husband and his own respect for her. So when he called, Trump told Mike, "I hear Karen is there, too? Can I talk to her?"[11]

After they got off the phone, instinctively, Mike and Karen prayed for Christie, Gingrich, and other hopefuls. Then they went back upstairs to the living room, where Charlotte and Sarah waited in anticipation for the news.

"They were holding hands, and he asked me to get Audrey on the phone," Charlotte recalls. "Sarah called Michael. With Audrey and Michael on speaker, all six of us huddled together around the phones. I fought the urge to yell, 'Just tell us already!' and let Dad take in the moment. 'We wanted to tell you all together,' he said, still holding Mom's hand, 'and now we can.'.... He took a deep breath and went on. 'Your dad was just asked to be the candidate for vice president of the United States.' His voice caught with emotion at the end."[12]

Sometime later, Mike called his brother, Gregory. The two wept and shared Scripture verses with one another. Quoting Matthew 25:21 (NLT), Gregory told Mike, "*Well done, my good and faithful servant.*"[13]

On July 14, 2016, Mike ended his gubernatorial reelection campaign and accepted Trump's offer to run as vice president. The next day, Trump announced his selection of Mike as his running mate. And on July 19, at the Republican National Convention, Indiana Lieutenant Governor Eric Holcomb nominated Mike as the party's candidate for vice president.

"On behalf of the great state of Indiana," Holcomb said, "I proudly nominate a great man of integrity, a proven conservative, an incredible husband and father, and one of my best friends. I nominate the great governor of Indiana, Mike Pence."

McIntosh recalls, "As soon as Trump announced Mike Pence was going to be his vice presidential pick, we were commenting on that and announced our support for Trump."

GOD HEARS US

Trump "made a great choice and probably a lot of people wonder why he made that choice," says Dr. Ronnie Floyd, senior pastor of Cross Church of Northwest Arkansas and member of Trump's spiritual advisory committee. "But I think God was involved in the choice. I really do believe the Sovereign God we call out to about our nation, I think He heard. He knew where we were going and I think that's really pivotal."

When Trump chose Mike, "it only strengthened our commitment and it underscored the fact that Mr. Trump was truly committed to conservative causes," says one adviser, the Rev. Dr. Jack Graham, pastor of Prestonwood Baptist Church in Plano, Texas. "His choice of Mike Pence had just validated our faith that Mr. Trump was truly going to fight for what we believe in."

"God doesn't always give us strong direction," says Bill Smith. "Sometimes He gives us peace to know that it's okay to move forward. That's what we saw when Mike was asked by President-elect Trump to join the ticket. He was offered an opportunity to serve and he had peace about it. If you're asked to serve, you better have a good reason to say no. And in this case, Mike Pence saw he had an opportunity to serve the president and the people."

With only a few days to work on an acceptance speech, Mike scrambled to craft one, meeting with writers and reworking their drafts. He wanted his first speech to reveal who he was at the core. Referencing several verses from Scripture, he told the thousands gathered at the Republican National Convention and the millions of Americans who watched on screens everywhere:

"Should I have the awesome privilege to serve as your vice president, I promise to keep faith with that conviction, to pray daily for a wise and discerning heart, for who is able to govern this great people of Yours without it? My fellow Americans, I believe we have come to another rendezvous with destiny. And I have faith, faith in the boundless capacity of the American people and faith that God can still heal our land."

TURNING POINTS FOR U.S.

Friends and colleagues say the selection of Mike for vice president was a turning point for America.

"There were three moments, hinge points or turning points, in the election with Trump when it comes to evangelicals and Catholics overcoming reservations with him—and there certainly were reservations," says Reed. "One was when he released the list of judges from which he promised to choose a replacement for the late [Justice Antonin] Scalia. The second was when he picked Mike Pence as his running mate. It was deeply revealing of Trump's priorities. There was no accidental way to pick him. It was revealing of Trump's character. Then, when Trump rather famously turned to Hillary Clinton and said, 'She just said she's okay with the baby being ripped from its mother's womb right before it's born. Maybe she's okay with that, but I'm not okay with that.' I don't think Mike closed the deal with evangelicals per se, but I think he advanced the ball. Trump ultimately got 81 percent of the evangelical vote. I don't think we would have got 81 percent before Pence was picked."

To express his love for Indiana and his willingness to be Trump's running mate, Mike used a sports metaphor.

"Now, if you know anything about Hoosiers, you know we love to suit up and compete," he said at the convention. "We play to win. That's why I joined this campaign in a heartbeat. You have nominated a man for president who never quits, who never backs down, a fighter, a winner."

But the media immediately jumped on Mike, saying he joined the Trump ticket out of desperation, claiming Mike wouldn't have won reelection as governor.

Mike's colleagues disagree.

"Mike probably would have won his reelection bid, but it wasn't going to be a cakewalk," says Blackwell. "He probably would have nosed it out, but it was going to be a dogfight. To make a strategic calculation of running for reelection and lose, or be number two on the ticket, even if it was a long-shot. Because if he won, the payout for the public good would be tremendous. To me, he made the right call."

Lake says he initially wanted to deter Mike from running.

"I have said all along, and particularly when he was chosen as the vice presidential candidate, that I wanted to say to Mike, 'Mike, turn your back on all of that and run as fast as you can,'" the pastor says. "'Don't take your family through all of that.' But I know it would be in vain because I don't think Mike feels it's predestined that he's going to be president, but I do think he has a commitment to his country to serve in whatever way he's called upon."

In the end, Lake says he's thankful Mike was chosen as Trump's vice presidential running mate.

"When I see so many people compromise their convictions according to the environment that they're in, or the people with whom they're associating, you have to admire someone who refuses to do that," Lake says.

ENDNOTES

1. Mayer.
2. Charlotte Pence, *Where You Go.*
3. Charlotte Pence, *Where You Go.*
4. "VP Mike Pence Shares Testimony at Church by the Glades," VFNtv.
5. Mayer.
6. McKay Coppins, "God's Plan for Mike Pence."
7. Mayer.
8. Charlotte Pence, *Where You Go.*
9. "Charlotte Pence On Her New Book, Family & More," *The View,* ABC, March 20, 2018.
10. "A Visit with Governor Mike and Karen Pence," *Dr. James Dobson's Family Talk,* October 5, 2016.
11. Parker.
12. Charlotte Pence, *Where You Go.*
13. Mahler and Johnson.

16

VICE PRESIDENT-ELECT

Whoever would be great among you must be your servant, and whoever would be first among you must be your slave, even as the Son of Man came not to be served but to serve, and to give his life as a ransom for many.
—Matthew 20:26–28 ESV

Karen and Charlotte were often by Mike's side as he hit the campaign trail with Trump. Charlotte's recent graduation from DePaul enabled her to travel with her parents and she would joke that it was her job to "babysit" them.

In reality, she was a great support to them, says Steger.

"Charlotte was there for both her mom and dad, so you really saw the serious part of Charlotte come out," says Steger. "She saw a need in the family and said, 'Wow, Mom and Dad are now both just covered over with stuff to do and if I can just pitch in here and be a good helper, it could be fun.' She looks to have the same servant's heart as her mom and dad."

While many media outlets continued their assault on Mike, perhaps none was as vehemently negative as the one written by Jane Mayer for *The New Yorker* in October 2017. It was headlined "The Danger of President Pence: Trump's critics yearn for his exit. But Mike Pence, the corporate right's inside man, poses his own risks."

Among other things, this piece, slugged as a "Letter from Washington," claimed Mike "never authored a single successful bill" as congressman. In fact, Mike co-sponsored a hundred pieces of legislation that became law and sponsored or co-sponsored more than sixteen hundred more. The article also called Mike "calculating" and "ambitious."[1]

Mike's friend Varvel came to his defense.

"Jane Mayer caricatures Pence so badly I didn't recognize him," Varvel wrote. "I'm a political cartoonist. I know caricatures. I also know Mike Pence, and *The New Yorker's* piece does not resemble him…. To start, the headline, 'The Danger of President Pence,' is an oxymoron. 'Danger?' 'Pence?' Before I read it, I thought the article either would be seriously funny or pretty ugly. It was the latter. Pence's sense of danger is limited to ordering a vanilla milk shake to chase his cheeseburger, hold the bacon. For most of his political career, Mike Pence has been knocked for playing it too safe. Now he's a threat to democracy?"[2]

MIKE'S MOTIVATIONS

Liberal national media outlets sought ways to join in the negative banter, criticizing Mike for having political ambition as though this was a sin and something no one else in politics ever had.

"Mike has a healthy ambition about him and that is altogether good in major leaders," says Steger. "But for Michael, there is an evangelical dimension to it. He is eager to do good. He is eager to help folks. The spiritual gift of help is a major part of him. He gets up in the morning and says, 'I have a meeting with so-and-so today. I want good to come from that. How can I be of service? How can I help others?' And he has the ability to have an instant rapport with people. He's affable; he's winsome; he sets people at ease. That helps make him highly effective. So in terms of his ambition, it has its root in his helper's heart."

Some have claimed that Mike is motivated by money. In 2016, Mike's Public Financial Disclosure Report indicated that he and Karen had one bank account valued at no more than $15,000—and perhaps as little as $1,001. When Steger hears people say Mike's in politics for the money, he laughs.

"You really ought to look at his financial piece," says Steger, who has his own business as a financial advisor. "The guy has raised a family of three and he hardly has a dime to his name. The kids have lived incredibly modest lives growing up, going wherever Dad needed to go and living in a very modest home back in the [Indiana congressional] district when he was in Congress and a very modest house in Washington, D.C. It's expensive to have two houses on a congressman's salary, let alone get three kids through college. So I think it's the most telling piece. Mike is not ambitious for power. He's not ambitious for wealth. Clearly, if he's ambitious for wealth, he's utterly failed."

Steger says Mike is able to calmly handle the personal attacks on him, his faith, and his character by looking at it from a biblical perspective. In the Beatitudes, Jesus tells His disciples, *"Blessed are you when people insult you, persecute you and falsely say all kinds of evil against you because of me"* (Matthew 5:11). Mike takes this concept to heart.

"People early in the Trump administration would say, 'How can he handle this?'" Steger recalls. "The political word for it would be being a 'happy warrior.' Somebody who goes into that political battle and he's just kind of happy and goes out there and it's a good fight."

THE EVANGELICAL DIVIDE

Evangelicals were somewhat split about the idea of a Trump-Pence ticket. Many were thrilled that there was a chance that an evangelical Christian with conservative views would be in the White House bending the president's ear. Others wondered: how can a godly man like Mike associate himself with someone who was known for making foul remarks, had been married three times, and was better known for funding gambling endeavors than being a Christian?

Those closest to Mike understand his reasons.

"Let's say you and I could come up with bullet points on why he would and why he would not join Mr. Trump," says Hubler. "And let's say one of them is that he sold out—sold out to the devil. But the other is, what about whispering in the man's ear? What about bringing Christianity into these offices? I think Mike has said, 'I'm going to position myself to be the purveyor of the conservative cause in the White House.'"

Dan Murphy's convinced conservatives are asking the wrong question.

"I don't think Mike sold out," he says. "The question is, 'What did he give up to run with Trump?' Nothing. Going back to the fraternity days, Mike is a guy who works with diverse people. We cannot forget that Jesus Himself sat down for dinner with tax collectors and other sinners. Mike is not one of these holier than thou, nose in the air kind of folks. I think he really did see a chance to work with this man and he saw something in him and a chance to do some good."

Simcox says Mike's heart of servanthood leads him politically.

"I think people try to make too much out of" Mike serving with Trump, says Simcox. "I think that he thought this is the best way he could serve his country. Ambition is not wrong and every U.S. senator, congressperson, state attorney general, and governor has thought about [becoming president]. When the opportunity came to him to be on a national ticket and to make an impact for the things he believes, there might have been reflection, but there wasn't any hesitation. I think he felt, 'I've prepared all my adult life to do this. I now have the opportunity to make a contribution to the things I believe that are in the best interest of the country and I'll not walk away from it.'"

Varvel talks about how he and a friend, who also knows Mike, discussed why Mike would even consider running with Trump.

"Pence often says, 'I'm a Christian, a conservative and a Republican, in that order.' So why would he partner with a man who many believe is none of these? As a Christian, conservative and a cartoonist, in that order, I think I know," Varvel says. "Many political observers think Pence has presidential ambitions. Because of that, some think he sold his soul and compromised his principles to be Trump's right hand man. After all, vice president of the United States certainly looks good on your resume."[3]

A BIBLICAL EXPLANATION

But Varvel argues, "I think there's a biblical explanation for why Pence agreed to become Trump's number two." Perhaps, like Esther, who saved the Jewish people, Mike "wondered if he was being given this position '*for such a time as this*'" (Esther 4:14). Perhaps Mike "recognized Trump's job offer as an opportunity to be like Joseph or Daniel and to be a godly influence to the future president."[4]

Deason maintains Trump needed Mike far more than Mike needed Trump.

"Trump needed a Mike Pence and there was just no one else like him," says Deason. "He wouldn't have won with Chris Christie. It had to be someone like Mike and Mike knew that and I think he really believed they had a chance to do it together. He brought Donald Trump credibility. In no way were we under the delusion that we were hiring Saint Trump. We were not looking to hire someone, a president, to come in and heal the moral ills of our country. We were hiring someone to go in and finally shake up Washington like it's never been shaken and truly change the way business is done. The great thing was that we were going to have this calm, cool, strong Christian, highly moral person there with him, to help him, to watch him, to influence him. And that's the role Mike Pence plays."

As Mike began campaigning with Trump, many evangelicals who were initially hesitant about Trump jumped on board in support of the team, encouraging others to do the same.Several of Mike's friends say they, too, had reservations about Trump until Mike was on the ticket, even though none of them wanted Hillary Clinton as president.

"I did not see Trump as a rock-solid Republican or true conservative," says Blackwell. "I saw him as somebody who had grown up and become successful running a family-controlled LLC and he never had to run a publicly traded corporation or deal with the complexities of a board of directors or shareholders. But I was surprised he survived the demolition derby known as the primary [election season]. At that point, having somebody that was close to him that at least stood a chance of influencing him in our direction on a day-to-day basis made me a champion of Mike right off the bat."

FRIENDS' THOUGHTS BEFOREHAND

For his part, Phipps "was originally supporting Ted Cruz," he says. "Vice presidents traditionally haven't had a lot of influence." Phipps cites the story of Alben Barkley, who served as vice president under President Harry Truman and often joked about the two brothers, one of whom "went off to sea and the other went to the office of the vice president and neither was heard from again."

Varvel, too, "was not a Trump supporter" in the beginning, he says. "But when he picked Mike Pence, that kind of verified, 'Okay, I can safely do this and stay true to my conscience.' I think a lot of evangelicals felt that way."

Dan Murphy says he leaned toward Rubio initially.

"I was not a Trump guy during the primaries," Murphy says. "I was a Rubio guy. Trump got it and I was going, 'Oh, my God, we're headed for a Hillary Clinton reign.' Mike joining on made sense. For me and for a lot of people, Mike normalized the ticket."

"I'm not sure I would have voted for the ticket [otherwise], but Mike being on it was absolutely an influence for helping me not feel disheartened about where we stood," says Piepgrass. "If you had to ask me, before, without knowing they were going to be running mates, to pick two more opposite people who are in politics, I probably would have said, other than the fact that they both identify as Republican, those two. They could not be more different."

Johnnie Moore, founder of The Kairos Company and a member of Trump's spiritual advisory committee, met Mike for the first time on the campaign trail. They immediately bonded and later met on several occasions.

Referring to a passage from Scripture that says, "*The Spirit himself bears witness with our spirit that we are children of God*" (Romans 8:16 ESV), Moore says he felt that spiritual connection with Mike. "I had that experience with him. The first time I shook his hand, I knew that this was someone who shared my faith and my values."

Mike is "someone who takes the Bible seriously, he takes his testimony seriously," says Moore. "Someone who's governed by a higher set of values, who tries to make a difference in the world not for his own personal reasons, [but] for his faith, which inspires his public service.

He's not trying to shimmy his faith into his public service or add his faith on to his public service. I think his faith inspired his public service from the beginning."

By the same token, Moore adds, "I think he has demonstrated that being a sincere Christian doesn't mean that you have to embrace a theocratic point of view either. I think he's been able to cut an effective balance between being a sincere believer, who is absolutely persuaded by the Judeo-Christian contribution to our Constitution and the founding ideals of our democracy, but never lapsing into sort of selective religious freedom or promoting establishing one religion over another."

Mike's "track record" is one of "a life of obedience to God and a willingness to work with everyone, to be kind to everyone, but yet live out his faith," says Graham, who served as the honorary chairman of the 2015 National Day of Prayer. "You see it in his marriage and family and the way he deals with people directly. He's a cool customer. His waters run very deep and that's clear. He's not a Johnnie-come-lately when it comes to the Christian faith. He's been at this for a while since he was a college student, when he committed his life to Christ, and he's very sincere and very deliberate and disciplined in his faith."

MIKE'S COMMITMENTS

Graham says when he and his wife, Deb, attended a small dinner party at the Pences' home, "I just watched their interaction as they hosted the dinner and as they spoke about each other, the long journey that they had shared, getting into the political world to begin with, and praying about those discussions. I see him respecting his wife and honoring her."

During the campaign, Mike didn't attempt to hide his admiration for Karen and his commitment to her and his family.

"I'm running for vice president of the United States, I'm governor of the state that I love," Mike said, "but the highest office I'll ever hold, the highest position I'll ever have, is D.A.D., and whatever I've been able to accomplish in our family is mostly due to [Karen]. She has been the architect of family life for our kids that even though we served on

Capitol Hill and served under two different administrations, Karen has always created a zone for our family of real normalcy."[5]

Mike's unusually close relationship with Karen didn't go unnoticed by either the press or Trump. Later, the latter would note the Pences have "one hell of a good marriage going."[6]

Steger, who knew Mike even before he met Karen, says their union has always been founded in Christ.

"We are taught that *'the two shall become one'* [Mark 10:8 ESV]. Karen and Michael are not perfect by any stretch, especially Mike, but after thirty-three years, through all kinds of turbulence, they are a lovely blend of patience and affection," Steger says. "It did not come easily, but they gently worked at it, protected it, but mostly, they desired it. It's a beautiful love story and God is at the center of that. It's really something special."

Simcox, who has witnessed the fraying marriages of countless politicians over the years, sees a great difference in Mike and Karen's.

"Mike has been an example, to me, as a man who has been faithful in the political arena and that is not easy to do," says Simcox. "But there's one way he has really, really set the example and that's in the relationship that he has with his wife. I've never seen a couple in public life who are more dedicated to each other, who have a better understanding and highly developed trust of one another, and who see their mission as not just one person and the other person supporting them, but as a team. I've known a lot of governors and I've watched the family dynamic and I think they are a couple who are just so devoted to one another and to public service in the right way for all the right reasons and that's really, really what impresses me about Mike and Karen."

Joining Mike on the campaign trail, Simcox says he saw several occasions in which Mike's love for Karen was publically displayed.

"In the campaign plane, every night on the way back, Mike would write a little thing that reflected on the experience of the day," Simcox recalls. "There's this team on the plane—his speech writer, his advance guys, friends, and a guy who was going to do some writing for him.

One day, he's sitting over there across the aisle from me and he writes this little thing, scribbles it out, and hands it to the stewardess to read over the public address system to everybody on the plane. The stewardess takes it and reads it. And it's a tribute to Karen. You're not around him very long before you see his absolute devotion to her."

Mike is known to pour out his affection for Karen and share with everyone how much he loves and appreciates her.

"She's the best part of my life," Mike says. "Everything we do in public life, we do together. I can't imagine it any other way."[7]

Others take note of the Pences' unity as a political team and Karen's conservatism.

"On social issues, I don't think you get any more conservative than these two," says Larry Sabato, director of the Center for Politics at the University of Virginia. "Karen Pence is much more conservative than Laura Bush. She's more conservative than Barbara Bush, or, for that matter, Nancy Reagan."[8]

WIVES TARGETED

During the campaign, Trump and Mike weren't the only ones being verbally assaulted. Their wives were also criticized and mistreated.

Jim Williams, former vice president of development at Riley Children's Foundation, recalls one event Karen hosted at the governor's mansion for Riley's art therapists. Guests had a bit of a walk because of the perimeter set up around the building. One told Karen, "After that walk, I'm voting for Hillary," Williams relates. "And she just smiled and said, 'Well, welcome to the residence.'… She's like, 'Ah, you know, it happens. People have their triggers and not everybody loves us and I understand that, but [we're] here to promote Riley and the art therapy program, and that's the most important thing this evening.'"[9]

Others on the campaign noted Karen's steel and impenetrable presence.

"She was a major part of our campaign, and she just never flinched," says Conway.[10]

Karen's strength was a major asset as the Trump/Pence campaign wasn't without its hiccups.

BANTER WITH BILLY BUSH

Three months after Trump and Mike began campaigning together, and just before the second presidential debate on October 9, 2016, *The Washington Post* published a video and accompanying article about Trump and *Access Hollywood* television host Billy Bush having a lewd conversation about women in 2005. Trump's choice of words were considered particularly offensive as was his view that women would let him "do anything" with them because he was "a star."[11]

The story and video provoked strong reactions everywhere—from other media outlets, women's rights organizations, conservatives, and politicians of both parties. Trump publicly apologized for his "foolish" words, asserting, "I've never said I'm a perfect person, nor pretended to be someone that I'm not. I've said and done things I regret, and the words released today on this more than a decade-old video are one of them. Anyone who knows me knows these words don't reflect who I am."[12]

By the next morning, however, several dozen Republicans had called for Trump to withdraw from the campaign and let Mike take over the Republican ticket. Mike's public schedule temporarily disappeared from the campaign website and the media waited intently to see what he'd say and do.

"It is clear that there was public silence from Mike for what seemed like a fairly long time given how fast the news cycle is," says Steger. "Usually the cycle just demands…'Where are you on this and we want to know right now.'"

By the end of the day, they had their answer.

"As a husband and father, I was offended by the words and actions described by Donald Trump in the eleven-year-old video released yesterday," Mike said. "I do not condone his remarks and cannot defend them." At the same time, Mike said he supported Trump and was "grateful" that he "has expressed remorse and apologized to the American people."[13]

Republicans and conservatives, who had been anxiously awaiting Mike's response to the video, let out a sigh of relief. Friends say it was Mike's spiritual wisdom and desire to do what was right for the nation that kept him on the ticket.

"A critical point for Trump was after the tape was released," says McIntosh. "Mike could have decided to walk away from it. They would have lost, but he'd kept his reputation intact. And he and Karen obviously felt called to stay there and continue to serve Trump. I remember Mike's statement very well because I realized it was prayerfully made. He said [in essence], 'I still support him. He clearly did something that was wrong and he knows it. And he's apologized to his wife and that's good enough for me. I think he'll be a good president and I'm supporting him.' That was a pivotal moment and basically signaled to Republicans that we should stay on board the Trump ticket. A lot of female candidates were saying, 'No, Trump should quit the ticket.' Paul Ryan announced he wasn't going to be on stage with him and Mike sent the opposite signal, a Reaganesque signal: 'We've got to stay united because the alternative of Hillary Clinton is unacceptable and terrible for the country.'"

McIntosh says Mike also had "a very personal, moral sense that, 'I believe somebody when they're sincerely regretting what they did and I believe in forgiveness and grace and his wife offered that to him so we should move on.' And that's how Mike's faith has guided him. He does think about every position he takes in terms of, 'Is it consistent with my faith?' I'm sure Mike and Karen were repulsed by the tape, but they found within their faith, and probably through prayer, that when someone asks for forgiveness, you should forgive them."

Rumors still circulated that Mike was going to either drop out of the race entirely or seek the presidency with former Secretary of State Condoleezza Rice as his running mate.

Mike repeatedly denied either option was a consideration, saying it was "absolutely false to suggest that at any point in time we considered dropping off this ticket. It's the greatest honor of my life to have been nominated by my party to be the next vice president."[14]

In private, aides say, Mike confronted Trump and he apologized personally to both him and Karen.

INNER STRENGTH FROM CHRIST

When considering the source of Mike's strength as he endured this trial, friends attribute it to something they've seen in Mike for years: an inner fortitude found with Christ.

"There is also a steel backbone inside Mike," says Steger. "He's had to navigate some pretty precarious situations. In many respects, he's a lot like Ronald Reagan in that way, kind of soft-spoken and affable day-to-day, but then [he] can be pretty tough when he has to be or feels he has to be. Then again, as a born-again Christian, Michael is going to be incredibly forgiving because his Christian faith is rooted so deeply in forgiveness. When you bring in the notion of forgiveness, Michael's perspective is, 'You are a child of God. I don't like what you did. I don't condone what you did, but I forgive you for what you've done and still love you as a person.'"

When Mike forgave Trump over the videotape incident, he was not condoning that behavior, Steger points out. "That gets really complex, especially for folks who just don't understand the Christian belief that we are all flawed. Mike takes that to heart. When you hear him using the word 'humble,' that's really the position he comes from: 'I'm still flawed. I still make mistakes. I'm forgiven and I'm forgiving my neighbor as well.'"

McIntosh believes Mike is one of few politicians who could work effectively with Trump and all of his flaws.

"Mike brings to the job the servant-leadership [perspective], which frankly I think means he's one of the few people who could be Trump's vice president," says McIntosh. "A prideful politician would start to distance himself from Trump and start to be an independent player and compete against him and that would then lead to Trump resenting them and it would start a downward spiral that would be very harmful to the administration. Mike's view is that he's there to serve the president and help him with implementing his agenda. That's what has led him to become very close to Trump and trusted by Trump. And it's not just a move to be vice president; it's sincerely who he is. He believes in servant-leadership and feels called to this role against all the odds and now wants to be faithful in implementing and serving in that capacity."

SINCERE BELIEF IN GOD'S POWER

Blackwell believes Mike's reasons for staying on the ticket and supporting Trump go beyond the basic Christian principle of forgiveness.

"At the end of the day, if you don't believe in the transformational powers of God, then there's something missing in your understanding of Christian faith," he says. "It isn't that you are the Michelangelo of Donald Trump's life, but you can be a paintbrush in God's hands. Mother Teresa was known to say she was a pen in God's hand, writing love letters to the world. And as sure as I'm saying this today, I know that Mike has asked God to be a pen or paintbrush in His hands to help [Trump] do the right thing, for the right reason, for the right time."

Many in the media took issue with the idea that Mike could forgive Trump for the things he'd said to Billy Bush, which Trump called "locker room talk." They questioned how Mike could stand by the crude presidential nominee.

"There's so much in the Christian faith that should be unifying for us," Steger says, trying to clarify the heart of God. "Maybe a better word is healing. There's a big piece of the American population that just doesn't flat-out know Christianity and what it's about; it's just a blank, so they're skeptical about it. Christianity isn't about damning people. There's a seeking of understanding and forgiveness and gentleness about it."

Instead of damning Trump, Mike's friends and colleagues say Christians need to consider where Trump is in his spiritual journey.

Like the apostle Paul, Blackwell says, "Donald Trump is on the road to Damascus, with a sort of transformation going on in his life."

He encourages believers and non-believers alike to be patient with both Mike and Trump.

Strack agrees with Blackwell's view that there's a spiritual transformation going on in Trump's life.

Referring to biblical heroes, Strack says there are some people like Daniel, Nehemiah, Nathan, and Deborah that Trump "has drawn around him to speak into" his life, as well as Mike and Karen's. The members of the spiritual advisory committee "share what we believe our convictions are and what the Scriptures say. Trump may push back a little bit and he'll say, 'I don't get that. Why is that? Where is that?' All the questions you want someone to ask. But it's been fascinating to watch [Mike and Trump's] relationship be this strong and the personal enjoyment they get out of being with each other. It really is a remarkable testimony and I think it further proves what a great choice it was to pick Pence."

ENDNOTES

1. Mayer.
2. Gary Varvel, "Varvel: Rebutting *The New Yorker* caricature of Mike Pence."
3. Gary Varvel, "A conservative's view: What motivated Mike Pence to run with Donald Trump?" *The Indianapolis Star*, August 30, 2017.
4. Ibid.
5. "A Visit with Governor Mike and Karen Pence," *Dr. James Dobson's Family Talk.*
6. Gabby Morrongiello, "Trump: Mike Pence 'has one hell of a good marriage going,'" *Washington Examiner*, March 31, 2017.
7. Shari Rudavsky, "Karen Pence is right at home," *The Indianapolis Star*, December 12, 2013.
8. Celeste Katz, "Karen Pence Is Playing the Mother of All Long Games," *Town & Country*, April 19, 2018.
9. Ibid.
10. Parker.
11. David A. Fahrenthold, "Trump recorded having extremely lewd conversation about women in 2005," *The Washington Post*, October 8, 2016.
12. Ibid.
13. Reena Flores, "Mike Pence: 'I cannot defend' Trump's words," CBS News, October 8, 2016.
14. Tom LoBianco and Alisyn Camerota, "Pence: I never considered leaving Trump ticket," CNN, October 10, 2016.

17

A NEW ERA DAWNING

Praise be to the name of God…. He changes times and seasons;
he sets up kings and deposes them. He gives wisdom to the wise
and knowledge to the discerning.
—Daniel 2:20–21

On Tuesday, November 8, 2016, Mike and Karen joined the Trumps at the Hilton in downtown Manhattan. They expected to celebrate the election before the night was over. With the exception of daughter Audrey, who was overseas, the entire Pence family was there, including Mike's mom, Nancy, and her husband, Basil; daughter Charlotte; son Michael and his fiancée, Sarah; all five of Mike's siblings; and several cousins, nieces, and nephews. Altogether, there were twenty-six members of the Pence family there.

The early polls didn't look favorable, but in the wee hours of the following morning, the Republican ticket crossed the threshold to claim a majority of Electoral College votes. Mike offered brief victory remarks before introducing the country's new president.

"This is a historic night," Mike said. "The American people have spoken and the American people have elected their new champion. America has elected a new president and it's almost hard for me to express the honor that I and my family feel that we will have the privilege to serve as your vice president of the United States of America."

After Trump gave his acceptance speech and the crowd dispersed, the Pence family all retired to Mike's brother Gregory's hotel room to celebrate and unwind. While celebrating, they received a text message from relatives in Doonbeg, Ireland, who hung a "Make America Great Again" hat outside the door to their pub with a note that read, "Gone celebrating."[1]

Mike immediately jumped into his new role and assumed control of Trump's transition efforts to build a solid group of individuals within the administration who would support their political and conservative goals.

SURROUNDED BY PEOPLE OF FAITH

"I think one of the reasons why I'm pleasantly surprised by what I see in the Trump administration is because of the fact that he replaced the governor of New Jersey (Christie) with Mike Pence as the chairman of transition," says Land. "That made a huge difference. One of the oldest rules in Washington is, 'Personnel is policy.' And because Mike Pence was in charge of the transition, there are more evangelical Christians and more deeply devoted Catholic Christians in this administration than any administration in my memory. And I've been dealing with administrations from Reagan on. In terms of numbers, percentagewise, there are more strong Christians in the Trump administration personnel I've dealt with and that's particularly because of Mike Pence in that transition."

"You cannot walk ten feet into the West Wing and not bump into a Christian and I'm talking about evangelical, Bible-believing Christians," says Graham. "This is a testimony to the president and vice president, who are putting people around them in this administration who have faith and are living and practicing their faith."

Others have also witnessed Mike's faith-based implementation of leadership.

"There's a faith-based component on every single department in the United States government now," says Steger. "It's staggering, refreshing."

Karen has continued to support Mike, sitting in on interviews and joining him for off-the-record briefings with reporters.

Mike brought in people who had worked for and with him for years, providing a firm foundation of loyal conservatives and Christians for the administration.

After Mike was elected, but before he was sworn in, Simcox had a conversation with Mike that revealed the heart of the nation's new vice president—and what had been his personal political motto from the very beginning.

"He said, 'Look, Ed, this is not about the president, it's not about me. It's about the country,'" Simcox relates. "It's simple, to the point, and profound. If you get up every day and say, 'I'm doing what I'm doing, despite the setbacks and difficulties and challenges, because I believe I'm here to serve the country and I believe I'm given this opportunity to write about policies that I think are important for the country, you can get through any difficult situation and deal with a lot of difficult people. I thought it was a profound mission statement for his tenure in this administration."

As the New Year came, Trump and Mike were both confident about the administration they'd assembled and were eager to begin their roles as the two most influential leaders in the world.

At 8:30 a.m. on January 20, 2017, before the inauguration, Mike and a small band of family and friends joined Dr. James Dobson for prayer at St. John's Episcopal Church. Dobson wanted to speak a blessing over Mike before he embarked on his journey as vice president of the United States.

Drawing a comparison to King Solomon, who the Bible says was the wisest man who ever lived, Dobson pointed out what he witnessed on Mike's faithful, spiritual walk over the previous twenty-five years, highlighting his humility and integrity. Dobson went on to pray that God would lay His hands on Mike, protect him, use him to lead the nation with righteousness, and grant him wisdom and knowledge.

As Mike and Karen went on to take part in other vice presidential traditions before the inauguration, their family and friends gathered for the inauguration in the main ballroom of the White House. Proud of Mike's accomplishment, the Pence family celebrated his new role as vice president, but also had some personal concerns.

THE FAMILY'S PEACEMAKER

"At the inauguration, the Pence family was right in front of me, so I sped up a little bit and caught [Mike's sister] Mary, who was kind of the caboose of the fairly long lineup of the big Pence family," recalls Steger. "We were walking together and I said, 'How are you guys doing?' Because all of this happened so fast. Mary just said, 'We've lost our peacemaker, we've lost our balance as a family.' And I looked at her like, 'What are you talking about?' She said, 'We have this huge Irish-Catholic family and we're all opinionated and Michael was the one who could just calm us all down and just kind of work things through and bring peace to the family.'"

Three hours after their intimate prayer service with Dobson, at exactly noon, Mike stood next to the Trumps, Karen, and their kids on the inauguration stage on the West Front of the United States Capitol Building in Washington, D.C., facing the National Mall with its iconic Washington Monument and the Lincoln Memorial in the distance.

With members of Congress, Supreme Court justices, high-ranking military officers, former presidents, living Medal of Honor recipients, other dignitaries, and hundreds of thousands of members of the public looking on, Trump was sworn in as the 45th president of the United States.

Afterward, Mike raised his right hand and placed it on the Ronald Reagan family Bible, more than a hundred years old, which had belonged to the former president's mother, Nell. Both had written notes and comments in its margins. Reagan used the Bible for his inaugurations as both governor of California and president, with it opened to 2 Chronicles 7:14: *"If my people, which are called by my name, shall humble themselves, and pray, and seek my face, and turn from their wicked ways; then will I hear from heaven, and will forgive their sin, and will heal their land"* (KJV).

Mike placed his personal Bible that he read every morning beneath the cherished relic from the Reagan family, handing them to Karen to hold while he placed his right hand on top of them. Supreme Court Justice Clarence Thomas administered the oath of office:

"I, Michael Richard Pence, do solemnly swear, that I will support and defend the Constitution of the United States against all enemies foreign and domestic...and that I will well and faithfully discharge the duties of the office on which I am about to enter. So help me, God."

Charlotte reflects that her father's voice caught on the last words of the oath. "It was a declaration, and admission he would not be able to do it without assistance," she says.[2]

Mike shook hands with Justice Thomas, embraced Karen and his three children, and then turned and waved to the cheering crowd.

REFLECTIONS ABOUT GRANDFATHER

Standing on the inaugural stage, Mike thought about his grandfather, Cawley.

"I kept thinking of what he would be thinking about looking down from glory," he says. "And I know two things for sure. Number one, knowing me as well as he did, he would be extremely surprised. Number two, I have to think he just thought he was right. He was right about America. He was right to summon the courage as generations did before and since to come here and follow their dreams, and make the contributions that they did. He was right to drive that bus for forty years in Chicago. He was right to raise that irascible redhead that would marry a fast-talking salesman and follow work down to a little, small farm town in southern Indiana and raise six kids with the same heritage and the same values that she had been raised with.... All that I am and all that I will ever be and all the service that I will ever render is owing to my Irish heritage."[3]

The following day, President Trump, First Lady Melania Trump, Vice President Pence, and Second Lady Karen Pence gathered at the Washington National Cathedral for the Interfaith Inaugural Prayer Service, giving them the opportunity to join the nation in prayer for America.

Just a week after the inauguration, with Karen and Charlotte by his side, Mike became the first vice president and the highest ranking official to ever speak in person at the annual March for Life.

"Life is winning again in America," he told the crowd, noting Trump promised his Supreme Court nominee would share that view. "Thank you for your love for the women and children of America. Be assured, along with you, we will not grow weary, we will not rest, until we restore a culture of life in America."[4]

SITTING FOR STATE PORTRAIT

Not long afterward, Mike was asked to sit for his statehouse portrait as a former governor of Indiana. The artist, Mark Dillman, and his wife, Lynn, traveled to Washington to take photos as Mike sat or stood in different poses. The plan was for the Pences to look through them and decide which one they preferred for the official portrait.

Mike sat for an hour, maintaining a professional appearance throughout. Things changed when Karen walked into the room.

"He said whenever Karen came by, he'd get a smile on his face," says Phipps. "He's very much in love with her."

On August 11, 2017, Mike, Karen, Audrey, Nancy, Indiana Governor Eric Holcomb and his wife, Janet, and state and local officials were among the three hundred people who attended the portrait's unveiling. Together, Nancy, Karen, and Audrey removed the drape covering it.

At times, Mike was overwhelmed by emotion as he talked about the portrait and the symbolism behind the different elements that were included.

In the portrait, Mike sits casually on his desk, flanked by the flags of the United States and the state of Indiana. He's wearing a tie designed by Karen. Atop the desk are a framed family photo, his father's old law books, and Mike's Bible, opened to one of his favorite passages: "*So give your servant a discerning heart to govern your people and to distinguish between right and wrong. For who is able to govern this great people of yours?*" (1 Kings 3:9).

"I always thought that was a particularly apt verse for the people in Indiana," Mike said in his remarks. The painting "is really just about paying tribute to all those who are not the subject of the portrait."[5]

During the photo session, Karen came downstairs. "I think she must have sensed that things weren't going well," Mike recalled.[6] But she stood behind Mrs. Dillman as the latter took another photo—and that was the one they ended up using for the portrait.

"Thank you for putting that smile on my face," Mike told Karen, his voice filled with emotion. "Thank you for bringing us here. Thank you for being the love of my life.… Lastly, I want to give glory to God for the opportunities in my small life."[7]

MAKING TIME FOR CHURCH

Although Mike and Karen's lives changed dramatically over the coming months, they still made time to go to church, Secret Service in tow. During an interview with Pastor David Hughes at Church at the Glades in Coral Springs, Florida, Hughes asked Pence about his commitment to attend services weekly.

"What you go through just to attend church is remarkable," said Hughes. "Why, even as you travel, is attending worship such a big thing for you?"

Mike didn't hesitate in answering. Citing the passage from Hebrews 10:25 in which people are encouraged to gather together in prayer, he said, "For me, it's always the best hour of the week. It's a time when we're refreshed. We just moved back to Washington, as you may have heard, so we've visited a few churches, and it's just an incredible blessing. But for me, it's just very important."[8]

As vice president, Mike has continued to stand for his convictions and encourages other believers to do the same, encouraging them in Christ to be a "voice for the voiceless."

"I urge you to continue to stand up, to speak out, to continue to be that voice for the voiceless that the church has been throughout its history," Mike said. "Continue to be the hands and feet of our Savior, reaching in with love and compassion, embracing the dignity of all people of every background and every experience."[9]

AN ATTACK ON CHRISTIAN FAITH

In February 2018, Mike was given an opportunity to speak for the often-misunderstood faith and practices of Christianity. It all started when reality TV show participant and former Trump staffer Omarosa Onee Manigault-Newman went on *Celebrity Big Brother* and slandered Mike for his faith.

"As bad as y'all think Trump is, you would be worried about Pence," Manigault-Newman told her housemates on the TV show on February 12. "We would be begging for days of Trump back if Pence became president, that's all I'm saying. He's extreme. I'm Christian, I love Jesus, but he thinks Jesus tells him to say things—I'm like, 'Jesus ain't sayin' that.' Scary."[10]

The next day on ABC's *The View*, the co-hosts talked about Manigault-Newman's comments after playing a video clip from *Celebrity Big Brother*.

"I think we're in a dangerous situation," said Sunny Hostin. "I don't know that I want my vice president speaking in tongues."[11]

Joy Behar responded, "It's one thing to talk to Jesus. It's another thing when Jesus talks to you. That's called mental illness, if I'm not correct, hearing voices."[12]

Sherri Shepherd came to Mike's defense, saying, "As a Christian, that's just par for the course. You talk to Jesus. Jesus talks back."[13]

Although Mike has never stated that he speaks in tongues or even shared his opinion on the topic, he was interviewed on C-SPAN on

Wednesday, February 14—which was not only Valentine's Day, but also the beginning of Lent—and stood up for his faith as well as the faith of Christians across America.

"I actually heard that ABC has a program that compared my Christianity to mental illness," Mike said. "And I'd like to laugh about it, but I really can't. I'm a believer. Like tens of millions of Americans today who will have ash on their foreheads to mark the beginning of Lent, an overwhelming majority of Americans cherish their faith. And we've all different types of faith in this country, but I have to tell you, to have ABC maintain a broadcast forum that compared Christianity to mental illness is just wrong. And it's an insult not to me, but to the vast majority of the American people who like me cherish their faith. I mean, my Christianity is the most important thing in my life. I try and start every day by opening the Good Book. My wife and I try to have a prayer together before I leave every morning. I can honestly tell you my faith sustains me in all that I do. And it's just a regular part of our lives. But I'm not unusual. I think I'm a very typical American. Whatever your faith tradition, people understand that. But I just think it demonstrates how out of touch some in the mainstream media are with the faith and values of the American people, that you could have a major network like ABC permit a forum for invective against religion like that. And I just call them out on it, not because of what was said about me, but it's just simply wrong for ABC to have a television program that expresses that kind of religious intolerance."[14]

Mike later repeated his concerns in an interview with *FOX & Friends*.

"When I heard that ABC had a program that likened my Christianity to mental illness, I just couldn't be silent," Mike said. "I think people of all different faith traditions cherish their faith in God and to have ABC have a forum that spoke in such demeaning terms, I think it's evidence of how out of touch some in the mainstream media are with the faith and values of the American people."[15]

A CAMPAIGN AGAINST ABC

Meanwhile, Behar's comments angered conservative groups and evangelicals. They joined forces to make sure ABC heard their disappointment and concerns. Brent Bozell, president of the Media Research Center (MRC), wrote to ABC News President James Goldston, calling on him to apologize for his network insulting Mike's faith.

"Bigotry against any group is hateful and ugly. Unfortunately, anti-Christian bigotry seems to be the last acceptable bigotry," Bozell wrote. "Make no mistake, the slurs against the Vice President's faith insult millions of Christians and are unacceptable."[16]

Within days, MRC's campaign had led to at least thirty thousand calls to ABC headquarters insisting that Behar apologize, as well as six thousand calls to the daytime show's advertisers.[17]

The pressure to apologize to people of faith apparently led Behar to make remarks that only stirred further controversy.

"Say what you will about Mike Pence and his religiosity and everything else," Behar said. "I don't think that he's mentally ill, even though he says he is hearing voices.… It was a joke."[18]

Devout believer and fellow host Meghan McCain said she was having "a very hard time" and was "so uncomfortable" over Behar's comments, noting her in-laws are evangelical and her whole family is "devoutly Christian." She then said she was a "great admirer" of Mike and his family and apologized on the air to him for her co-host's remarks.[19]

The controversy was still brewing nearly a month later. On FOX's *Hannity* show, host Sean Hannity asked Mike about the news that Behar had called him privately to apologize although her original comments were made publicly.

"Well, my Christian faith is the most important thing in my life," Mike said. "I think tens of millions of Americans cherish their faith, and so when I heard that ABC had a program where my Christian faith had been described as a mental illness, I thought it was important for me to speak out. Not on my own behalf…criticism comes with public life. But I felt it was important that I defend the faith of tens of millions of Americans against that kind of slander and I did so."[20]

Mike said he gave Joy Behar "a lot of credit. She picked up the phone, she called me, she was very sincere, and she apologized. And one of the things my faith teaches me is grace, forgive as you've been forgiven."[21]

"So does mine," Hannity responded, "but I'm just not as good at it as you are."[22]

Mike said he told Behar, "Of course, I forgive you, that's part of my faith experience." He also encouraged her "to use the forum of that program…to apologize to tens of millions of Americans who were equally offended by what she said.… For me, it was never about me. I didn't take it personally.… My hope is that Joy and others on the airwaves will come to appreciate the meaning and, if I can say, the joy of faith and come to respect that."[23]

Mark Bailey shares something he read about Mike that summarizes why he's been attacked so viciously in the media regarding his faith. On the conservative Christian website, The Stream, Michael Brown wrote: "According to everything I know, Vice President Mike Pence is not a religious fanatic. Rather, he is like millions of other Americans: a God-fearing, Bible-believing Christian. Yet large segments of our population have become so anti-Christian (and even anti-God) that a committed believer like Pence is now vilified as a religious nutcase."[24]

SIMPLY LIVING OUT HIS FAITH

Bailey says this is "a pretty good summation" of the problem. "It's not that Mike's a radical," he says. "Mike is just a very devout person who lives out his faith and that shouldn't be that unusual in our society, but it is."

Other supporters of religious freedom agree. Just a couple of years before Behar made her remarks, Mike's faith was under attack while he campaigned with Trump.

"What bothers the left about Pence seems to be that he is a man of strong religious conviction," said preacher and author Peter Heck, noting Mike had referred to Scripture thrice in a twelve-minute speech. "Such behavior is disquieting to an embarrassingly biblically illiterate state and national press corps that convinces itself such behavior is a telltale characteristic of a closet theocrat. They are far more comfortable with politicians who use their faith as a prop, and who allow their politics to shape and mold their 'beliefs.'"[25]

Friends say Mike's goal is not to convert the world to Christianity.

"Unlike the caricature of these people who are always attacking him, he is not some sort of Christian fundamentalist, zealot, Christian jihad," says Dan Murphy. "He's not trying to create a theocratic state. He's simply living out his faith."

Mike is "the real deal," says Varvel. "If you have a testimony for Christ, you're going to get mocked—and he does. I've heard people say he's a fake. He's not a fake—this is who he is. He lives it. He believes it. For people who are not believers, that scares the daylights out of them. They think he's on some kind of mission to turn us into a theocracy and force everyone into Christians. That's not what he wants anyway. He just thinks a godly influence would be good for everyone."

Mike "looks at life through a Christian prism," says Simcox. "He has a highly developed sense of the Christian worldview. People will totally misinterpret what I'm saying. That does *not* mean he wants America to be a theocracy. That does not mean that he's intent on converting people to Christianity. It does not mean he has less respect for other religions than his own. He is guided in who he is, he's guided in what he believes, he's guided in reasons he believes it.

"Mike is a deep thinker," Simcox adds. "He goes to the perceptible reason why he takes a political stand on any given vote or on any given issue and his principles are governed by his faith. There are certain foundational things going on there. One is the equality of all people before the eyes of God. The ground is level at the base of the cross. Another is Matthew 25—visit the prisoner, tend [to] the sick, feed the hungry, clothe the naked. Those are things that Christ directs His followers to do and Mike has a mature sense of obligation in government to care for those who cannot care for themselves."

STANDING FOR RELIGIOUS FREEDOM

Mike's convictions for religious freedom extend beyond America's borders. Speaking at the World Summit in Defense of Persecuted Christians, Mike said, "The Bible tells us, 'All who desire to live a godly life in Christ Jesus will be persecuted.'...The Christian faith is under siege. Throughout the world, no people of faith today face greater hostility or hatred than the followers of Christ."[26]

The sincerity of Mike's faith "has really inspired his personal involvement in issues of religious freedom abroad," says Johnnie Moore. "At the president's directive, he's been deeply, deeply involved in promoting religious freedom and speaking up for persecuted religious minorities around the world. I think that's not only a commitment to a constitutional value of the United States, but that it comes from a person who is a sincere believer himself. When you're a sincere believer and you see sincere believers being persecuted against or discriminated against or marginalized because of their belief, it speaks to you in a different way with a greater level of empathy. I think he'll definitely go down in modern American history as a celebrated champion of the rights of those persecuted around the world."

"The heartbreaking truth is that believers of so many backgrounds are under assault across the wider world," Mike shared at Focus on the Family's fortieth anniversary celebration. "Nowhere is this more evident than the Middle East in the very land where our faith was first given life. Nearly 2,000 years ago the disciples of Jesus Christ fanned out from Israel in every direction, spreading the Good News that we proclaim to this day. All across that ancient land… the fathers of our faith planted seeds of belief that blossomed and have borne fruit ever since. But today, these Christian communities face unspeakable atrocities at the hands of radical Islamic terrorism. The terrorists seek to stamp out all religions that are not their own, or not even a version of their own, and believers of many backgrounds have suffered grievously, especially at the hands of the barbarians known as ISIS. The brutal regime shows a savagery unseen in the Middle East since the Middle Ages."[27]

FIGHTS FOR OTHER RELIGIONS, TOO

Colleagues say Mike's fight for religious freedom extends to other religions as well.

"I've seen him interact with one of the top Muslim leaders of the world, a leader of a sixty-million-person Islamic organization in Indonesia," says Moore. "It's a modern organization that has helped a lot of persecuted Christians. This was just days after a series of bombings in Indonesia. And to sit down and watch [the] most influential evangelical ever in American public life, as the vice president of the United States, have such a congenial, constructive conversation with a Muslim leader of such renown, talking together about combating extremism and making the world safe, where co-existence between religions is the status quo and not an exception...that's something I admire about him.... His sincerity and depth of his faith have not made it difficult for him to interact with people who are not like him, who don't believe like him."

ENDNOTES

1. Charlotte Pence, *Where You Go.*
2. Charlotte Pence, *Where You Go.*
3. "Remarks by Vice President Pence to the American Ireland Fund National Gala," March 15, 2017 (Whitehouse.gov).
4. "Vice President Mike Pence Speech March For Life 2017 Washington DC," FOX News Network/FOX 10 Phoenix, Jan 27, 2017.
5. Elena Mejia Lutz, "Bible, family picture grace Vice President Mike Pence's official portrait as governor," *The Indianapolis Star*, August 11, 2017.
6. Ibid.
7. Ibid.
8. "VP Mike Pence Shares Testimony at Church by the Glades," VFNtv.
9. Matt Hadro and Adelaide Mena, "Vice President at Catholic Prayer Breakfast: 'Continue to Be Hands, Feet of Our Savior,'" *National Catholic Register*, June 6, 2017.
10. "Omarosa says 'we would be begging' for Trump if Pence became president," CBS News, February 12, 2018.
11. "Omarosa Overshares About Pence On 'Big Brother,'" *The View*, ABC, February 13, 2018.

12. Ibid.

13. Ibid.

14. "Axios Interview with Vice President Pence," C-SPAN, February 14, 2018 (www.c-span.org/video/?441176-1/vice-president-pence-expresses-confidence-white-house-chief-staff).

15. "Pence: Behar's Comments About Faith Show How Out of Touch Some in the Media Are," *FOX & Friends*, Fox News, February 19, 2018.

16. Craig Bannister, "Bozell Calls on ABC News President to Apologize for Insults to Pence's Christian Faith on 'The View,'" CNSNews, February 15, 2018.

17. Brian Flood, "ABC News silent after more than 30,000 calls over 'View' star Joy Behar's 'anti-Christian bigotry,'" FOX News, February 28, 2018.

18. "'The View' Co-Hosts Respond To Criticism Of Comments On Vice Pres. Pence," *The View*, ABC, February 15, 2018.

19. Ibid.

20. "One-on-One with Vice President Pence," *Hannity*, FOX News, March 12, 2018.

21. Ibid.

22. "One-on-One with Vice President Pence," *Hannity*, FOX News, March 12, 2018.

23. Ibid.

24. Michael Brown, "America Needs the Faith of Mike Pence," *The Stream*, February 19, 2018.

25. Peter Heck, "Pete Heck: Mike Pence is a man of true faith," *The Indianapolis Star*, July 18, 2016.

26. "Remarks by Vice President Pence at the World Summit in Defense of Persecuted Christians," May 11, 2017 (whitehouse.gov).

27. "Remarks by the Vice President at the Focus on the Family 40th Anniversary Celebration."

18

VICE PRESIDENT PENCE

Let us not become weary in doing good, for at the proper time we
will reap a harvest if we do not give up.
—Galatians 6:9

One of the first things Mike did upon becoming vice president was implement a Wednesday morning Bible study group for ten Cabinet members, asking evangelical pastor and retired professional basketball player Ralph Drollinger to lead it. Drollinger has been instrumental in providing Bible studies, evangelism, and discipleship to political leaders since founding Capitol Ministries in Washington, D.C., in 1997. His influence is such that at the president's request, he provides Bible study printouts for Trump on a weekly basis.

In addition to attending the weekly Bible study, Mike meets with long-time friend Bill Smith and three other friends regularly for accountability.

"The vice president and I have a personal time, every couple of weeks or so, of prayer and Bible study," says Smith.

For her part, Karen has continued to be invested in art therapy, committing her time and resources to raising awareness and educating the public about the mental health arts profession in the United States and around the world. She has observed art therapy programs in Canada, Japan, Germany, Belgium, Indonesia, Australia, South Korea,

Asia, and across the United States. Karen has continued to support Riley Hospital for Children, Tracy's Kids, and other programs and has received awards for her efforts. In July 2017, Sister Cities International named her an honorary vice chairwoman.

In October 2017, Karen launched her own art therapy initiative, "Art Therapy: Healing with the HeART." She notes this innovative mental health and human services profession is not arts and crafts, but requires at least a master's degree in the field. Art therapy "enriches the lives of individuals, families, and communities," she says. Among the many people who can benefit are children with cancer, struggling teens, grieving families, and soldiers experiencing post-traumatic stress disorder.[1] Karen has also hosted and participated in numerous events to honor and recognize all of those in the armed forces.

FINDING A JUSTICE NOMINEE

Following through on a campaign promise to find a Supreme Court justice who opposed abortion and held other conservative views, Mike helped Trump narrow down the president's original list of twenty-one candidates to three judges from the U.S. Court of Appeals who could potentially fill the vacant seat: Thomas M. Hardiman of the Third Circuit, William H. Pryor Jr. of the Eleventh Circuit, and Neil M. Gorsuch of the Tenth Circuit.

Both Trump and Mike knew the individual they picked would have influential and life-changing effects on the United States judicial system. After personally interviewing all three men, Reed says Mike came up with a brilliant idea on how to settle on one final candidate.

Mike's idea was "we should ask all three of the finalists, aside from themselves, who they would pick out of the other two finalists," says Reed. "The [other] two guys both picked Gorsuch."

Ironically, like Mike, Gorsuch was inducted into the Phi Gamma Delta fraternity while attending Columbia University for his bachelor's degree. He and former President Barack Obama were also classmates while attending Harvard Law. Gorsuch's conservative values have been a hallmark of his career. Thus, selecting him for Supreme Court was a move that spoke volumes.

STILL A PEACEMAKER

Friends say Mike has found his way as the moral compass and peacemaker within the Trump administration, delicately balancing the ups and downs that have come with that role.

"From the very beginning, Jim [Dodson] and I and other friends who know and love the Pences have watched him and we feel like he is involved in the things he really endorses and he kind of stands back in the shadow and stays out of things where it would demand compromise," says Pastor Lake. "And I am impressed in what I believe is the masterful way in which he's done that. I'm just amazed that he's been able to keep himself unscathed up to this point."

Simcox agrees, saying Mike's role is precarious, requiring a steady hand and a spiritual foundation.

"There are many examples in Scripture of the importance of counselors to the king," Simcox points out. "The king may be right sometimes, or never right, but the Bible tends to focus on those who counseled the kings and who therefore made impacts as a result of it without characterizing the king. I think Mike can be compared to those who counseled the king. Mike has had a positive influence on the president and set a very good example to the president."

A PERFECT BALANCE

Several people who have worked side-by-side with Mike and Trump say they have the perfect balance of give and take.

"I've had several personal moments with the vice president and I've made a point to tell him that I'm obviously praying for him, but [also] how glad I am that he's standing next to the president and speaking words of faith and God's Word in Scripture and praying with the president," Graham says. "It gives me a great deal of comfort and gratitude that Mike Pence is standing by and with our president at this very critical time in our nation."

Reed, speaking "as someone who has been able to observe it first-hand," says Trump and Mike "have a tremendous relationship. I know that they talk all the time and they are able to talk really honestly with one another. I know that they pray together. Pence has proven to be a very smart, wise, capable member of the president's team, as well as an advisor and counselor to the president."

As one of Trump's spiritual advisers, Strack has been with the president and Mike both together and separately. He says he's witnessed "the deep respect that the president has for Pence. He's said, 'I want to thank my partner, my friend, this real gift, Vice President Pence. You know, he's a man of prayer, a man of faith. Trust me—he wants to pray all the time. Every time we get together, there's a prayer meeting.'"

Friends say Mike's ability to bring solidity to the team that unites the two men and gives hope to people of faith.

"I think Pence so stabilizes the team that it's comforting to people of faith, that he's right there in the battle with the president," says Floyd. "I can't underestimate that and the value of that and only history will record what it really meant and what it really will mean."

Friends and colleagues from both sides of the aisle praise Mike for his strong leadership within the walls of the White House and his heart of servanthood on behalf of our nation. Many believe that Mike has been given to America during this crucial time to be an instrument in God's hands.

The son of famed evangelist Billy Graham, Franklin Graham is the CEO of the Billy Graham Evangelistic Association and Samaritan's Purse. He says he has known Mike for over a quarter of a century.

"I am grateful we still have politicians who are not ashamed of their faith, who are pro-life, and have a conservative agenda," says Franklin Graham. "Mike and Karen Pence have been outspoken on their Christian faith and live their faith for all to see. My wife, Jane, and I have had the privilege to be with the vice president on a number of occasions and we appreciate his willingness to serve the people of this great country."

The Rev. Jack Graham notes he's close to George W. Bush and the former president "opened God's Word every morning—I know that for a fact—and he sought God on the sanctity of life and other issues we care about. I believe President Bush lived out his faith. But Mike Pence is very unique. He's his own man and God's man in the West Wing."

Elsass says it's "a great joy to see someone you know who is so good and decent succeed. I'm convinced that God put him there to share his faith with the president and have a great, positive impact because of the way Mike thinks and lives his life. It's just consistent with who he is and what he does, all based on the person he is because he's someone who places the Lord first and he really makes decisions on that basis. He trusts God."

Elsass chuckles over the idea, held by many in the mainstream media as well as political opponents, that Mike has climbed the ladder of success for selfish reasons.

"It's always funny to watch people step over each other to climb the political pole," he says. "All Mike Pence had to do was go to work every day, love the Lord, be led where the Spirit leads him, and answer the call of service, and that's what he's done. And he's done it without all the anxiety of people who have to plot and plan a course of life. He just made himself available and let God place him where He could use him the greatest. I think that's why he's where he is today."

Mike says he truly believes his life is not his own. "Most especially, as a Christian, when I made a decision to put my life in God's hands, it was part of what I think is really a transaction in which a believer says, 'I will endeavor now both on my knees and opening up the [Bible] to discern what you want me to do' as opposed to getting up every day and deciding what I want to do," Mike explains. "For me and my house, we serve the Lord. And we will always make every effort, with deep humility, to discern whenever we can what God require of us, what our faith requires of us in any situation, and then put feet on that and make that real."[2]

LOVED BY GOD

Mike believes that God cherishes the United States, Phipps points out. "Mike Pence believes our nation has been blessed of God...that God has shown grace to our nation that we started as a Christian nation. And I believe he tries to live his life with that in view."

Although the United States has gone through great trials, Mike believes there is hope for America.

"You know, God's love really eclipses our failing and, as always, He's been a source of renewal and strengthening for this nation and for people of faith throughout our history," Mike says. Those who cherish faith, freedom, the sanctity of life, "and all the liberties enshrined in our Constitution should step forward and heed the call to action."[3]

American history shows "that the strength of our nation has come from our communities of faith," Mike says. "It's been the voices of faith that, more often than not, have driven our nation to a more perfect union. It was the pulpits around the American founding that thundered against the tyranny of King George. It was the pulpits around America that spoke of the evils of slavery and brought an end to the scourge of slavery in America, even through a great civil conflict. And it was voices of faith and communities of faith that transformed our nation through the civil rights movement in our own lifetime and we're a better nation for it."[4]

Mike reminds people of God's promise in 2 Chronicles 7:14: "*If my people, who are called by my name, will humble themselves and pray...then I will hear from heaven, and I will forgive their sin and will heal their land.*"

He encourages people to "pray for our country. But as you do so, please pray, as Lincoln said with his prayer, not so much that God would be on our side, but that we would be, in his words, on God's side."[5]

Friends and colleagues say Mike Pence is steadfast in his spiritual convictions, conservative views, and desire to serve our nation. The whispers in Washington are that he will one day seek the presidency. That's certainly the desire of many who know him personally. If it's God's will, Mike will surrender to it, they say. And they echo the words of his long-time friend, Doug Deason:

"He's going to be a great president."

ENDNOTES

1. "Second Lady Karen Pence's Initiative, Healing with the HeART," The White House YouTube channel, October 18, 2017.
2. C-SPAN, "Q&A with Mike Pence," January 19, 2006.
3. "Trump and Pence Send Video Messages to the Nation's Churches."
4. Ibid.
5. Ibid.

ABOUT THE AUTHOR

Leslie Montgomery is the author and ghostwriter of over a dozen books. She is best known for writing the spiritual biography *The Faith of Condoleezza Rice* when Rice was serving our nation as secretary of state in the George W. Bush administration.

Leslie has been a writer for Focus on the Family for more than twenty years and is the former director of publications for the American Association of Christian Counselors.

She is also the founder of Yeshu'a Ministries, with the goal of helping people gain a better and closer relationship with the Lord through her writing, speaking, and teaching ministry. She has traveled to churches and conferences around the world through her evangelical ministry, sharing the Word of God.

Leslie has four children and six grandchildren. She resides in Boise, Idaho.

Leslie Montgomery
Yeshu'a Ministries
P.O. Box 45104
Boise, Idaho 83711
Email: leslie@authorlesliemontgomery.com
Web: www.authorlesliemontgomery.com
Facebook: Author Leslie Montgomery
Twitter: LGMontgomery
Pinterest: Leslieginevramontgomery
LinkedIn: Leslie Montgomery